AF897739

THE POLITICS OF JUDICIAL SELECTION IN IRELAND

For my family
Hugo, Isabella, Georgia and James

The Politics of Judicial Selection in Ireland

Jennifer Carroll MacNeill

FOUR COURTS PRESS

Typeset in 10.5 pt on 12.5 pt EhrhardtMTPro by
Carrigboy Typesetting Services for
FOUR COURTS PRESS LTD
7 Malpas Street, Dublin 8, Ireland
www.fourcourtspress.ie
and in North America for
FOUR COURTS PRESS
c/o ISBS, 920 NE 58th Avenue, Suite 300, Portland, OR 97213.

© Jennifer Carroll MacNeill and Four Courts Press 2016

A catalogue record for this title is available
from the British Library.

ISBN 978-1-84682-597-2

All rights reserved.
Without limiting the rights under copyright
reserved alone, no part of this publication may be
reproduced, stored in or introduced into a retrieval system,
or transmitted, in any form or by any means (electronic, mechanical,
photocopying, recording or otherwise), without the prior
written permission of both the copyright owner and
publisher of this book.

Printed in England
by Antony Rowe, Bumpers Farm, Chippenham.

Contents

Acknowledgments

I wish to thank a number of people who helped me with this book. Chief among these is Professor Niamh Hardiman of the School of Politics and International Relations, University College Dublin. I thank her for her support and commitment, as well as her patience and kindness. I also wish to thank Professor David Feldman of Downing College, University of Cambridge, Professor John Coakley, Dr Iseult Honohan, John O'Dowd BCL, Professor David Farrell and Professor Tom Garvin – all of University College Dublin – for their assistance, questions and insights. I also wish to thank Dr Jacqueline Hayden of Trinity College Dublin and Professor Kevin T. McGuire of the University of North Carolina at Chapel Hill for prompting my initial research interest into the judiciary.

The real value of this book is in the richness of the contributions made by the senior political and legal office-holders in Ireland since 1982. I am deeply grateful to them for their generosity in sharing their experiences and contributing to this thirty-four-year analysis. Only the bounds of my guarantee of confidentiality prevent me from enthusiastically thanking them in turn. However, I do wish to give special thanks to Harry Whelehan SC for contributing to this study. I am grateful to him for sharing his unique experience and for doing so in a way that allowed this experience to be understood and identified.

I have been most fortunate to have had the support of my employers during the completion of this research and I want to thank Enda Kenny, Frances Fitzgerald and Alan Shatter in this regard. For the respective periods of my employment with them, each gave me the time and intellectual space required to produce this independent academic research.

Brendan Ryan, CEO of the Courts Service and Secretary to the Judicial Appointments Advisory Board, has been the target of my incessant questions and unsolicited suggestions for over ten years. I am very thankful to him for engaging with this work and for providing such kind assistance to me throughout my research.

I am grateful to the Irish Research Council for Humanities and Social Sciences (IRCHSS) for the award of a Government of Ireland PhD Scholarship, from which I benefited greatly until such time as my work commitments made it impossible for me to hold a full-time scholarship.

I wish to thank most especially my family and friends for their love, support and companionship and for reading and re-reading this book, especially my wonderful husband Hugo MacNeill, my great friends Lori Hellkamp and David McRedmond, and my parents Denis Carroll and the very lovely Mary Carroll.

Preface

There is a political difficulty as to how political involvement in judicial selection is to be managed. This book examines different institutional arrangements for the selection of judges and the conditions under which politicians feel it necessary to consider changing those judicial selection systems. Do changes to judicial selection systems happen in ways that reduce political influence in judicial selection or does political involvement in judicial selection remain static? What instruments do politicians use to distance judicial selection from politics and how robust are those instruments over time? Why are we concerned at all about the level of political influence in the selection of judges in stable democracies with political acountability? This book provides a comprehensive comparative analysis of the political pressures in managing the role of politicians in judicial selection.

The judiciary is an important body in systems of constitutional government. The credibility of constitutional governance rests on the separation of powers between the executive and the judiciary and the independence of the judiciary is one of its most highly prized features. Judicial systems that are too directly subordinated to the political preferences of the government of the day quickly lose their capacity to protect core constitutional freedoms. Yet there is a necessary link between the executive and the judiciary. The executive must provide the administrative supports to the judiciary but, more than this, the executive must play some role in their appointment. Even in an entirely self-selecting judicial appointments system, some responsibility for institutional design still rests with the executive since it is implicitly responsible for facilitating and supporting such a system. In some systems, the power of judicial appointment is explicitly delegated to a non-political body to insulate judicial appointments from political influence. But in these cases too, an explanatory puzzle is present since the government must both voluntarily cede power over a key function while retaining responsibility for the actual outcome of the appointments system. The analytical challenge is to account for why countries opt for particular types of institutional solutions. A core argument of this book is that the circumstances that lead to change in judicial selection systems are critical in understanding the outcomes.

From this analysis, we can draw important lessons about the institutional design of certain delegated bodies. The institutional design of a delegated body can have profound effects on the institutional functioning of that body over time. This is something of real importance in the modern polity where many government functions are delegated, to various degrees, to independent non-majoritarian bodies. Suitable oversight of the functioning of such institutions is important to ensure that they are, in fact, operating as designed and meeting the objectives of their establishment. Poor institutional design can lead to outcomes that are at variance with the objectives of the establishment of the institution. Equally, sub-optimal institutional functioning through institutional drift can lead to outcomes at variance with the purpose of the establishment of the institution. This can have very serious effects. In Ireland, a parliamentary report on the banking crisis of 2008 found that the Central Bank and Financial Regulator – both delegated institutions – had sufficient powers to intervene to protect the financial stability in the state but did not use them.[1]

This book demonstrates the centrally important role of political commitment in bringing about institutional reform. It examines the impact of government preferences in the introduction and implementation of institutional change that has the effect of reducing the power of governments in functions that are important to them. It explores these issues through an analysis of the distinctive Irish experience and by situating this in a broader comparative framework. The comparative analysis performed in this book demonstrates that when major reform is undertaken to delegate powers to a non-political institution, two key trends emerge – explicit political commitment to major institutional change and a consultation process involving external stakeholders and public debate.

This book systematically examines the mode of appointing senior judges in common law systems in a cross-national comparative context. The focus is on common law systems because, in general, judges are chosen by a politically governed process from the ranks of senior lawyers as opposed to civil law systems where, in general, people may become judges as a career in itself, separate to the experience of legal practice and separate to political influence. The common law systems examined include Australia, England and Wales, Scotland, Ireland, Israel, New Zealand, Northern Ireland and the United States.

The book identifies the key explanatory variables that shape 'successful and effective' institutional change and presents an index of reforms to show how political commitment affects outcomes. This same model is used to explain the reforms undertaken to the system for appointing judges in Ireland. These inferences are then tested against two complementary cases of political reform, which permits some counterfactual reasoning. These case studies – one in Ireland and another in Scotland – strengthen the arguments about the central role of political commitment in explaining the nature of institutional change and design.

1 Report of the Joint Oireachtas Committee of Inquiry on the Banking Crisis, January 2016, p. 10. 'Once the new structure, which represented a material change in the delivery of financial supervision in Ireland, was in place, the government should have carried out an independent review and assessment of its effectiveness and the delivery of its functions. However, it was the execution by the CBFSAI of their mandate and the absence of interventions that directly contributed to the crisis.'

OVERVIEW OF THE BOOK

Chapter 1 describes the different methods of appointing judges in democratic common law countries, and why, and under what conditions, political authorities initiated and, in some cases, introduced institutional change. The comparative survey presented in Chapter 1 reveals that the Irish mode of undertaking reform was quite distinctive. Chapter 1 also presents a systematic index of indicators of political commitment to institutional reform. This enables us to isolate the drivers of reform in Ireland that resulted in a hybrid judicial selection model and raises the puzzle as to what drivers of such reform may be.

Chapter 2 goes into more detail about the background to reform in Ireland and what is so distinctive about the Irish case. In fact, reform initiatives were triggered by a crisis of trust between coalition partners. Judicial appointments were the flashpoint of tensions that had been building up for some time. The crisis over judicial appointments casts new light on the unsatisfactory aspects of the then-Irish processes of judicial selection. The major outcome of this crisis was a long drawn-out legislative process involving two drafts of legislation to delegate the power to a non-political body of delegated governance to screen and recommend judges for appointment. Each draft of this legislation would afford a different degree of influence to the non-political body of delegated governance and, as a consequence, a different degree of discretion to future governments in judicial selection.

The outcome of these political processes enables us to understand the outcomes of the new institutional design adopted in 1995 – a hybrid model of judicial selection that combines elements of a system dominated by the power of government and a system that had been delegated to a non-political body of delegated governance. But the consequences of institutional design are important for the functioning of delegated bodies. The critical juncture occurred in 1995 when the legislation that gave effect to the new system was enacted. The years post-1995 were a period during which the consequences of that statutory change were worked out but also a period during which actors within the institutions responded to often conflicting concerns about how to best perform their functions.

Chapter 3 examines the mixed experience of the Judicial Appointments Advisory Board ('JAAB' or 'the Board') – the non-political body of delegated governance charged with preparing recommendations for judicial appointments. It is based on interviews with the members of the JAAB and the key government decision-makers involved in judicial selection. This in-depth investigation of institutional reform in Ireland reveals the particular form of institutional design had consequences that permitted a drift in the practice of the JAAB such that the scope for political discretion in judicial selection was widened to levels close to those before institutional change was introduced. However, there are also aspects of the design that serve as examples of well-planned reforms with consistent institutional design and institutional functioning.

Chapter 4 presents two counterfactual cases as examples of successful institutional design and institutional functioning. In 1974 the Irish government established a body with delegated powers in another area of political sensitivity related to the administration of justice – that of criminal prosecutions – taking it out of the hands of government. An analogous examination of reform in Scotland reveals consistent and far reaching institutional reform of judicial appointments.

Chapter 5 presents the current political picture regarding judicial selection in Ireland and examines the calls made for further reform. It presents some of the implications for future institutional change to judicial selection in Ireland and charts a path for process and statute based developments for the Irish judicial selection system that may incrementally enhance institutional functioning.

Introduction

THE JUDICIARY AND EXECUTIVE IN CONSTITUTIONAL DEMOCRACIES

Constitutional democracy is based on two simultaneous but competing principles: a commitment to the will of the majority and a commitment to limit the potential excesses of the popular majority by recourse to a set of fundamental laws (Grimm, 2012). Each institution, while recognizing the boundaries of their respective powers, plays a role in ensuring that the other institution does not overstep the limits of its constitutional role. By checking and balancing the exercise of power by the other institution, each ensures the other will stay within its constitutionally defined parameters (Dahl, 2000; Kokott and Kasper, 2012).

Courts are an integral part of any political system (Koopmans, 2003). At the most general level, the function of the courts is to resolve disputes, either between citizens or private entities or between the state and citizens or private entities. However, the decisions of courts may affect the interests of parties far beyond those related to the original action. While an action can only be taken by individuals with the requisite standing, the judgment delivered by a court has the potential to affect a much wider societal group or indeed the actions of the state itself.

Occasionally, courts examine questions that have important political and social consequences for society. Through their interpretation of the constitution, they may make value judgments on behalf of society. Courts can articulate human rights, can constrain human rights, can protect individuals from the government and protect the government from its own transgressions through *a priori* review of legislation for its constitutionality. In this way, courts and judges can act as policy makers (Dahl, 1958; Casper, 1976). Accordingly, in constitutional politics, the function of judges can be as a 'passive legislator' with transformative effects on parliamentary governance and the law-making process (Stone, 2007; Roesler, 2007). The role of the judiciary in the constitutional and political system is deeply important to the conduct of the democratic political order – eventually questions of policy may come to be decided by the judiciary, as opposed to being decided by the law-making majority (Frankenberg, 2012; Bickel, 1975). The growth of political jurisprudence as a discipline has emerged as a response to the discovery of how 'un-court like' some courts can be or how much they behave like other political actors (Shapiro, 1986). Judicial power is a significant political force that can produce outcomes that are at variance with the will of the law-making majority – the 'counter-majoritarian difficulty'. Essentially, the counter-majoritarian difficulty concerns the exercise of power by judges who are neither appointed by the popular majority, nor accountable to it (Bickel, 1975).

Notwithstanding the rule of law, judicial discretion and different forms of constitutional interpretation mean that different individuals, in certain identical cases, can produce non-identical decisions (Epstein, Knight and Shvetsova, 2002; Morgan, 2001). We know this to be correct by observing the fact that judges on the same court (such as a multi-member Supreme Court), faced with the same facts and legal issues can give rulings that favour different parties or can give the same ruling but on different grounds. Governments, conscious of these possibilities, are concerned by who becomes a judge and how they might affect the administration of justice or decisions in certain cases of interest to government. Control of membership of the judiciary becomes, therefore, highly important to political actors because judicial discretion in decision-making can have profound consequences for the constitutional politics of the day and the development of constitutional jurisprudence over time (Burbank and Friedman, 2002). It is argued that the selection of judges clearly marks the point where politics and courts most visibly intersect (Volcansek, 2007). It is for these reasons that the choice of the method governing how judges are selected and retained is so important – politicians and the public alike believe that how we choose our judges plays a part in determining which types of men and women will serve as judges and, in turn, the choices they may make in their post (Epstein and Segal, 2005).

Judicial selection is of concern to governments for another reason – it is a potential source of political patronage. Judgeships are highly prestigious appointments: this is reflected in their position and powerful function in the constitutional order, particularly in common law countries where judges are appointed from the ranks of senior lawyers, and the fact that they are often seen to represent the pinnacle of the legal hierarchy in which senior legal practitioners have made their careers. There is also a traditional link between the activities of politicians and lawyers because they both operate as practitioners in different spheres of the constitutional order. To the extent that lawyers may support a particular political party, judgeships are often, correctly or not, perceived to be a means by which political parties distribute patronage among their supporters.

JUDICIAL SELECTION SYSTEMS VARY: AND SOMETIMES THEY CHANGE

The patterns of judicial selection and appointment vary across societies (Epstein, Knight and Shvetsova 2002; Lee, 2011). Many judicial selection systems involve politicians to varying degrees and in different ways. Some systems are exclusively based on the preferences of the executive, some systems require approval of judicial nominations by the legislature, some appoint judges according to a quota by different branches of the political system and some restrict the involvement of politicians to selecting among individuals that have been pre-screened by an independent body comprising judges and representatives of the legal profession (Burbank and Friedman, 2002). Whatever selection system is used, it is the government that controls the rules administering that system and therefore any change to that system.

The role of politics in judicial selection is perennially contested and the acceptable boundaries of politics in judicial selection vary among countries and over time (Malleson and Russell, 2006; Burbank and Friedman, 2002; Bell, 2006). What is interesting is when these questions or pressures to change the judicial selection system reach a point where the existing system is perceived to be unsatisfactory, and, for whatever reasons, politicians share this view. It may be that politicians share the view that the domestic constitutional politics of a country would be better served by a distancing of politics from judicial selection or it may be that political pressure reaches a point at which changing the judicial selection system becomes an imperative for political survival. At these moments the shape of the judicial selection system within a given jurisdiction comes into focus and, in certain cases, may undergo change.

Changes to the judicial selection institutions can occur for different reasons. Three kinds of incentives may be identified, though these may not be exhaustive. Change can arise as a function of broader political change, it can occur as a response to specific concerns about representativeness in divided societies or it can be linked to concerns about the role of politics in judicial selection. The academic debate surrounding reform of judicial selection has focused on three issues: removing political influence from judicial selection, improving the quality of the judiciary and providing for a measure of accountability of the judiciary (Volcansek, 1982; DuBois, 1980; Malleson and Russell, 2006).

In certain jurisdictions the expanded role of the judiciary through the adoption of international human rights, norms and legal processes has given the judiciary the capacity to impact on the actions of government. This has led to a renewed interest in who becomes a judge and how they are chosen. The political and constitutional contexts of the global expansion of judicial power vary considerably but a common feature of this trend is that it is accompanied by a growing public and political interest in who judges are and how they are chosen (Malleson and Russell, 2006). While the judiciary is not required to be directly accountable socially, political actors have sought to ensure that, in countries with clearly identifiable social cleavages, the composition of the judiciary will reflect the diversity in society – often as an effort to overcome past marginalization of certain social groups in a country under a different political regime (Ashenfelter et al., 1995; Du Bois, 2006; Salzberger, 2006).

Institutional change to judicial selection systems can also arise from a concern that politics and the judiciary should be further separated and that the removal of political actors from judicial selection is desirable. Whether as a concern about the link between political parties and judicial appointments or a concern that traditional methods of appointment to the judiciary overly relied on the operation of networks between senior legal professionals and political actors, there has been increased scrutiny of the role of politics in judicial selection systems in the past two decades; for example, Australia in the mid-1990s, Ireland in 1994 and England and Wales between 1998 and 2005. These are among the cases that will be examined in detail in Chapter 1. Governments engaged in public debate about changing judicial selection systems and some opted to make changes to their judicial selection system that removed the process from political control or diminished the influence of political control. This could be motivated by governments seeking credibility gains on the question of the politicization of the judiciary or through political reform generally. These are the questions that will be explored in this study.

What is interesting about change to judicial selection systems is that it must be introduced by the government, which is both the agent of institutional change (through the introduction of new processes for judicial selection) and a participant in the judicial selection process. What is especially interesting is that, in general, institutional change to judicial selection systems has put the government in a less favourable position as regards the judicial selection process following the change. The government may make a decision that, by reducing their power in judicial selection systems, it is achieving some other benefit, whether through credibility gains or some other political objective.

In the context of this puzzle, what is particularly interesting is the degree of discretion governments allow themselves in a changed judicial selection model. When the institutional change is being initiated we might expect a range of outcomes to be possible. What sort of institutional design do governments opt for? What shape does reform take? To what degree are institutions distanced from government or powers delegated more completely to a delegated body such that government endorses what they recommend?

One of the ways in which the problem of political involvement in judicial selection is managed is the explicit delegation of the governance of the judicial selection function – or a part of it – to a non-political body. Judicial selection commissions are an example of such 'non-majoritarian institutions' – that is, a non-political body of delegated governance that is not subject to political control or answerable to an elected forum (Thatcher and Stone, 2003).

There are good reasons why non-political bodies of delegated governance exist and are used by governments to keep political distance from certain public functions. But how does government weigh the decision to utilize such non-political bodies? Are short-term credibility gains a sufficient trade-off for long-term loss of power? (North, 1990a). Is the government motivated by other policy considerations and happy to accept the ensuing loss of influence?

A core argument of this book is that the political circumstances that lead to the introduction of new judicial selection models are critical in understanding the level of political commitment behind the decision to introduce change and the nature of that change. Government has the power to control the rules governing judicial selection and the power to control the institutional design of any change to those rules. Governments can introduce an institutional design that is very effective at reducing the power of government in judicial selection, or an institutional design that is much less effective at reducing such government power. Understanding the motivation of the government in introducing institutional change is central to understanding the form of that institutional change and its impact on future government power in the selection of judges.

THE THEORY OF INSTITUTIONS AND INSTITUTIONALISM

Institutions are the rules that organize the conduct of political actors. In doing so, institutions shape political behaviour and we study institutions in order to answer real world questions about how political behaviour, strategies, outcomes and preferences are structured in different situations (Lewis and Steinmo, 2012).

If institutions are the rules by which actors and processes are organized, then any change to those rules has implications for the participants to that institution. These participants may encourage institutional change or may resist institutional change. In general, it is perceived that institutional change is difficult – either because humans are habitual creatures who dislike change or because humans have invested time, effort or money into learning to use the existing institution. Resistance to institutional change can also occur where the introduction of such change will, or is perceived to, remove some advantage from a group of actors and confer that advantage to some other group of actors. In playing the role of both participant and agent of change, government plays a unique, and possibly conflicting, role in the institutional change of judicial selection systems. But given that it is the government, within the popularly elected law-making majority of the day, that has the democratic authority to initiate or resist institutional change of one kind or another, who else could legitimately introduce such change?

Institutional change can occur in different ways – either as a slow, gradual evolution of the institution or as a sudden and distinct institutional change. Historical institutionalism traditionally viewed institutions as static, with long periods of continuity punctuated by critical junctures where substantial institutional change occurred (Collier and Collier, 1991; Thelen and Mahoney,

2010; Peters, 2000; Lewis and Steinmo, 2012). This 'punctuated equilibrium' at critical junctures was, for many years, the dominant explanation for institutional change. This view of institutional change saw change as a response to some external factor that had shifted, such as an economic or military factor. However, in recent years, historical institutionalists have also understood institutional change as being something that can occur slowly, gradually and as a response to internal pressures (Thelen and Streeck, 2005; Thelen and Mahoney, 2010). Institutional change has been recognized as occurring in terms of institutional drift, institutional conversion and institutional layering – all of which generally refer to the different means by which an institution can change slowly and subtly (Thelen and Mahoney, 2010). Humans have 'agency' in institutional change (Lewis and Steinmo, 2012; Peters et al., 2005; Peters, 2000). The role of government as agent of institutional change to judicial selection systems is central to this study.

In providing an explanation for this, historical institutionalists will look back to the events, environmental issues and circumstances of the day to understand the context in which decisions were made. This study leans on the historical institutional approach by analysing the events and political circumstances of the period that led to the introduction of institutional change of different judicial selection systems. It also employs the rational choice approach in seeking to explain the motivation of political actors in government who introduced change that seems, on the surface, to have been against the interests of government.

Chapter 1 provides this analysis and describes the circumstances in which politicians implement institutional change through new rules that constrain their capacity to choose their preferred candidate for appointment to the judiciary. It examines whether the circumstances that surround the introduction of institutional change can explain the level of political commitment to that change.

IRELAND

The Irish case presents a unique explanatory challenge for two reasons. First, unlike the other countries examined in this book where governments introduced planned institutional change of the judicial selection system, the Irish experience emerged from a political crisis rather than a planned programme of reform. Second, the institutional change proposed was a system that would reduce government discretion in future judicial appointments, but by a smaller degree than the other countries that would introduce similar reforms in the years to follow.

In 1994, the issue of reform of the judicial appointments system suddenly emerged on the political agenda as a consequence of a political crisis between two political parties in a coalition government. This set in motion a set of reforms that were eventually enacted in legislation in 1995. Over time, however, the functioning of the new Irish system displayed remarkably little substantive change after the reforms, compared with the practices in place prior to the legislation being enacted. Far from granting powers to a non-political body of delegated governance, the Irish system involved setting up a body with statutory screening powers, but retained discretionary political powers of appointment in the hands of the government. Crucially, this discretionary power of government was further, and rather widely, enhanced by an overly narrow application of these new statutory screening powers by the new non-political body. As will be shown in Chapter 4, the combination of these two factors meant that the apparent reforms had scope for meaningful reduction in the discretion of government, especially for appointments to District Court, but this reduction was all but set aside by the interpretation of the new institutional rules by the non-political body, the Judicial Appointments Advisory Board.

In Ireland, as in many other constitutional systems, the judiciary occupies a central role in governance. The Irish Constitution expressly acknowledges the powers of judicial review of the judiciary. This has been used to identify unenumerated rights of Irish citizens in the Constitution, such as the right to bodily integrity or the right to earn a livelihood. Judicial review in Ireland has resulted in the judiciary setting rules for the conduct of referendums and elections, the rules relating to the investigative powers of the legislature and its capacity to censure its members. The judiciary in Ireland has the capacity to review the decision-making process of members of government and of administrative bodies of the State to ensure that they comply with the principles of constitutional justice. Since it is manifestly a vitally important branch of the constitutional order, the manner in which judges are appointed in Ireland is a subject of keen political, as well as constitutional, interest.

This book situates the Irish experience in a wider range of experiences of how institutions are designed to appoint judges and under what circumstances and, with what effect, reform is undertaken. The central argument is that institutional reform that reduces the discretion of government requires intentionally fashioned institutional design that is backed by strong political commitment. The incentives set up at the moment of institutional reform shape the practices of the judicial appointments body. But, over time, mixed or unclear incentives can give rise to a shift in institutional practice. In the Irish case, this has resulted in the further dilution of control of the delegated body over political discretion in judicial appointments.

This book builds on earlier work conducted on the Irish judiciary, including a 2004 study conducted by this author of the judges of the Irish High Court and Supreme Court that sought to answer the question 'Who is an Irish judge?' This study examined the social backgrounds of the senior judiciary, their career profiles, the mode of their appointment and their perceptions of the judicial appointments system. That study, in turn, built on seminal work conducted in 1969 by Professor Bartholomew from Notre Dame University who interviewed most of the members of the judiciary, as well as retired members of the judiciary, to answer the same question, 'Who is an Irish judge?' Drawing on his research design, the same questions were asked of the judges in 2004 to develop a picture of how the profile of the senior judges had changed in the intervening period. In the course of that study, the nature of the judicial appointments process began to emerge as an issue and consequently the judges were asked about their experiences of the judicial selection process and why they thought they had been appointed as a judge. Having conducted interviews with the 'selected', that is, those who had been appointed to judicial positions, the next stage was to explore the question of judicial selection in Ireland from the perspectives of the 'selectors'. The analysis conducted is done in a way that could make a contribution both to the comparative study of judicial appointments and to the legal and political literature in Ireland in relation to the judicial institution – about which very little scholarly work has been conducted. There is a broad international literature about the selection and retention of judges to domestic and international courts and a very detailed literature on the composition and decision-making of the US Supreme Court and its influences. The case of Ireland is not well reflected in this comparative international literature.

The key original data resource for this study consists of forty lengthy and detailed individual interviews with key office-holders largely from the period between 1982 and 2007.[2] Full details of the interview schedule and coding are included in Appendix 1. The study is also based on other primary sources such as legislation and government reports and a range of secondary sources.

This book comes at a timely moment in Ireland in 2016. The issue of change to the judicial selection system has appeared once again on the political agenda in the past three years. In 2013 the Minister for Justice and Equality elicited submissions in a consultation process to help inform that process. The question of judicial selection reform remained 'live' on the government legislative programme for the remainder of the lifetime of the 31st Dáil. It was also an issue for two political parties and an independent candidate in the election of 2016.

2 This study of the Irish case covers the years between 1982 and 2007. It encompasses a twelve-year period on either side of the pivotal institutional change introduced in 1995, while spanning all the major variations in government composition that have had a role in judicial appointments in recent decades. It was supplemented by interviews and data gathered on the operation of the JAAB and the Cabinet process for judicial selection in Ireland up to 2016.

This book may contribute to the debate about any reform of judicial selection processes in Ireland in the future by telling the story of institutional change and institutional drift of judicial selection in Ireland between 1994 and the present day and setting out a path of incremental institutional development to help achieve an enhanced selection model that encompasses the best elements of independent scrutiny of judicial candidates combined with popular participation in judicial selection through political involvement in judicial appointments.

CHAPTER 1

Institutional change to judicial selection systems

Judicial selection is undertaken through a variety of institutional mechanisms. Judicial selection systems can also vary depending on the naure of the court to which the judge is being appointed. Of principal concern to political actors is the membership of courts that have the power to overturn the actions of the legislature through judicial review. This is because of the particular influence individuals may have on the decision-making of the court. For this reason, the focus in this chapter and in this study is on judicial selection systems for these, more senior courts.

This chapter examines the role of governments in judicial selection systems in nine developed, democratic countries and jurisdictions that use the common law legal system and instances where that role has been contested or changed. These countries and jurisdictions are Australia, Canada, England and Wales, Ireland, Israel, New Zealand, Northern Ireland, Scotland and the United States. The cases of Israel and the United States are included. Israel is included because, although it is not a purely common law country as such, it appoints judges in a similar manner to common law systems – judges are appointed from the ranks of senior lawyers and have the same capacity to interfere with the actions of government through constitutional review. Second, Israel experienced comparable institutional change to the type of institutional change discussed and introduced in the common law countries examined.

The United States is included because judicial selection is a visible and perennially contested issue that occupies considerable space in the law and politics discourse and is the subject of significant domestic political interest. In 1977, President Carter introduced some changes to the appointments mechanism for Federal Court judges but these changes did not extend to Supreme Court judges. On that rationale, the United States could be excluded from this study but, unlike other common law countries, judicial review operates slightly differently in the United States where Federal Courts also have the capacity to declare an act unconstitutional through judicial review.

Therefore, although neither country is a direct comparator, they have sufficient similarities and are of sufficient importance to the analysis of institutional change and the role of government in judicial selection to ensure their inclusion contributes to the overall analysis of institutional change of judicial selection systems.

The period of such change ranges from the date of the first such institutional change in Israel in 1953 to the current day. The power of governments in judicial selection can vary considerably with some governments exerting complete control over all aspects of the selection of a judge – from choosing a nominee to ensuring that nominee fills a given vacancy. Other systems provide power for government to choose the nominee but are then dependent on the legislature for approval of the nomination before the vacancy can be filled. Other systems restrict the capacity of government to nominate people for appointment to the judiciary by providing that the government must choose from a list of candidates recommended by an external, independent non-governmental body. There is no single best model of judicial selection and different countries employ different methods.

In the range of countries examined there were different political perspectives on whether institutional change of judicial selection processes is desirable. Some governments actively sponsored and promoted institutional change. Others were resistant to change and did not favour changes to judicial selection processes. In each of these countries, political debate about judicial selection systems arose as a result of something external to government – a series of controversies involving the judiciary or broader constitutional change that thrust the role of the judiciary into light. What is clear, however, is that the perspective of government was crucial in determining whether or not institutional change was introduced. Where government favoured change, change generally occurred; where government did not favour change, change generally did not occur.

What is common about the majority of these countries is that, whether or not institutional change was introduced, there was extensive debate about whether there should be change and how such change should be shaped. The only place where this did not occur was in Ireland. Changes to the judicial selection process in Ireland were introduced quickly and without any of the policy change processes that characterized the debate in other countries, such as consultation papers or parliamentary or academic reports.

This chapter sets out the different judicial selection systems used for the senior courts capable of judicial review in the group of countries examined. It does this by assessing the role and power of the government in each system. This book presents a typology of three different judicial selection systems used in these common law countries based on the role and discretion of government in judicial selection and then examines the political debate about judicial selection processes. All of the countries (except Ireland) experienced some level of debate about the need for change or the form that change should take. This chapter will present the factors that triggered that political debate in the different countries. We can assess whether there were common features of these debates across countries – whether the debate was linked to other institutional changes and whether it arose as a result of political activity by government. For example, what common features did the debates have and were they protracted or did they happen quickly?

This helps us to understand where the pressures to introduce institutional change may originate and how they may gain strength. It also helps us to understand the motivation of government either in introducing change or resisting calls for change. Where institutional reform became a political issue, what were the triggers for this? Were there common issues that led to institutional change of judicial selection systems becoming a priority of politicians? Not all political debate results in institutional change. What we want to know is whether there was a link between the government's preferences and whether or not change occurred.

Where institutional change was introduced, it generally took the form of the establishment of an independent screening commission to perform part of the process of judicial selection. The structure of such commissions can vary but the general purpose is to create some separation between judicial selection and politics. However, different institutional designs of judicial screening commissions can result in different outcomes for the separation of judicial selection and politics.

It is important to remember that governments control the shape of any new institutional design. Depending on their motivation in introducing institutional change, political actors may have incentives to set the boundaries at different points of the spectrum of possible institutional design and boundary management. This chapter examines how the different systems introduced impacted on the discretion of governments in choosing judges under changed institutional processes. Having examined the circumstances behind the introduction of institutional change, we can see whether there is a link between the motivation of government and the effectiveness of the institutional change in separating judicial selection from politics. Did governments who unwillingly introduced institutional change introduce weak institutional change that would not materially impact on their power to choose judges? Did governments who were committed to reducing political power in judicial selection introduce strong institutional change that would fundamentally change the role of future governments in judicial selection?

This chapter examines institutional change of judicial selection systems using the following analytical structure:

1. What is the role of government in judicial selection systems in common law countries?
2. Why do politicians introduce institutional change to judicial selection systems?
    a. What triggers exist for creating political debate on the possibility of institutional change of judicial selection systems?

   b What triggers exist for the introduction by government of institutional change of judicial selection systems?
   c What explanations exist for governments' resistance to institutional change of judicial selection systems where there has been political debate on the possibility of such change?
3 In countries that have experienced institutional change to judicial selection systems, what is the nature of that change?
   a What was the purpose of institutional change?
   b How did the design of the new institutional process achieve this?
   c Was the institutional change effective in achieving its purpose?

The next section categorizes types of judicial selection systems according to the power of government at each stage of the process of judicial selection. It then examines each country to determine which judicial selection system operates in that country and describes how that system works in each country. In doing this we will answer the first question of the analytical framework in this chapter: what is the role of government in judicial selection systems in common law countries?

ROLE OF GOVERNMENT IN JUDICIAL SELECTION SYSTEMS IN COMMON LAW COUNTRIES

Government rarely has complete discretion in judicial selection – either in choosing the system or in choosing the judges. The role of government in judicial selection is generally governed by the constitution or by statute, or both. While government can sponsor either constitutional or legislative change to amend the rules in relation to its role in judicial selection, it must do so within constitutional parameters. Changes to judicial selection systems are an unusual occurrence in the established democracies examined in this study and, indeed, in each case where there were changes to the judicial selection system, it was generally the first time such major structural change took place.

There are certain minimum technical qualifications and/or experience that are required before a person is eligible for consideration for judicial appointment. Of course, governments also control the rules governing eligibility for appointment in addition to all other elements of the rules governing judicial selection. With the exception of the United States, all of the countries in this analysis have long-standing minimum criteria.

Once the basic eligibility requirements are satisfied, the power of governments in the judicial selection process has two important elements: first, the power to nominate an individual for a given vacancy and, second, the power to ensure that the nominated individual becomes the judge that fills the vacancy in question. Both of these phases are important for the government but, of the two phases, the power to nominate a judicial candidate must be the more important. Failure to have a nomination appointed is a blow for the political credibility of a government but to have no role in the nomination of a candidate can entirely remove the influence of government in judicial selection.

Based on the role of government in the process, judicial selection systems can be broadly categorized as follows:

1 executive nomination and appointment
2 executive nomination with legislature approval for appointment
3 executive nomination following application by candidate and independent judicial screening commission (JSC) recommendation.

Table 1.1 summarizes the power of the government at the different stages of the judicial selection process in each of the three systems. We can see while the government retains full control of the process in the first system, the second and third systems place constraints on the capacity of the government to nominate a judicial candidate or ensure that a nominee can be appointed.

Table 1.1: Power of governments in judicial selection systems

Judicial selection system	Power of government in nomination	Power of government in appointment	Power of government in judicial selection
1. Executive nomination and appointment	Can nominate any eligible candidate.	Government nomination appointed by Head of State.	Complete power.
2. Executive nomination with legislature approval for appointment	Can nominate any eligible candidate.	Government nomination dependent on legislature to approve nomination for appointment.	Power to nominate but overall power constrained by having to secure parliamentary approval.
3. Executive nomination following application by candidate and independent judicial screening commission (JSC) recommendation	Can nominate a candidate that has been recommended by the JSC.	Government nomination appointed by Head of State.	Government nomination will be approved, but power to nominate constrained by the number of recommendations of the JSC and whether the government is bound by those recommendations.

Executive appointment

Judicial selection systems based on executive appointment are ones in which the selection of judges is entirely controlled by the executive. In this system judges are appointed or nominated for appointment by the head of government – typically acting on the advice of the Attorney General. Government has control of all aspects of the judicial selection process – they have the freedom to choose a person for nomination for a judicial vacancy and the political power to ensure that their nomination becomes the judge. It is important to note that the position of Attorney General is usually a political position. In parliamentary systems, the Attorney General may or may not be a member of legislature but is chosen for the position of Attorney General by the government (usually the head of government) and, because of the political nature of the appointment, the term of the Attorney General is generally coterminous with the government of the day. The Attorney General acts as legal adviser to the government but is not a detached advisory position – it is a political appointment.

The executive appointment judicial selection system emerged from the historical influence of the Commonwealth judicial appointment system of strong Westminster-type executives controlling appointments to the courts, free from outside interference or constraints. It is not public, is not required to

Table 1.2: Procedures in countries that use the executive nomination and appointments system

Country	Constitutional court	Minimum eligibility requirements	Procedure for nomination	Procedure for appointment
Australia	High Court of Australia	Must be a member of another court.	Cabinet makes decision for nomination, following advice of Attorney General.	Nomination is appointed by Governor General.
Canada	Supreme Court of Canada	Minimum ten years' experience as a legal practitioner or must be a member of another court.	Cabinet makes decision for nomination, following advice of Minister for Justice. Supreme Court nominees take questions from parliamentary committee, but committee cannot veto nomination of government.	Nomination is appointed by Governor General.
New Zealand	Supreme Court New Zealand	Minimum seven years' experience as a legal practitioner.	Cabinet makes decision for nomination, following advice of Attorney General.	Nomination is appointed by Governor General.

Source: High Court of Australia Act 1979; Supreme Court Act 1985; Supreme Court Act 2003.

engage the views of the opposition, judiciary or other bodies and leaves a wide discretion open to the individual, usually the Attorney General, Minister for Justice or Lord Chancellor, to conduct the process as they see fit. Government power in judicial selection is greatest under the executive appointment system. The only constraints on a government in making its decision are any statutory requirements as to professional background and experience or obligations to consult, in a non-binding way, with the legal profession or other actors. However, the government is also in control of these rules and has the political power to change them.

Countries that use executive appointments systems today include Australia, New Zealand and Canada. Table 1.2 presents an overview of how each system operates before we discuss each system in more detail.

Australia

In Australia, for an individual to be considered for a judicial post, they must meet minimum statutory qualifications. To be qualified for appointment as a judge to the High Court of Australia, a person must have been a legal practitioner of at least five years' standing and have been a judge of another court (High Court of Australia Act 1979). In addition, to be eligible for appointment as a judge of the Family Court, a person must be a suitable person to manage family law matters by reason of training, experience and personality.

Chapter III of the Commonwealth of Australia Constitution Act 1900 provides that judges of the High Court must be appointed by the Governor General in Council. In practice, this means that the Cabinet will make a decision on the recommendation of the Attorney General. The decision of the Cabinet is taken to the Federal Executive Council, in which the Constitution vests the actual judicial appointment function. The process leading up to Cabinet consideration of a candidate involves the Attorney General's consultation with the head of the court involved and with the legal professional bodies such as the Law Council or the relevant State Bar Associations or Law Societies. The Attorney General may also consult serving and former judges in respect of new judicial appointments (High Court of Australia Act 1979). At the time of the drafting of the Act the object of this requirement was said 'to ensure that the Court continues to be truly national in character and fully equipped to discharge its constitutional functions as a federal Supreme Court' (Mr Ian Viner MP, Minister for Employment and Youth Affairs, House of Representatives, 25 October 1978, p. 2500).

However, the consultation procedure is not required as a matter of law and the form and extent of any such consultation is at the discretion of the serving Attorney General. The government in Australia retains full power to nominate candidates for vacant positions on the High Court of Australia and to ensure those nominees are appointed.

Canada

In Canada, the Governor General appoints judges to the Supreme Court, acting on the advice of the federal Cabinet. The Minister for Justice makes a recommendation to Cabinet with respect to judicial appointment. Before recommending an appointment to Cabinet, the Minister may consult with members of the judiciary and the Bar, with his or her appropriate provincial or territorial counterparts as well as with members of the public. With respect to provincial and territorial court judges who apply for appointment to a superior court, the Minister may consult with that candidate's current Chief Judge as well as with the Chief Justice of the court for which the candidate is being considered (Ziegel, 2006; Morton, 2002).

While the Canadian government enjoys near total discretion in respect of the majority of its judicial appointments, it faces one restriction in relation to the Supreme Court and that is to ensure the regional balance on the court of nine judges. Three of the judges are required to come from Quebec (Supreme Court Act 1985). An informal tradition has emerged around the regional balance on the rest of the court, but this does not restrict the power of the government to choose candidates in the same way as the requirement in respect of Quebec.

In 2006, the Canadian Prime Minister announced a change in the process of appointing Supreme Court judges. Today, Supreme Court nominees are required to take questions from an all-party committee of the House of Commons. Critically, the committee does not have the power to veto a nominee. The final decision on whether to go ahead with the appointment or withdraw a nominee's name rests with the Prime Minister. The government in Canada retains full power to nominate candidates for vacant positions on the Supreme Court of Canada and to ensure those nominations are appointed. The revised processes were introduced by the government but have not been put on a statutory footing.

New Zealand

In New Zealand judges are appointed by the Governor General on the recommendation of the Attorney General (Judicature Act 1908). Eligibility for judicial selection is restricted to barristers or solicitors of not less than seven years' practice experience (section 6 of the Judicature Act 1908). There is also a minimum age of 28 years for appointment to the judiciary, but in reality appointees will be considerably older (Hodder, 1974).

The Attorney General identifies a pool of possible candidates for appointment to the Supreme Court of New Zealand by consulting with a broad range of judges and legal professional representatives (McGrath, 1998). Allan (2006) comments that the longlist produced from this process is shortened at a second stage involving a meeting between the Attorney General, the Chief Justice, the President of the Court of Appeal and the Solicitor

General. It is ultimately the Attorney General who decides on the shortlist and the ranking of candidates thereon. The Attorney General then makes recommendations to Cabinet. In reality, power is concentrated in the hands of the Attorney General in making senior judicial appointments. There are transparent published standards for making expressions of interest, for conducting consultations and for shortlisting candidates. Nevertheless, the Attorney General is appointed on the recommendation of the Prime Minister, is a Minister of the Crown, usually holds a Cabinet post and is invariably a member of parliament (The Governance of Britain: A Consultation on the Role of the Attorney General, 2007). The Attorney General's role in judicial selection processes must be considered in that overall context. Institutionally, the political office-holders of the day hold power at each stage of the selection process.

Summary

Governments have strong power in the judicial selection process under the executive nomination and appointment model of judicial selection. This system allows the government nearly full discretion to appoint their preferred candidate, and enables governments to appoint candidates who are familiar to them and about whom they have a degree of knowledge, experience or confidence. In theory, this makes the government accountable for their judicial selection, but in reality judicial selection tends not to be an issue that typically dominates election campaigns in these countries. Nevertheless, a series of poorly regarded appointments could bring unwanted political difficulty to a government in a way that could force a response by politicians.

Executive nomination with legislature approval for appointment

United States

In this system the executive has control over the nomination of a person for judicial office, although the nomination cannot proceed unless the legislature approves it. Therefore, the executive has full control over the first stage of the process but not the second. In reality, the executive is restricted in its freedom to choose individuals for judicial nomination because of the political dynamics inherent in securing the approval of the legislature for that nomination. Table 1.3 gives an overview of the operation of this model of judicial selection.

As mentioned, recent Supreme Court appointments in Canada have been required to attend before an ad hoc parliamentary committee to answer questions in relation to their suitability for office. The appointment does not depend on the outcome of this hearing and no formal role for the committee is included in the appointment process. This change in the system is not on a statutory footing and, crucially, the government is not dependent on its outcome to appoint the judge. There is on-going review of the Supreme Court judicial selection process in Canada and it may be possible that a more formal

Table 1.3: Executive nomination with legislature approval for appointment

Country	Constitutional court	Minimum eligibility requirements	Procedure for nomination	Procedure for appointment
United States of America	Supreme Court of United States of America and Federal Courts of the United States of America.	None, but in practice nominations are restricted to experienced legal professionals.	President nominates candidate by giving name to Senate.	Senate Judiciary Committee considers candidate, including questioning of candidate and makes recommendation. Senate votes on approval of candidate.

Source: Segal and Spaeth (2002); Article 2, section 2, Constitution of the United States of America.

role for this form of hearing be incorporated in statute in the future.[1] From the comments of committee members, it is clear that any such role for a committee is not intended to mirror the more 'aggressive' format of the Senate Committee hearings in the United States.[2]

The United States is the only common law country in this study not to have mandated minimum qualification or experience requirements to become a judge – one need not even be a lawyer to be appointed to the Supreme Court, though no Supreme Court justice has lacked at least some informal training in law (Epstein and Segal, 2005) and it is considered politically inconceivable for a President in the modern era to nominate a person without legal training and experience. The President faces constraints in nominating a candidate: these constraints arise because the President knows that the nominated candidate will have to be approved by legislature (King, 1987).[3] In the United States, the Supreme Court confirmation process has become one of the most contentious aspects of American politics – representing a 'seismic struggle' between the President and the Senate over the ideological composition of the Court

1 As we will see later in this chapter, a comparable model was also mooted in Israel in 2011. 2 (Canada. Department of Justice. (2013) 'Ad hoc committee on the appointment of Supreme Court of Canada justices'. Available at http://www.justice.gc.ca/eng/news-nouv/ja-nj/2013/doc_32972.html (accessed 16 Jan. 2014). 3 Segal and Spaeth (2002) offer some competing explanations of presidential choice, commenting that while it may be possible to explain a president's choice after the nomination, a priori accounts of presidential behaviour in nominating justices are far more difficult. According to one account, presidents interested in maintaining their popularity and prestige will attempt to avoid losing a confirmation battle if at all possible (Cameron et al., 1990). Therefore, if one places the median senator, the president and potential nominees on a liberal-conservative ideological spectrum, the president should always nominate someone in the space between himself and the Senate, rather than a nominee outside that range (Segal and Spaeth, 2002).

(Johnson and Roberts, 2004; Strauss and Sunstein, 1992).[4] In 2016, the death of Supreme Court Justice Antonin Scalia has reignited debate about the 'struggle' to fill vacancies – a Democrat President with the opportunity to fill a Supreme Court vacancy in his last months in office versus a Republican majority Senate with no desire to facilitate the filling of the vacancy in advance of the inauguration of the incoming President in 2017.

In framing the Constitution of the United States, the debate over how judges should be selected was remarkable both for its intensity and importance to the goal of achieving an independent judiciary (Epstein and Segal, 2005). The compromise that was finally resolved gave the appointing power to the executive on the 'advice and consent of the Senate'.[5]

After a vacancy arises on the Supreme Court, the first step in the judicial selection process is for the executive office to identify a list of possible candidates for the post. Typically, Presidents will tend to delegate the initial stages of the nomination process to senior staff or the Attorney General who generate a list of names. Names are also obtained from recommendations submitted to the Justice Department. The shortlist is passed to the FBI for exhaustive investigative checks on personal background. Prior to 2001, the American Bar Association (ABA) pre-screened nominees but this now occurs immediately prior to the Senate vote. The ABA ranks candidates along a 'well qualified', 'qualified' or 'not qualified' dimension. Its ranking is regarded as a basic barometer of competence and only 1.5 per cent of nominations since Eisenhower's administration received a 'not qualified' rating (Goldman, 2005). Segal and Spaeth (2002) note that although the final choice is the President's, the influence of others can be felt.[6]

Once the President gives his nominee's name to the Senate, the Senate Judiciary Committee convenes to discuss the candidate. The purpose of this exercise is to provide a review and recommendation system for the Senate prior to going to a vote. The composition of the Senate Judiciary Committee

4 In 'The Bork effect', Epstein et al. (2006) examined all of the Supreme Court appointments until 2006 to determine if the consensus that the nomination of Bork in 1987 triggered a new, ideologically based regime in the Senate's voting over presidential nominees – 'a regime that deemphasizes ethics, competence, and integrity and stresses instead politics, philosophy and ideology' (Epstein et al., 2006). They found that while Supreme Court confirmation processes have always been highly politically contentious the intensity of the Bork confirmation process galvanized politics in judicial appointments to a hitherto unseen proportion and extended controversy over federal appointments from the Supreme Court down through the lower Federal Courts. Also, on the impact of the Bork nomination on the writings of Supreme Court justices see Gaille (1997) and on the decision by Supreme Court judges to time their retirement strategically see Squire (1988). 5 The words 'advice and consent' were never defined, and the intent of the framers as to the extent and scope of this process never established. Shapiro (1980). 6 See also Szmer and Songer (2005) on Presidential assessments of nominees.

reflects the partisan balance in the Senate and its powers include conducting hearings with the Supreme Court nominee. In reality, candidates submit themselves voluntarily for such hearings rather than waiting for an invitation from the committee. However, while the candidates voluntarily submit themselves for questioning they have in the past two decades become 'strategically silent' on salient issues (such as abortion) that might come before the Court (Epstein and Segal, 2005). Such silence, while perhaps frustrating to senators, can serve to keep nominees out of political trouble – for example, had Supreme Court nominee Clarence Thomas stated his view on abortion it is argued that he would have alienated half the Senate (Epstein and Segal, 2005). This change can be tracked to the failed nomination of Robert Bork in 1987, who was quite willing to answer questions on his views:

> perhaps unavoidably so since he had criticized certain Supreme Court decisions in such strong terms that he could not avoid telling senators under oath what he had repeatedly told the rest of the world in articles and speeches. (Esptein and Segal, 2005, p. 97)

The role of the Senate Judiciary Committee is important in the judicial selection process, and, in practice, the vote of the Judiciary Committee is critical to the candidate's chances of success.[7]

The final stage of the judicial selection process is the full Senate vote. As has been discussed, partisan and ideological concerns are central to the Senators' decision on a candidate. However, there may also be other influences affecting the decision of a Senator to confirm or reject a Supreme Court nominee. The Senate Confirmation process for US Supreme Court nominees was tested (Overby et al., 1992) for the level of 'constituent influence' experienced by individual Senators when voting to confirm or reject the President's Supreme Court nominee. Overby et al. (1992) argue that, traditionally, Senate confirmation votes are determined by the individual Senators' partisan loyalties but that the constituency concerns of the Senator may prove to be extremely important.[8] This is especially true if the nomination is made by

7 One of the important elements of the Committee hearing process is the exposure it generates for media scrutiny of the candidate. Epstein and Segal comment that this has increased dramatically in the past two decades (Epstein and Segal, 2005). 'Between the time of Ruth Bader Ginsburg's nomination on 14 June 1993 and her confirmation on 3 August 1993, the *New York Times* ran forty-two more stories on her than it did in 1962 about her predecessor Byron White' (Epstein and Segal, 2006). 8 Overby et al. (1992) conducted a study of Senators' voting behaviours in the Supreme Court nomination of Clarence Thomas. This highly salient case involved a clearly identifiable political constituency important to key 'swing' Senators – the African-American constituency. They found that Senators with a large African-American constituency who would soon be up for re-election were significantly more likely to confirm Thomas' nomination, irrespective of their partisan commitments, thus illustrating how the appointments process can become highly politicized

a 'weak' President – one who is not elected,[9] who faces a Senate controlled by the opposition or who is in their terminal year of office (Maltese, 1995).

Summary

This system is one in which the legislature has significant power over judicial selection. It has the power to approve or veto a nomination by the President, including the power to publicly question the candidate in Committee. Although the executive office has full power to nominate a candidate, the President will be acutely conscious of the political need to nominate a person who is likely to be approved by the Senate.

Executive nomination following application by candidate and independent judicial screening commission recommendation

An executive nomination following judicial screening commission recommendation system is a two-stage process involving an initial screening of applicants for judicial vacancies by a body that is independent of the executive or legislature, followed by the nomination by the government for appointment – typically by the head of state. Candidates for judicial office apply for consideration for judicial office and are pre-screened by an independent body before the executive considers their application. On foot of the screening system, candidates' names are either rejected by the screening body or forwarded by that body to the government. The government then chooses the nominee from the recommended candidates and the head of government or head of state makes the appointment.

Judicial screening commissions vary in terms of their function, powers and composition. The model operates by establishing an independent body, separate from government, to consider candidates for judicial office and make recommendations. Some of the systems have more extensive powers than others, particularly in relation to their power to recommend or select and their power to generate their own candidates. Some judicial selection commissions have been incorporated at constitutional level, while others are established by legislation. Institutional design of these bodies is important and each element of that design has an effect on the actual role of the commission vis-à-vis the government and in the balance of power between the two institutions as to control of judicial appointments.

This judicial selection system is now used in various forms in England and Wales, Ireland, Israel, Northern Ireland and Scotland. Table 1.4 presents an overview of the nomination and appointment procedures in each country.

(Overby et al., 1992). The ideological relationship between the President, the nominee and the Senate will play a key role in the President's decision of who to shortlist for nomination (Nemacheck, 2008). 9 A vice-president who has become president on the death of a president.

Table 1.4: Judicial screening commission nomination with executive appointment – procedures for nomination and appointment of judges

Country	Constitutional court	Minimum eligibility requirements	Procedure for nomination	Procedure for appointment
England and Wales	High Court, Court of Appeal and Supreme Court of United Kingdom	Minimum 15 years' experience as a legal practitioner or 2 years' as a member of a senior court.	Prime Minister nominated candidate that has been selected by Judicial Appointments Commission.	Nomination is appointed by Queen.
Ireland	High Court, Court of Appeal and Supreme Court of Ireland	Minimum 12 years' experience as a legal practitioner.	Cabinet makes decision for nomination, following receipt of JSC recommendations and on advice of Minister for Justice, Attorney General and with consent of Taoiseach (Prime Minister).	Nomination is appointed by President.
Israel	Supreme Court of Israel	Minimum 10 years' experience as a legal practitioner and must be an Israeli national.	Members of Judicial Selection Committee may nominate candidates.	Appointed by Judicial Selection Committee.
Northern Ireland	High Court and Court of Appeal of Northern Ireland[10]	Minimum 10 years' experience as a legal practitioner.	Office of First Minister and Deputy First Minister, acting jointly, recommend names of candidates selected by Northern Ireland Judicial Appointments Commission.	Nomination is appointed by Queen.
Scotland	Supreme Courts of Scotland (High Court of Justiciary and Court of Session)[11]	An advocate or solicitor with rights of audience before the Supreme Courts of Scotland of 5 years' standing or a sheriff for a period of at least 5 years continuously.	Cabinet makes decision for nomination, following receipt of JSC recommendations.	Nomination is appointed by Queen.

Source: Crime and Courts Act 2013 and Constitutional Reform Act 2005; Courts and Court Officers Act 1995 and 2002; Judges Act 1953; Justice (Northern Ireland) Acts 2002 & 2004; Judiciary and Courts (Scotland) Act 2008.

10 The Court of Appeal of Northern Ireland has power of judicial review. However, its judgments can be appealed to the Supreme Court of the United Kingdom and it is subordinate to the Supreme Court of the United Kingdom on constitutional matters. 11 The Court of Session in Scotland has power of judicial review. However, its judgments can be appealed to the Supreme Court of the United Kingdom and it is subordinate to the Supreme Court of the United Kingdom on constitutional matters. Constitutional Reform

England and Wales

In England and Wales, following a nomination from the Prime Minister, the Queen appoints judges to the High Court and the Supreme Court. The Prime Minister nominates an individual for appointment as a judge of the High Court following receipt of the recommendation of the Judicial Appointments Commission.

For Supreme Court vacancies, a special selection commission is convened including the Court President and Deputy President (the two most senior members of the Court) and a member each of the judicial appointments commissions in England and Wales, Scotland and Northern Ireland, with at least one of these people being a lay person. The Prime Minister has no discretion in these appointments and must recommend, for appointment by the Queen, the person who is recommended by this process (Section 26, Constitutional Reform Act 2005).

Under section 27(9) of the Constitutional Reform Act 2005, the commission must have regard to any guidance given by the Lord Chancellor as to matters to be taken into account (subject to any other provision in the Act) in making a selection.[12]

Israel

Supreme Court judges are appointed by the Judicial Selection Committee. The Committee is composed of three judges of the Supreme Court, two members of Cabinet, two members of legislature and two representatives of the Israel Bar Association. The Chairman, the President of the Supreme Court or any three members of the Committee may propose a candidate. A majority vote of the members of the Committee is required to appoint a candidate.

Supreme Court judges in Israel are required to have at least ten years' legal practice experience and must be an Israeli national. There is also a provision for a significant jurist to be appointed to the Supreme Court.[13] For example, Aharon Barak, who was President of the Supreme Court, was a law professor who was appointed to the position of Attorney General in 1975 and to the Supreme Court in 1979. However, the practice is regarded as very rare (Salzberger, 2006).

There is pressure to reflect the critical social cleavages of Israel in the composition of the Supreme Court of Israel. Since the 1950s there have been calls to have an Israeli Arab judge on the Supreme Court bench, while the religious parties of the Knesset have always called for the reservation of a seat for an Orthodox judge. In practice, there has usually been a member of the Supreme Court, albeit unofficially, each from an Orthodox and Spharadic

Act 2005 s 40 (3). 12 As amended by the Crime and Courts Act 2013. See Gee, Hazell, Malleson and O'Brien (2005), Chapter 7, for a detailed description of the process of the Judicial Appointments Commission in England and Wales. 13 The Attorney General can also be appointed but there is a statutory 'cooling off' period of 18 months before he or she can be appointed.

background. The first appointment of an Israeli Arab to the Supreme Court was in 1999 – this was for a fixed nine-month term. In May 2004 an Israeli Arab appointed as a temporary judge was given a permanent Supreme Court seat (Salzberger, 2006). There has been one woman member of the Supreme Court since 1977. These representative considerations operate as informal constraints on the selection of judges and have no official or binding status.

Israeli scholars take the view that over the last fifty years the Judicial Selection Committee has broadly been a great success. The judiciary established a long-standing reputation for independence and integrity in its early years (Edelman, 2001). The judicial selection system is viewed as having contributed strongly to that reputation. The Committee is also used for judicial promotions, which is also a matter outside of direct party political control. In a country concerned about respect for the rule of law, in a heavily partisan environment and in politically tense geo-political conditions, the politics (real or perceived) of judicial promotion may be an even greater risk to the independence to the judiciary than the initial selection of judges.

Ireland

In Ireland, the President appoints judges on the advice of the government. In most instances, government makes the nomination following receipt of recommendations from the Judicial Appointments Advisory Board.

Where a vacancy arises, the government may make a decision to refer the vacancy to the Judicial Appointments Advisory Board (JAAB) or it may decide not to do so. If the vacancy is so referred, the JAAB begins its process. It may cause the vacancy to be advertised or it may rely on applications it has received in the past twelve months. The JAAB then meets to consider the applications and the candidates on file and makes a recommendation to the government concerning all of the candidates that are suitable for appointment. Although the legislation says that the JAAB is to recommend at least seven names in respect of each vacancy, there is no limit to the number of applicants that the JAAB can recommend. In practice, the JAAB tends to recommend all of those people who are suitable (which can be greater than seven).

Whether or not the vacancy is referred to the JAAB for consideration, the government retains its discretion to fill the vacancy in one of two other ways. It may promote a judge from another court. This is the most common way of filling vacancies on the Supreme Court in Ireland. Alternatively, the government may fill the vacancy by appointing a practising lawyer of at least twelve years' experience, who may not have applied to the JAAB for consideration.

Thus, unlike England and Wales (where the Judicial Appointments Commission recommends one name to government) and unlike Israel (where the Judicial Selection Committee selects the judge), the Irish government retains significant discretion to choose any person to fill a judicial vacancy.

Northern Ireland

Judges of the High Court of Northern Ireland are appointed by the Queen upon recommendation by the First Minister and Deputy First Minister acting jointly. The First Minister and Deputy First Minister recommend the persons selected and recommended by the Northern Ireland Judicial Appointments Commission (NIJAC). NIJAC is composed of five judicial members, two representatives of the legal profession and four lay members (who are appointed through the public appointment service).

Where a vacancy arises on the High Court, the NIJAC advertises the vacancy and receives applications. It reviews applications and may require applicants to take a test or attend an interview or role-play exercise at an assessment centre. The NIJAC may also consult with individuals selected by the applicant. The NIJAC makes a recommendation to the Office of the First Minister and Deputy First Minister in respect of judicial appointments, who may choose not to refer the recommended candidate for appointment by the Queen. However, if so, they must write to the NIJAC giving their reasons. NIJAC may then make a further recommendation having considered the reasons given. NIJAC can then recommend the same individual or a different individual for appointment.

The NIJAC is specifically concerned with ensuring that the members of the judiciary in Northern Ireland are representative of the communities they serve. There is no binding rule as to quotas, but it is a key theme of the judicial selection considerations in that jurisdiction.[14]

Scotland

Judicial appointments are made by the Queen following a recommendation by the First Minister of Scotland. The First Minister of Scotland receives the name of the candidate selected for nomination by the Judicial Appointment Board for Scotland (JABS). There are ten members of JABS: three judicial and two legal members and five lay members including the lay Chairing Member.

The First Minister may refuse the recommendation made by the Judicial Appointment Board for Scotland, but, if so, he or she must write to the Board giving their reasons. The Judicial Appointment Board for Scotland may then make a further recommendation having considered the reasons of the First Minister. However, the second recommendation of the Judicial Appointment Board for Scotland may be the same individual.

Summary

In this form of judicial selection system, governments generally have less power than in the other systems analysed in this chapter. Earlier, we described the power of government in judicial selection systems as having two elements:

14 See Gee, Hazell, Malleson and O'Brien (2015), Chapter 9, on judicial selection processes in Northern Ireland and Scotland.

the power to choose a nomination for judicial office and the power to ensure that the nomination of government is appointed and fills a given vacancy on the constitutional court.

The impact of the judicial screening commission model is that it reduces the pool of individuals from which the government can choose a nomination. However, as we saw with the case of Ireland, there may be elements of the institutional design of the system that preserves government power to choose a preferred candidate. How much government discretion is reduced is directly dependent on the institutional design of the judicial screening commission. This will be discussed in detail later in this chapter.

WHY DO POLITICIANS INTRODUCE INSTITUTIONAL CHANGE TO JUDICIAL SELECTION SYSTEMS?

Institutional change can occur in different ways and for different reasons and can occur slowly or quickly, and can arise as a result of internal or external factors. We need to establish why political debate on institutional change of judicial selection systems begins and what factors ultimately lead to an initiation of institutional change by governments or resistance by governments to institutional change. This section addresses the second point in the analytical framework of this chapter and presents the following questions:

a What triggers led to political debate on the possibility of institutional change of judicial selection systems?
b What triggers led to the introduction of institutional change of judicial selection systems?
c Where there has been political debate on the possibility of such change, what explanations exist for failure to introduce institutional change?

Table 1.5 presents an overview of the triggers for political debate and institutional change in each country.

England and Wales

Institutional change in England and Wales was the product of long-term debate and incremental change of the judicial selection system, combined with major constitutional reform. The arguments for change had been made over many years and by the mid-1990s, there was widespread support for reform of the process among lawyers, interest groups and politicians (Malleson, 1999).

The judicial selection process had been the focus of a good deal of attention in the 1990s and there were a number of minor reforms in the years preceding the establishment of the Judicial Appointments Commission. From 1994, all those appointed to the positions of more junior judicial appointments (such as

Table 1.5: Political debate and institutional change

Country	Period of political debate	Trigger for political debate	Trigger for institutional change of judicial selection system	Date of introduction of institutional change of judicial selection system
Australia	1993–5	Concern about conduct of judges, gender imbalance on the court and the increasing power of judges.	Not applicable.	Not applicable.
Canada	1982–2006	Charter of Rights expanded role of Supreme Court; institutional changes to judicial selection systems at provincial level.	Not applicable.	Not applicable.
England and Wales	1991–2005	Political initiative to separate judicial selection and politics and to enhance diversity of judiciary.	Major programme of constitutional and legal reform initiated by incoming government in 1997.	2005
Ireland	1994–5	Political crisis relating to two senior judicial appointments.	Threat by minor coalition partner to collapse government unless institutional change introduced.	1995
Israel	1948–53	Protection of the rule of law in a fledgling State with significant domestic political conflict by separating judicial selection from political control.	Enactment by government of Judges Act 1953.	1953
New Zealand	2002–4	Preparation for establishment of new Supreme Court to replace Privy Council appeals.	Not applicable.	Not applicable.
Northern Ireland	1998–2002	Belfast Agreement (1998) committed to reviewing all aspects of administration of justice.	Recommendation of Northern Ireland Criminal Justice Review to establish judicial screening commission.	2002
Scotland	1998–2002	Political initiative to separate judicial selection and politics and to enhance diversity of judiciary.	Commitment by new Scottish government to change judicial selection systems in 1999 Programme for Government.	2002
US	1977	United States Circuit Judge Nominating Commission.	No institutional change introduced for Supreme Court appointments but temporary institutional change for Federal Courts of Appeal.	1977

Source: Malleson, K. (1999); New Zealand Ministry of Justice (2004); Northern Ireland Office, Secretary of State Ireland. (2000); Scotland. Judicial Appointments Board for Scotland (2009); Gerhardt (2003); Morton (2006); Edelman (1994).

District Court judges and recorders) had to be interviewed by a new system of interview panels (Malleson, 1999). In 1997, the role of these interview panels was expanded to examine initial applications and screen them for suitability.

Other reforms included the introduction of advertising of judicial posts up to High Court level and job descriptions for each judicial rank. The changes were led by the Lord Chancellor's Department, starting with the publication in 1986 of a guide to how judicial appointments were to be conducted (Lord Chancellor's Department, 1986). These changes, which were continued by the next two Lord Chancellors, were 'partly a response to the practical demands of the increasing numbers of judges, but they were also an attempt to address the growing criticisms of the process in the light of the expansion of judicial power' (Malleson, 1999) and, in particular, a concern about the lack of transparency in judicial appointments.

The institutional change had clear political backing even if it was some time before it was finally implemented. In 1995, the Labour Party supported the judicial screening commission model in its policy document 'Access to Justice' (Labour Party, 1995). The election of that party to government in 1997 meant it would be firmly on the policy agenda. The new Lord Chancellor quickly announced that his Department would conduct a consultation on the merits of such a system, including research on comparable systems (Thomas, 1997; Malleson, 1997). In 1998, the first indication of substantive reform of the judicial appointments process for senior judges in England and Wales occurred when the Lord Chancellor issued an advertisement inviting applicants to apply for judicial appointment to the High Court.

In 2003, a former Appeal Court judge, Sir Iain Glidewell, conducted a review (on behalf of the Bar Council – the representative group of barristers) of the judicial appointments process for High Court judges, following the enactment of the Human Rights Act 1998 and the perceived increased role of the judiciary in administrative matters (Slapper and Kelly, 2013). This review suggested that, given the perception of an increased role for the judiciary in matters relating to human rights, review of administrative decisions and devolution issues, it was no longer constitutionally acceptable for judges to be directly appointed by the government of the day (Slapper and Kelly, 2013). In June 2003, the new Lord Chancellor issued a consultation paper on the establishment of a judicial appointments commission, which subsequently formed the basis for the new institutional model adopted in the Constitutional Reform Act 2005. It is important to note that this occurred in the context of a highly politicized atmosphere involving controversy between the Prime Minister and the Lord Chancellor.[15] The seeds of reform had been sown by the

15 See Stevens (2005) on the tension around this institutional change. 'Politically, New Labour, when it was returned in 1997, promised constitutional reform and joined-up government ... In June 2003, as part of a Cabinet reshuffle, the Prime Minister – Tony Blair – announced that the Office of the Lord Chancellor would be abolished, a judicial

work done both in the Lord Chancellor's office in the 1980s and the political commitment of the Labour Party in the 1990s. Nevertheless, the actual impetus for introducing such reform was as a product of political events of the day.

This Act created a new Supreme Court and established a judicial screening commission. The decision of the government brought England and Wales into line with the other jurisdictions of the United Kingdom, that is Northern Ireland and Scotland, both of which had established similar judicial selection models in the preceding years.

Notwithstanding the institutional changes of 2005, there remains political concern about the judicial selection system in England and Wales. This concern relates particularly to questions of diversity of the members of the judiciary (Thomas, 2005). The Lord Chancellor established an Advisory Panel on Judicial Diversity to identify barriers to judicial diversity and make recommendations to the Lord Chancellor.[16] In November 2011, the Ministry of Justice published a paper on judicial appointments and diversity which followed a public consultation in relation to the judicial selection process and how to make the judiciary more representative (Ministry of Justice, 2012).[17]

In March 2012, the House of Lords Constitution Committee published a review of the judicial appointments system.[18] Arguing that the process by which judges are appointed is of 'significant constitutional interest' the Committee concluded that, six years after the introduction of the new model, there was a broad consensus that it was working well and no fundamental change was recommended but that steps needed to be taken to enhance diversity of the judiciary through the implementation of recommendations of the Advisory Panel on Judicial Diversity.[19] In December 2012, a former leading Labour Party politician, Jack Straw, criticized the judicial appointments commission model introduced by his immediate predecessor as Lord Chancellor and Secretary for State for Justice. Straw argued that the 'tap on

appointments commission would be established, and, perhaps most significantly, there would be a Supreme Court, with the law lords no longer being members of the legislature. These changes, while supported by many, were seriously undercut by the inept and inexcusable method of their announcement. Consultation had been non-existent. Working out the solutions was to take nearly two years.' (2005; i). 16 United Kingdom. Judiciary. (2010) *Report of the Advisory Panel on Judicial Diversity*. Available at http://www.judiciary.gov.uk/Resources/JCO/Documents/Reports/advisory-panel-judicial-diversity-2010.pdf (accessed 11 Nov. 2015). 17 The response was published in May 2012 and legislative changes were made through the Crime and Courts Act 2013 (Schedule 13). The change introduced enabled a form of affirmative action in choosing between two candidates of equal merit for the purposes of enhancing the diversity of the group of persons who are members of the court. http://www.legislation.gov.uk/ukpga/2013/22/schedule/13/enacted (accessed 15 Jan. 2014). 18 United Kingdom. House of Lords Constitution Committee. (2012) *Twenty-Fifth Report of Session 2010–12: Judicial Appointments*. Available at http://www.publications. parliament.uk/pa/ld201012/ldselect/ldconst/272/272.pdf (accessed 16 Jan. 2016). 19 United Kingdom. Judiciary. (2010) *Report of the Advisory Panel on Judicial Diversity*.

the shoulder' system enabled the government to appoint minority groups to the judiciary and that the judicial appointments commission model, introduced by Labour, had failed to deliver the expected improvements on this system in relation to diversity on the bench.[20] There is on-going concern that the reforms have failed to enhance diversity on the bench and it remains a core part of the debate on judicial selection in England and Wales. In October 2015, the Lord Chief Justice, in a speech on judicial diversity in England and Wales, highlighted the efforts being made by the Diversity Committee of the Judges' Council to widen as far as possible the pool of lawyers from which senior judicial appointments may be made.

> We introduced a new route to the High Court. Historically, judges have been appointed to the High Court by first undertaking a part-time role in the judiciary, usually as a Recorder. I did so myself. It became apparent that this route was not suitable for all and meant that it was difficult for some, for instance, a legal academic or a senior lawyer in a City law firm, to aspire to become a High Court Judge. That has now changed and, relying on provisions in the Senior Courts Act, in the recent competition for deputy High Court Judges the requirement for prior judicial experience was removed. We have thereby opened up the competition to a wider range of applicants. Successful candidates will then be given any necessary training in the relevant jurisdiction before sitting as a deputy High Court Judge; when the time comes, they can compete on a level playing field for appointment as a judge of the High Court. (Lord Chief Justice John Thomas, 19 October 2015)[21]

Ireland

Institutional change of judicial selection systems occurred in 1995 with the establishment of a judicial screening commission – the Judicial Appointments Advisory Board (JAAB). Political debate in Ireland about judicial selection systems began in 1994 following a crisis in the coalition government created by disagreement between the two coalition partners about two senior judicial appointments.

Prior to this institutional change, judicial appointments had been solely the preserve of the government and, more particularly, of the Prime Minister (Taoiseach) and the Attorney General. The resolution of the political crisis in 1994 depended on a new system of judicial selection being introduced immediately to satisfy the minor political party in the coalition. The political

20 Rozenberg, J. (2012) 'Jack Straw on judicial appointments "Labour went too far"', *The Guardian*, 4 December. Available at http://www.theguardian.com/law/2012/dec/04/jack-straw-judicial-appointments-diversity (accessed 15 Jan. 2014). **21** https://www.judiciary.gov.uk/wp-content/uploads/2015/10/temple-womens-event-leeds-oct-2015.pdf (accessed

debate about judicial selection was not connected to any other series of legal or constitutional reforms, nor was the change the product of public criticism of the judiciary or its governance. There is little evidence of public, academic or media debate on judicial selection in the years before institutional change was introduced.

The institutional change occurred quickly: legislation was drafted and introduced to the legislature within weeks of the crisis in November 1994. Despite the efforts of the coalition, the relationship had deteriorated beyond repair and a new government was formed before the legislation introducing the new system could be processed through the legislature. Institutional change of judicial selection was enacted one year later.

Neither the politicians nor the civil service had expected institutional change to the judicial selection systems to be introduced at this time. There had been one reference to the possibility of setting up a judicial selection commission in a report in 1990,[22] but this did not result in any political debate about the merits of such a system or about problems with the existing system. All of the other documents that debate reform of the judicial selection model do so in the years following the introduction of statutory change in 1995 and do not contribute to the policy rationale for changing the system.[23]

The changes in Ireland were exclusively a product of the political crisis that erupted directly as a result of two particular judicial appointments. It occurred quickly and without the usual policy processes found in other countries such as consultation exercises, or reports by law reform bodies or parliamentary committees.

There are important considerations in the development of any alternative system in Ireland. As shown in Chapter 2, the Irish Constitution is prescriptive in relation to judicial selection and it acts as an important part of the consideration of any judicial selection model in Ireland. Article 35.1 of the Constitution provides: 'The judges of the Supreme Court, the High Court and all other Courts established in pursuance of Article 34 hereof shall be appointed by the President.' Judicial selection processes are affected by Article 13.9 of the Irish Constitution and it is this provision that creates a requirement for government to have discretion in judicial selection.

Article 13.9 of the Irish Constitution requires that the government advise the President in certain functions, including judicial appointments. It is essential that the government retains its discretion in this process; another body cannot, constitutionally, perform this function on behalf of the government. As we will see in Chapter 2, the two Bills that provided for the

11 Nov. 2015). **22** Ireland. Fair Trade Commission (1990) p. 299. **23** Constitution Review Group 1996; Oireachtas Committee on the Constitution 1999, Report of the Working Group 1999.

establishment of the JAAB took different views of the number of candidates to be recommended by the JAAB. The 1994 Bill provided that the JAAB would recommend not less than three and not more than five candidates; on the other hand, the 1995 Bill provided that the JAAB would recommend at least ten candidates in respect of each vacancy, although this was reduced to seven names during the Committee and Report stage of the enactment of the Bill. The government enjoys a presumption of constitutionality in the passage of legislation through the Houses of the Oireachtas. The role of the Attorney General is critical in this presumption and in the development of the legislation. As will be shown in Chapter 2, two different Attorneys General signed off on Bills with different implications for the role of the JAAB in judicial selection under the Constitution and each of these Attorneys General, and their officials, presumably took the view that their version of the Bill was within suitable constitutional parameters.

The subsequent change in process by the JAAB which led to it recommending 'all of those who were not unsuitable' was based on a further constitutional view that not to do so could encroach on the constitutional prerogative of the government in judicial selection. This seems like a substantially overly narrow interpretation of the role of the JAAB in the Courts and Court Officers Act 1995, which established the JAAB expressly to make recommendations to government of a comparatively small number of judicial candidates. Indeed, this was the way it had been operating in the first few years immediately after its establishment 1995.

Different political and legal actors interpreted the minimum constitutional standard in different ways. It is an important issue from the perspective of government and for the political system generally, as the prerogative of the government to advise the President in the exercise of his functions under Article 13.9 applies to all of the President's functions other than those explicitly stated in the Constitution. The Irish government took the view that the JAAB could recommend as few as three candidates to the Minister and not be said to unconstitutionally usurp the role of the government under Article 13.9.

In summary, Ireland is different from the other countries that introduced institutional change in the judicial selection system. Policy change occurred quickly and without the debate that took place in other countries. Institutional change to judicial selection processes was introduced although there was little evidence of political commitment to such change. The trigger for institutional change was the need to find a solution to a political crisis that might prevent the coalition government from breaking up. That is not to say that the change introduced was good or bad, better or worse than in other systems; it is simply to acknowledge that the circumstances of the introduction of institutional change in Ireland are different from the rest of the countries considered.

Israel

Institutional change of the judicial selection system in Israel occurred in 1953 when the government introduced a judicial screening commission model to replace the government-controlled executive appointment systems that had been inherited from the period of British rule. It was the first country to introduce reform of this sort. As we have seen, the judiciary in Israel has held an important place in the establishment and stability of the democratic nature of the state since its creation in 1948 (Edelman, 2001). Compounded by heavily partisan political conditions in a fragile and fledgling state, the government consciously decided to insulate the judiciary from the political environment in order to protect the rule of law in Israel (Edelman, 1994; Shetreet, 1994). This was a particular concern because of the extraordinary political circumstances associated with the foundation and stabilization of a new state in contrast to the more stable domestic political environments of most of the other countries assessed in this study.

When the State of Israel was established in 1948, the process of judicial appointment was the responsibility of the Provisional Government (Salzberger, 2006; Allan, 2006). With the enactment of the Judges Act 1953, the Ben-Gurion government removed control over judicial selection from the government by the establishment of a statutory committee to perform the function of selecting judges, who would then be formally appointed by the President. In 1984, the status of the committee was upgraded when it was included in the Basic Law (Constitution).[24] The composition of this Committee originally contained a legal academic and the Attorney General, but was ultimately comprised of three Supreme Court judges, two representative of the Bar, two Cabinet ministers and two Knesset members (Judges Act 1953; Allan, 2006).

Israel differs from the other countries that introduced institutional change. It did so much earlier than any other country and in a different domestic and geo-political environment. Institutional change occurred in Israel in 1953 – some forty-two years before institutional change occurred in the other countries. It had only a seven-year period during which the government had control of the judicial selection process. Israel was a newly established state, experiencing significant threats to its existence. The military played an important role in national politics and support for the military was high. The judgments of the Supreme Court could have had (and indeed have had) a significant impact on the conduct of security forces in Israel.[25] In these circumstances, it is easy to imagine how the selection of judges of the Supreme Court would be a key political concern such that politicians would want to retain control. Notwithstanding this, the government in Israel took steps to

24 Basic Law: The Judiciary (1984). **25** *Public Committee Against Torture v. State of Israel HCJ* (Israeli Supreme Court) 5100/94, July 15, 1999.

divest itself of political power in judicial selection in order to preserve the rule of law and to insulate the judiciary from politics.

Israel is an example of institutional change sponsored by and supported by the government. The initiative for institutional change arose because of the concerns and policy preferences of the government in relation to judicial selection systems. This is an example of a government deliberately reducing its discretion in judicial selection to achieve gains in another area of concern.

Northern Ireland

Institutional change in Northern Ireland in 2002 was the result of three contemporaneous drivers of reform: incremental changes to judicial selection that mirrored those changes in England and Wales and Scotland, the influence of broader political trends in the United Kingdom and a review of the criminal justice system that formed part of the outcomes of the Belfast Agreement.

The Justice (Northern Ireland) Acts 2002 & 2004 provided for the establishment of a judicial screening commission.[26] These Acts implemented the recommendations of the Northern Ireland Criminal Justice Review, which flowed from the Belfast Agreement (1998). The Belfast Agreement was a major constitutional and legal event in Northern Ireland. It also provided for a wide-ranging review of criminal justice in Northern Ireland which was conducted immediately after the Agreement and which involved broad consultation with stakeholders in the criminal justice process and with the wider public in Northern Ireland. The Northern Ireland Criminal Justice Review was tasked with examining the judicial selection system in Northern Ireland because 'these matters impact upon the crucial issues of judicial independence and public confidence' (2000, p. 107).

Similarly to England and Wales, institutional change of judicial selection began incrementally with a trend towards greater openness in the procedures for selecting people to be recommended for appointment. A key element of the reform was the introduction of a transparent application process, accountable to the Lord Chancellor. However, following the Review of the Criminal Justice System, this was superseded by the introduction of NIJAC to remove political involvement in judicial selection altogether.

Institutional change of the judicial selection system in Northern Ireland was put on the political agenda as a consequence of significant broader political institutional change that provided for new political institutions and power-sharing arrangements in post-conflict Northern Ireland. The Belfast Agreement provided for a Review of the criminal justice system. This Review recommended changes to the judicial selection system to enhance public

26 This was further underpinned by the Justice (Northern Ireland) Act 2009, which provided for the devolution of the Justice function from the Westminster to Belfast legislature.

confidence in the judiciary. The Review expressly recommended the creation of a judicial appointments commission to separate the judiciary from politics and to enhance transparency and openness in the judicial selection process. This template was used in the institutional design of the new judicial selection system as provided for in the Justice (Northern Ireland) Acts 2002 & 2004. The Northern Ireland Judicial Appointments Commission was one of the key innovations.

In 2012 the Committee for Justice of the Northern Ireland Assembly published a review of the judicial appointments process. This review was required by the Justice (Northern Ireland) Act 2009. The review included written submissions and held three oral evidence sessions with the Attorney General for Northern Ireland, the Lord Chief Justice in his capacity as Chairman of the NI Judicial Appointments Commission (NIJAC), along with other NIJAC representatives, a representative from the Office of the Lord Chief Justice, and the NI Judicial Appointments Ombudsman. It recommended that no change be introduced to the judicial selection system.

Responsibility for judicial selection, along with other elements of the administration of justice, was, at the time of institutional change, still vested in the Lord Chancellor and had not been devolved to the Northern Ireland Executive. The reforms introduced were a response to the Northern Ireland Criminal Justice Review, but they were reforms that mirrored the changes in England and Wales and the institutional change introduced at the same time in Scotland.

Scotland

Institutional change in Scotland took place in 2002 with the establishment of a judicial screening commission. The Scottish government sponsored the institutional change, having made a formal commitment to consult on the judicial appointments system in their programme for government in 1999.

Following the change of government in Westminster in 1997, which resulted in a landslide victory for the Labour Party, Scottish politicians began to talk publicly about reform of judicial selection, including the possibility of introducing a judicial appointments commission. As we have seen, the government elected in England in 1997 championed a range of legal and constitutional reforms, including institutional changes to judicial selection processes. This provided the political space in Scotland to discuss similar possible institutional change. Political debate in Scotland about judicial selection systems took place in tandem with the institutional changes being mooted by the government in England. These institutional changes were given further momentum by members of the newly devolved Scottish government in 1999.

In 2000 the Scottish government initiated a consultation process on institutional change of judicial selection systems.[27] The responses were heavily in favour of the establishment of an independent body. In March 2001, the Deputy First Minister (who was also the Minister for Justice) announced that a 'Judicial Appointments Board' would be established (Paterson, 2006). The Judicial Appointments Board for Scotland was duly established in 2002. At the outset the Scottish ministers gave an undertaking that the Board would be put on a statutory footing once it had been set up and had been in operation for a time. This occurred in June 2009 under the Judiciary and Courts (Scotland) Act 2008 when it became an Advisory Non-Departmental Public Body.

Politicians initiated institutional change of judicial selection systems in Scotland. They drove a public consultation exercise about the shape of any such change and provided important supports to the new Judicial Appointments Board for Scotland both at its inception and later when they underpinned it in statute.

Summary

We have assessed the circumstances that led to political debate on institutional change of judicial selection systems and institutional change of judicial selection systems in five jurisdictions. In two jurisdictions (England and Wales and Scotland), institutional change of judicial selection was linked to a series of constitutional and legal reforms broadly emanating from the same political event – the election of a new government in 1997. It was further underpinned by the public commitment of political leaders to institutional change. The institutional change in Northern Ireland mirrored the institutional design of the new institutional arrangements in Scotland, introduced in the same year (2002), but was driven by the broader progamme of political change in Northern Ireland at that time. Institutional change in Israel was linked to the concerns of the government that the judicial institution needed to be protected from the difficult and partisan party politics of the day in a delicate new State. In Ireland, institutional change was introduced following a political argument between coalition partners on two senior judicial appointments. Each change, with the exception of Ireland, was preceded by public and political debate on separating politics from judicial selection.

Ireland stands out in several ways:

1 There was no evidence of incremental change to the judicial selection system prior to institutional change in 1995,
2 Institutional change of judicial selection processes followed significant legal and political changes in each of other cases examined,

27 Scotland. Scottish Government. (2000) *Judicial appointments: an inclusive approach*. Available at http://www.scotland.gov.uk/Publications/ 2000/04/5626/ File-1 (accessed 16 Jan. 2014).

3 Policy change occurred quickly and without the policy change processes that characterized debate about policy change in other countries,
4 Institutional change to judicial selection processes was introduced even though there was little evidence of political commitment to such change.

We now turn to those cases where there was political debate about institutional change, but where no change was introduced.

CASES OF RESISTANCE TO POLITICAL DEBATE ABOUT INSTITUTIONAL CHANGE

Political debate does not necessarily lead to institutional change. Politicians who do not favour institutional change can resist pressure, unless that pressure reaches a point where it may be more politically expedient to change the system than to remain static.

The following cases are examples where there was political debate about the desirability of institutional change of judicial selection systems, but where such pressure was resisted for different reasons. We saw that institutional change returned to the political agenda of countries that had already experienced formal institutional change. In Northern Ireland (2012), Scotland (2008) and England and Wales (2012) reviews of the new judicial selection systems were conducted. Although, in each case, suggestions for improvements were made, none of these considerations recommended or resulted in substantive institutional change. In 2011 there was political debate in Israel about possible further institutional change to the Judicial Selection Committee, but it did not progress to actual change. In Ireland in 2013 and 2014 there was political debate about possible institutional change, but so far no change has been proposed by government. Table 1.6 summarizes the experiences of the cases where pressure to introduce institutional change was resisted.

Australia

In the 1990s, Australia experienced considerable debate about the manner in which its senior judges were chosen. A series of controversies about the conduct of judges, their comments while on the bench and the role of the senior courts in the political system generally prompted a burst of activity and debate around the judicial selection process and especially in respect of appointments to its highest courts.

In the 1980s, there was a series of prosecutions of judicial officers for crimes against the administration of justice (Handsley, 2006). The most high-profile of these, the 'Murphy affair', involved a judge of the federal High Court of Australia, the highest court in the country. Justice Murphy was charged with attempting to pervert the course of justice in the case of a solicitor friend of his

Table 1.6: Resistance to institutional change

Country	Trigger for political debate on institutional change	Tools used by government to respond to political debate	Reason for no institutional change
Australia	Controversial judicial decisions brought membership of judiciary into focus.	Parliamentary committee and law reform commission discussion papers on judicial issues.	No consensus from these reports that appointments system should be changed removed pressure from government; no political commitment to fundamental change.
Canada	Adoption of Charter of Rights 1982 and enhanced role for judiciary.	Parliamentary committee reports.	No evidence of political commitment to fundamental change.
New Zealand	Establishment of Supreme Court.	Report conducted by former Attorney General and Prime Minister on desirability of institutional change.	No consensus from these reports that appointments system should be changed. Removed pressure from government and no evidence of political commitment to fundamental change.
USA	Initiative by President to establish judicial nominating commissions for certain Federal Court judges.	Consultation with stakeholders who were opposed to change.	Opposition by Senate Judiciary Committee chair ensured no legislation was passed to implement this initiative. However, President signed an executive order to give effect to the proposal for Federal Courts of Appeal. This was overturned by his successor.

Source: Davis and Williams (2003); Morton (2006); Malleson and Russell (2006); Palmer (2002); Hall and McGuire (2005).

who was charged with fraud. Justice Murphy was subsequently acquitted. However, the affair led to debate about judicial selection processes – not just because of his conduct but because of the manner in which he was appointed. Handsley (2006) states that Justice Murphy had been appointed at a much younger age than was traditional and he was considered not to have spent sufficient time in practice to have the kind of experience appropriate for judicial appointment. He had strong connections with the appointing government as he had previously served as Attorney General in the Labour government; his appointment was widely regarded as 'political'.

Separately, the question of gender imbalance on the bench arose during this same period as a consequence of unfortunate comments made by some judges in sex crime cases – comments that suggested that some held women to bear responsibility for their experience of sexual crimes. The implication was that women do not know their own minds and that their non-consent remained unproven. The most high profile of these cases was *R. v. Johns*[28] where Justice Bollen, in a case involving sexual violence between a married couple, made certain comments about the acceptability of 'rougher than usual handling' by a man in persuading his wife to have sex with him.[29] There was sustained public criticism of the judge's conduct in the handling of this case, leading to questions about the accountability of judges and further questions about how judges are appointed.

At the same time, there was increasing public comment about the power of the courts and the individuals wielding that power, following the landmark case of Mabo v. Queensland (No. 2) (1992), 175 CLR 1 connected to the historical nature of law in Australia. The effect of the ruling in Mabo was that the granting of a lease did not extinguish the native title of the land (which by implication would have belonged to the Aborigines). This was 'new law' that the High Court had made. The concern was that if the High Court was suddenly going to start to make new law in this way, then 'we had to be much more careful about who we put on the Bench' (Handsley, 2006, p. 128).

All of these issues happened within a short space of time, within three years. Each on its own might have generated public debate, but the quick succession of contentious issues related to the judiciary generated substantial political pressure to reform the judicial selection system. The response of the government (who made no statements in favour of reform) was to refer the issue to various law reform bodies including the independent Law Reform Commission, a parliamentary committee and the Attorney General's office. These bodies published a series of reports on the question of judicial appointments, gender, and the legal system generally, over a period from 1993 to 1995, as set out in Table 1.7 below.

None of the reports recommended institutional change of the judicial selection system. The only change that was recommended was that a broader range of candidates should be encouraged to identify themselves as judicial candidates, but without any institutional reform of the judicial selection process or the role of the government in that process. Ultimately no institutional change was introduced by the government.[30]

28 Unreported, 26 August 1992, Supreme Court of South Australia, Bollen J. 29 Furthermore, in his instructions to the jury, he told an anecdote about the fabrication of sexual misconduct charges against a man that ultimately led to his suicide. 30 Handsley (2006) argues that the establishment of a judicial appointments commission in any Australian jurisdiction is highly unlikely, 'unless there is another wave of controversies sufficient to convince a government that there is political capital to be made' (p. 136) and that even in those circumstances a government would be likely to focus on issues such as judicial training and education, rather than judicial selection, in as far as they could because of the highly valuable political prize of being able to patron such valuable state appointments.

Table 1.7: Reports on judicial selection reform in Australia, 1993–5

Date	Department	Report	Recommendations
1993	Attorney General's Department Discussion Paper	Judicial Appointments: Procedure and Criteria	Highlighted the limited nature of the consultation that generally occurs before the appointment of judges and noted that the selection process draws from a narrow field of possible candidates for judicial appointment, largely in the private Bar.
1994	Commonwealth Attorney General's Department	Judicial Appointments: Procedures and Criteria	Makes no recommendations as to reform of system other than a reference to an assumption that there is a need to review the existing system. Outlines criteria for appointment, which had hitherto been unpublished.
1994	Senate Standing Committee on Legal and Constitutional Affairs	Gender Bias and the Judiciary	Followed public consultations by the Committee in three major Australian cities and written submission from public. Report concluded a need for reform of judicial selection processes, but limited it to widening eligibility criteria, rather than recommending a fundamentally different process. Recommended a committee to advise the Attorney General on prospective appointments, but not in any binding sense.
1995	Attorney General's Department Justice Statement	Justice Statement	Noted that judicial appointments must continue to be made on merit, but that the government would find new ways of attracting a broader range of eligible candidates to come forward for selection.

Source: Reports are cited directly in Table 1.7.

As stated earlier, this book takes no view about the relative merits of different judicial selection methods. It is the democratic prerogative of the elected political leaders of the day to take the view that the status quo is an acceptable system and that reform is not necessary or desirable. What is of interest is that there was political debate and political pressure to change the system and the government resisted that pressure. Whether or not they could have continued to do so in the face of further problems with the judiciary is unknown. Their solution to the political pressure was to use consultative mechanisms to defer and displace discussion about institutional change of judicial selection processes. In the end, these reports did not come down in favour of change. The passage of time eased the pressure on the government to introduce change.

Canada

The Supreme Court of Canada has had a broader role in rights-based issues since the adoption of the Charter of Rights in 1982. Cases such as *R. v. Morgentaler,*[31] which struck down Canada's abortion law, drew public attention in terms of the extent of the Court's new powers. Morton (2006) argues that the Court had an expanded role and that public awareness of the Court, and its new powers, had increased.[32]

This public attention brought the judicial selection system for the Canadian Supreme Court into focus. Appointment processes attracted considerable and sustained debate from academia, the media and interest groups.[33] Provincial legislatures in Canada introduced institutional change of judicial selection systems through the establishment of judicial screening commissions for the appointment of provincial judges. The courts to which they are appointed though, do not have powers over federal government or the capacity to restrict or reverse government acts as being inconsistent with the Charter. Federal government retains discretion in the selection of judges for the Supreme Court, other than the regional quota mentioned earlier in this chapter.

Political pressure for institutional change emerged from provincial groups that were keen to have a greater role in the appointment process to ensure a more representative court. Morton (2006) comments that, in 1987, the Mulroney government accepted some of these reforms, through the Meech Lake Accord. This proposed that the federal government would be required to appoint Supreme Court judges from lists submitted by the provinces. However, public debate on this reform was so divisive that the Accord never came into operation.

Subsequent calls for reform included calls from newspaper editors and legal academics[34] to bring the process of appointment 'out into the open'. In 2003 the Prime Minister, Paul Martin, indicated his support for reforming the process of Supreme Court appointments. In the same year, the House of Commons gave all-party support for a private member's motion to authorize a parliamentary committee to study the process by which judges are appointed to the courts of appeal and to the Supreme Court of Canada (Morton, 2006).

The report proposed that, in the long term, a nominating committee would be created to send lists of three to five names to government in respect of an appointment, but that the final choice would rest with the Minister who could be called before the committee to explain his or her decision.[35] There was significant opposition to the proposals, although for different reasons; some arguing that they were too federally-dominated, others that they were too timid.

31 R. Morgentaler [1988] 1 S.C.R. 30. 32 Morton (2006) cites a 2003 Ipsos-Reid poll that reported that 71 per cent of Canadians agreed that 'it should be up to Parliament and provincial legislatures, not the courts, to make laws in Canada'. See also Riddell (1994). 33 Ziegel (2003); Ziegel (2006); Russell and Ziegel (1991). 34 Ziegel (2005). 35 Canada. House of Commons. (2004) *Improving the Supreme Court of Canada Appointments process:*

Ultimately, no institutional change was introduced by the government to judicial selection processes for the Supreme Court in Canada. This, too, was an example of government resistance to pressure for institutional change.

New Zealand

Debate in New Zealand about institutional change for judicial selection systems arose in the context of broader institutional change. In 2004, New Zealand introduced significant constitutional and legal changes with the abolition of the right of appeal to the Privy Council in London and its replacement with a domestic Supreme Court as the final court of appeal in the land. The New Zealand Supreme Court was established to 'recognize New Zealand as an independent nation with its own history and traditions and improve access to justice and enable important legal matters, including those relating to the Treaty of Waitangi, to be resolved with an understanding of New Zealand conditions, history and traditions' (Supreme Court Act 2003).

This change presented a significant opportunity for contemporaneous institutional change to the judicial selection system. The creation of four new senior judicial posts brought the appointments mechanism into sharp political and public focus. The primary concern was that, under the existing system, the appointments to the new Supreme Court would all be made by a single person (Nevill, 2005). While it would be a unique situation in time, the prevailing view was that to give one person control over the full composition of a new court would be undesirable.

As we have seen, judicial selection in New Zealand operates according to the executive appointment model, where government has full control of judicial selection. In 1998, the Ministry of Justice in New Zealand established a Judicial Appointments Unit to publicize judicial vacancies and receive applications. The question was whether the government would come under political pressure to introduce more significant institutional change to judicial selection as part of the broader constitutional and legal reforms and, if so, whether the government would support such demands.

Pressure came from lawyers, business groups and the media to consider reform of the judicial selection process. The issue was rooted in a concern that the country would not have sufficient legal talent to replace the judges of the Privy Council – a concern not shared by the Attorney General.[36] The response of the government was to ask an eminent lawyer and former politicians to

report of the Standing Committee on Justice, Human Rights, Public Safety and Emergency Preparedness. Available at http://www.parl.gc.ca/HousePublications/Publication.aspx?DocId=1350880&Language=E&Mode=1&Parl=37&Ses=3 (accessed 16 Jan. 2014). **36** In an editorial to mark the establishment of the Supreme Court of New Zealand, the *New Zealand Herald Tribune* noted, 'The concern of many lawyers that this country might not possess a sufficient pool of high judicial talent has not swayed the select committee or the report on the issue and this was followed by a consultation paper sponsored by the Attorney General.

In September 2002, when the constitutional reform process was beginning in earnest, the government asked Sir Geoffrey Palmer to review the current appointment procedures in New Zealand. He was a former Attorney General and a former Prime Minister of New Zealand. His report strongly rejected the notion of an independent commission to make judicial appointments and recommended that this power should remain with the Executive (Palmer, 2002). The report did, however, recommend the establishment of a new Judicial Appointments and Liaison Office, but this office was to fulfil a purely administrative role in the recruitment process and other issues then shared by several government agencies, such as judicial terms and conditions of service. Palmer's report does not give any reasons for his rejection of a judicial appointments commission. The report simply states that there is no support and, in his view, no justification for an appointments commission and it is recommended that judges should continue to be appointed by the Governor-General. (Palmer, 2002)

In April 2004, the Attorney General published a paper on the establishment of a judicial appointments commission (New Zealand Ministry of Justice, 2004). Ultimately, at the time of the establishment of the Supreme Court in 2005, the government did not include any changes to the judicial selection system as part of the constitutional and legal reforms. The immediate issue of the appointment of the four new judges was resolved by the promotion of judges from the Court of Appeal.[37] The government had invested significant political effort into the establishment of the new court structure through the constitutional and legal reforms. Writing in the *New Zealand Herald Tribune* on 10 October 2003, Prime Minister Helen Clark commented, 'Few proposals that come before Legislature have been consulted on more thoroughly than this one'.[38]

government. But they, of course, are not the most frequent litigants. Commercial disputes give rise to most of the Privy Council's work from this country and business organisations sound not at all confident about the quality of decisions they will receive from an indigenous substitute. The government and the select committee have ignored those concerns too. Ms Wilson simply proclaims "the nation's ability to produce legal talent on a par with any in the world". That is not the quality of argument that should precede a decision of this kind.' Editorial. (2003) 'Not too late for poll on new court'. *New Zealand Herald*. Available at http://www.nzherald.co.nz/nz/news/article.cfm?c_id=1&objectid=3523814 (accessed 15 Jan. 2014). **37** Allan (2006) contends that even in such a highly anomalous situation the open, direct status quo appointments process was preferable because everyone could see it for what it was; hence political and grassroots opposition could be mobilized against an Attorney General prepared to argue that she was entitled to choose all the new judges to a new highest court. 'And that same political and grassroots opposition to the Attorney General doing anything other than the most senior existing judges ultimately succeeded' (Allan, 2006, p. 115). **38** Clark, H. (2003) 'Nation ready for

The issue of institutional change to judicial selection processes had been avoided by the government – notwithstanding the pressure to introduce institutional change and the level of consultation that had occurred. Here again we find an example of resistance to institutional change. The government responded to political pressure by ensuring the issue was debated and considered, but ultimately resisted pressure to change judicial selection.

Since then, change of judicial selection systems has remained a live issue in New Zealand's legal and political discourse. In November 2012, the New Zealand Law Commission[39] submitted a review of the Judicature Act 1908 to the Prime Minister. This review recommended that the Attorney General should follow a more structured and transparent process in identifying candidates suitable for judicial appointments and that they should consult on their suitability with other legal officers and representatives of the legal profession. Ultimately, the Commission made no recommendation to change the process by which the Attorney General made recommendations to their Cabinet colleagues, who would make the decision in relation to judicial appointments. Notwithstanding the scrutiny of the judicial selection process over a ten-year period, including through the establishment of a new court structure for New Zealand, no institutional change to the judicial selection process has been introduced and the role of the government in choosing judges remains unaltered.

United States

The United States is a unique case. As we have seen, its judicial selection processes are heavily politicized – especially for judicial vacancies on the Supreme Court where a combination of polarized political perspectives and life tenure makes choosing Supreme Court judges one of the most important functions of a President. Institutional change to the appointment of Supreme Court judges has never been mooted seriously in the United States.

There was one attempt to introduce institutional change to judicial selection processes to lower Federal Courts and it is worth mentioning in this analysis. In 1977 President Carter attempted to introduce institutional change that could have had the effect of reducing the importance of the role of both the President and the Senate in judicial selection. The President attempted to introduce judicial nominating commissions for Federal Court vacancies on the District Courts and Courts of Appeal. He encountered resistance from the then Senate Judiciary Committee Chairman and no legislation was ever passed

its own highest court'. *New Zealand Herald*, 10 October. Available at http://www.nzherald.co.nz/nz/news/article.cfm?c_id=1&objectid= 3527954 (accessed 15 Jan. 2014). **39** An independent, government funded body, established by the Law Commission Act 1975, that reviews laws in need of updating (http://www.lawcom.govt.nz/).

to give effect to the commissions (Gerhardt, 2003). By Executive Order in 1977, President Carter introduced the commissions for Courts of Appeal.[40] In May 1981, President Reagan 'abruptly' overturned this Order (Hall and McGuire, 2005, p. 147).[41]

It is relevant because the impact of the proposed institutional change would have introduced a reduction in the discretion of the powerful actors in judicial selection for some Federal Courts. The President, and by extension the Senate, would be guided by the deliberations of a judicial nominating commission. In this way, the discretion of the President would be partly reduced. Critically, the role of the Senate Judiciary Committee would also be diminished because it would be much more difficult for this Committee to reject or find fault with a nominee who had been approved by a nominating commission and not simply the product of the President's preferences.

Summary

In summary, we have seen three examples of governments resisting pressures to introduce institutional change to judicial selection systems. With the exception of the United States, pressure to introduce institutional change came from sources external to government. There was little evidence of government commitment to institutional change in each instance where political debate led to calls for reformed judicial selection processes. We have also seen one example where institutional change was driven by the executive but resisted by the legislature (and by the successor executive) that held the balance of power in judicial appointments.

The experiences of Australia, New Zealand and Canada demonstrate how political pressure for institutional change can develop and can be resisted by politicians. In each case, the government responded to the political debate with a political response – a political commitment to implement a report and the establishment of a working group or consultation process to consider institutional change. In each case, no institutional change was introduced.

The case of Australia is distinctive among these cases in the sense that calls for institutional change of judicial selection systems emerged following sustained criticism of the judiciary in a number of high profile cases. In Canada and New Zealand, the pressure for political debate on institutional change arose as a consequence of broader legal changes affecting the constitutional court – the establishment of a Supreme Court in New Zealand and the adoption of the Charter of Rights in Canada. The cases differ in terms

40 Executive Order 11972 and 12059. Available at http://www.presidency.ucsb.edu/ws/?pid=6588; http://www.presidency.ucsb.edu/ws/?pid=30796 (accessed 15 Jan. 2014).
41 Associated Press (1981) 'Reagan ends Carter's judge selection system', *The Telegraph*, 7 May. Available at http://news.google.com/newspapers?nid=2209&dat=19810507&id=NqkrAAAAIBAJ&sjid =IPoFAAAAIBAJ&pg=5485,1473422 (accessed 15 Jan. 2014).

of timing. Calls for institutional change to the judicial selection system in Canada arose after the adoption of the Charter in 1982 and following institutional change of judicial selection systems at the provincial level. In New Zealand, debate about institutional change of judicial selection arose before the legislation to establish the Supreme Court had been completed.

Political debate on institutional change does not necessarily beget institutional change. Politicians can resist calls for institutional change simply because they are the body that governs the rules regarding the institution and governs the rules regarding institutional change. Institutional change must be both supported by politicians, but also, crucially, sponsored by politicians. Politicians can respond to political pressure in a variety of ways including introducing institutional change, ignoring political pressure to introduce institutional change, or taking steps to respond to political debate that fall short of introducing institutional change. In the cases of Australia, New Zealand and Canada, pressure to change was resisted. While they commissioned working groups and consultation papers, politicians in each case were seen to respond to calls for institutional change. Government considered the issues over a period of years. However, the reports produced did not promote significant institutional change and no proposals for change emerged from government.

Had the governments favoured institutional change of judicial selection systems, these critical junctures would have provided a useful moment to introduce institutional change. Certainly, government would have had the political cover necessary through the sustained political debate and, particularly in New Zealand, the creation of entirely new legal structures. Where there is no evidence that governments favoured institutional change to judicial selection systems, institutional change was not introduced. Where political pressure to introduce institutional change was insufficient to force the government to adopt institutional change, institutional change was not introduced.

IMPLICATIONS: POLITICAL DEBATE AND INSTITUTIONAL CHANGE

Table 1.8 summarizes the circumstances of the debates about institutional change and the actions of governments in response to political debate on institutional change of judicial selection systems. It is interesting to note that, in some cases, there has been review of the new system and it has been further embedded in statute or, in the case of Israel, in the Basic Law of Israel. We do not need to read too much into this, but where governments have taken steps to further embed the new process into law, it provides evidence of ongoing political support for the changed institutional arrangements. It is also interesting to note that, irrespective of the outcome of the political debate, all

Table 1.8: Summary of circumstances of policy change process

Country	Political commitments or statements in support of institutional change	Consultation processes	Other contemporaneou s constitutional or legal reforms?	Post- Debate	Duration of debate
Australia	None.	Four discussion/ consultation papers.	None.	Not applicable.	1993–5
Canada	None.	One major report which could not be agreed – Meech Lake Accord.	Adoption of Charter of Rights in 1982.	On-going review of judicial selection mechanism.	On-going and sporadic from adoption of Charter of Rights in 1982.
England and Wales	Statements by new government in support of changed institutional arrangements for judicial selection.	Home Affairs Select Committee Report 1996; academic research commissioned by government 1997.	Enactment of Bill of Rights, which could change nature of judicial role.	On-going concern regarding diversity of judiciary.	1997–2005
Israel	Institutional changes initiated by the government.	Peoples Assembly 1947 but this did not directly inform the 1953 Act.	None.	1984 – Elevated to Basic Law; political attempts to change system in 2000 and 2011.	1948–53
Ireland	None.	None.	Establishment of administrative body to manage courts function.	Minister announced review of judicial selection system in 2013.	2 weeks
New Zealand	None.	Palmer Commission in 2002 on whether to change judicial appointments system.	Abolition of Privy Council and establishment of Supreme Court of New Zealand.	Not applicable.	2004–5
Northern Ireland	Institutional change driven by Lord Chancellor in England whose political party was committed to such change.	Review of the Criminal Justice System as required by the Belfast Agreement.	No.	Legislation refined in 2004 and 2009.	2002–4
Scotland	Statements by new government in support of changed institutional arrangements for judicial selection.	Yes.	Yes – devolution from Westminster legislature.	Upgraded to statutory body in 2009.	2000–2
United States	Institutional change proposal initiated with the President.	Consultation with Senate Judiciary Committee Chairperson.	None.	Overturned in 1981 by successor executive.	1977

Source: Edelman (1994), Davis and Williams (2003); Morton (2006); Malleson and Russell (2006); Palmer (2002); Paterson (2006); Hall and McGuire (2005).

countries (except Ireland) experienced the debate for a period of at least two years. In Ireland, the political debate began in October 1994 and the original legislation was published in November 1994. We will explore this in more detail in Chapter 2.

Ireland stands out as being different from the other countries. Table 1.8 highlights how little consultation and debate there was in Ireland prior to the introduction of institutional change. The next stage of this analysis is to determine whether there is a link between indicators of political commitment of a government to institutional change and the likelihood of introducing institutional change. In the countries examined, it appears that there is indeed such a link.

Summary

The purpose of this study is to examine how and why politicians reduce or appear to reduce their discretion in functions where they prize their power and where the loss of that power could impact negatively on them. Earlier we said that politicians are interested in the outcome of judicial selection processes because the individuals appointed can overturn the actions of government through judicial review. We also noted how, in common law systems, where government appoints judges from the ranks of senior lawyers, judicial appointments can be used as a means of disbursing political patronage. Reducing one's power in judicial selection therefore seems to be somewhat counter-intuitive and we want to know why it happens. The reason we want to know is that it may tell us something about the conditions that are necessary for governments to introduce what seem like counter-intuitive policy proposals.

Ireland looks different to all of the other countries in this analysis – different in terms of the circumstances of the introduction of institutional change and different in the impact of institutional change on the power of future governments under the revised institutional processes for judicial selection. What is it about Ireland that makes it stand out from its comparators? We now seek to comparatively measure the levels of political commitment to institutional change (to the extent publicly knowable) and the outcomes of that change on judicial selection for governments in the future in the range of countries that introduced institutional change.

VARIATION IN POLITICAL COMMITMENT TO INSTITUTIONAL CHANGE

Political commitment to institutional change is difficult to measure. It is necessarily subjective and subject to differences in human personalities. We are not trying to measure political commitment with mathematical precision, but rather to see if there are common trends among groups of experiences that can help us understand the background to institutional change.

We can identify certain indicators that can show evidence of political commitment. For example, political commitment to institutional change can be signalled if the measure is contained in the election manifesto or programme for government. This is a clear indicator of voluntary and proactive support (or lack of support) by a political party or political leader of a particular initiative.

Consultative processes – whether through parliamentary committees, law reform bodies or other mechanisms – are a less helpful indicator of political commitment. They can sometimes be evidence of political commitment, but they can equally be used to give the appearance of action while, in reality, it is a tool by government to defer or stall proposed change that it does not favour. However, in cases where there is an expressed political commitment to institutional change (such as where the measure is included in a manifesto or programme for government) we can assess the use of consultative processes by government differently – in these instances consultative processes are more likely to be used by government to reinforce and increase support for an institutional change already favoured by government.

In the preceding section, a likely indicator of political commitment to institutional change appeared to be the expressed preference of the government itself. Negative statements or the absence of comment by government are likely to be indicative of a lack of support for a particular initiative. We should expect that where there is strong political commitment to institutional change we will see evidence of long-term planning and consultation prior to change. Where there is low commitment to institutional change, we should expect to see little evidence of long-term concern about judicial selection, or evidence of consultation or other standard change processes.

To determine the level of political commitment to the institutional change initiatives discussed in this chapter, each country is assessed in terms of its approach to the process of changing the judicial selection system and the following criteria are considered:

- Whether the measure was expressed in an election manifesto, programme for government or in a statement by a government politician,
- Whether any formal government consultation occurred or formal government sponsored research was commissioned on how systems could or should be changed.

Table 1.9 summarizes the links between political commitment to change and the eventual implementation of change. Each positive response is given a score of 1 allowing us to determine the relative commitment of different countries to institutional change.

Table 1.9: Political commitment, institutional change processes and outcome of political debate on institutional change

Country	Evidence of political commitment in manifesto or PFG or government statement	Was there consultation on change	Political commitment score	Outcome of political debate
Australia	No	Yes	1	No institutional change
Canada	No	Yes	1	No institutional change
England and Wales	Yes	Yes	2	Institutional change
Ireland	No	No	0	Institutional change
Israel	Yes	Yes	2	Institutional change
New Zealand	No	Yes	1	No institutional change
Northern Ireland	Yes	Yes	2	Institutional change
Scotland	Yes	Yes	2	Institutional change

Table 1.9 presents the political commitment score. We can see that all of the countries that obtained political commitment scores of 2 were countries that introduced institutional change. Those countries that obtained political commitment scores of 1 were countries that did not implement institutional change despite political pressure to do so.

It is immediately apparent that there is something different about Ireland. Ireland gets the lowest political commitment score. In this analysis, Ireland receives a score of 0. This outcome is quite distinct from the other countries and raises further questions about what were the circumstances of institutional change in Ireland.[43] The only discussion of a possible judicial selection commission in Ireland was contained in a report published in 1990 by the Fair Trade Commission on restrictive practices in the legal profession which suggested the establishment of a judicial screening commission. This recommendation did not stimulate any further political debate in Ireland on this issue. It was not the basis for the decision of the government in 1994 to introduce such a model. As will be shown in Chapter 2, the introduction of institutional change to judicial selection commissions had not formed part of the policy preferences of either political party in the government.

42 Ireland. Fair Trade Commission (1990) *Report of Study into Restrictive Practices in the Legal Profession*. Dublin: Stationery Office.

Table 1.9 also presents the political commitment score and the outcome of the political debate on institutional change. In this table, Ireland is again different from the other countries. Other countries that introduced institutional change have political commitment scores of 2, whereas Ireland has a score of 0.

This raises another question about Ireland – if the way in which institutional change was introduced in Ireland was different to its comparators, is there also something different about the form of institutional change introduced in Ireland?

POLITICAL COMMITMENT AND INSTITUTIONAL DESIGN – COMPARING JUDICIAL SELECTION COMMISSIONS

The next step in the analysis is to examine the institutional design of the judicial selection commissions. The functions and powers of the different judicial screening commissions introduced in England and Wales, Ireland, Israel, Northern Ireland and Scotland vary according to their institutional design. The purpose of their establishment was, to a greater or lesser extent depending on the country (or jurisdiction), to separate politics from judicial selection. It was shown earlier in this chapter that certain institutional design has the effect of constraining the capacity of the government to choose a preferred judicial nominee. The test for effective (or successful) institutional reform of this sort is the degree to which government is bound by the recommendations of the judicial selection commission.

Table 1.10 presents an overview of the impetus for institutional change and the purpose of the institutional design. The table shows that the case of Ireland is different – institutional design of the judicial selection commissions in the other political authorities is such that the government is bound by the recommendations of the delegated body. In Ireland, the institutional design is such that the delegated body makes recommendations to government, but the government is not bound by these recommendations. The institutional design of screening bodies may vary considerably.

At the initial application stage, candidates may be required to submit information of their professional qualification, experience, details of cases and earnings for specified period prior to appointment, references, photographs, tax clearance information and other such information to assist the screening body in making an initial determination. Some screening bodies take the view that candidates should be screened 'blind' with no identifying information or photographs, others take the view that 'being known' to a member of the screening board is essential for a recommendation to government.

The institutional design of the body may also vary at the stage of consideration of the candidates for recommendations. Some bodies may take formal or informal soundings from professional bodies or colleagues, some

Table 1.10: Cases where political debate led to institutional change

Country	Impetus for change	Purpose of change	Institutional design
England and Wales	Part of a series of constitutional and legal reform sponsored by government.	Reduce political involvement In judicial selection and enhance diversity.	Independent commission to screen and interview judicial applicants and make recommendation to government, which must be accepted.
Israel	To insulate the judiciary from politics and enhance public confidence in the judiciary.	To separate judicial selection and politics.	Judges to be chosen by Judicial Selection Commission, instead of government.
Ireland	Political crisis related to high profile judicial appointment.	To reduce political discretion in judicial selection.	Names of suitable candidates to be recommended to government following screening process. Government not bound by recommendations.
Northern Ireland	Part of a broader set of changes arising from a review of the criminal justice system following the Belfast agreement.	To reduce political involvement in judicial selection, to promote a judiciary that was reflective of the community of Northern Ireland and to foster better public confidence in the judiciary.	Independent commission to screen and interview judicial applicants and make recommendation to government, which must be accepted.
Scotland	Part of a series of constitutional and legal reform sponsored by government.	Reduce political involvement in judicial selection and enhance transparency and diversity.	Independent commission to screen and interview judicial applicants and make recommendation to government, which must be accepted (unless the Minister writes to the Board to explain why not).

Sources: Constitutional Reform Act 2005; Courts and Court Officers Act 1995; Judges Act 1953; Justice (Northern Ireland) Acts 2002 & 2004; Judiciary and Courts (Scotland) Act 2008.

may require candidates to attend for interview, some may require candidates to undergo medical testing.

Judicial screening commissions can vary in their composition. They are generally comprised of legal, judicial and lay members to varying degrees. They may be chaired either by a legal person or by a lay person.

Furthermore, some institutional design features may have a major impact on the discretion of future governments in judicial selection. In particular it matters whether the government has to refer all vacancies to the commission or whether the government can make appointments without reference to the commission at all. Of critical importance is the extent to which the output of the judicial screening commissions' processes restricts the capacity of government to make nominations for judicial appointment by the head of state.

We are interested in the important elements of institutional design that result in a reduction of government discretion. In examining different institutional designs of judicial selection commissions, what we are looking for is evidence that the government is constrained in its actions and choices by the existence and the operation of a judicial screening commission.

Judicial screening commission systems can vary from a requirement that they recommend a specified number of candidates (in total or per vacancy), recommend only one name or express candidates in order of preference of the commission. Some systems may have no formal limit on the number of candidates to be recommended to government. Some systems may demand a response from government if their recommended candidate is not appointed, others expect and receive no feedback from government in relation to their recommendations or the subsequent appointments made. Some systems may also apply to the promotion of judges between courts and others may not.

The variation inherent in the range of institutional design of such screening bodies is important because it can directly affect the professed purpose of the establishment of that body – to reduce political influence on the appointment of judges. Depending on the design of the screening body, that discretion can be reduced considerably.

To understand the operation of judicial screening commissions and their impact on government in judicial selection, we consider the functions and powers of the commissions. The objective is to determine what restrictions are placed on government in appointing judges and the degree to which the output of the commission is binding on governments. The following four indicators are used to assess the functions and powers of a judicial screening commission and its impact on the discretion of government in judicial selection:

1 are all judicial appointments governed by the commission?
2 what is the output of the commission and does this constrain government discretion – does the commission select the appointees or does it recommend candidates for appointment and how many names are given to government in each case?
3 is the government bound to accept the recommended name(s)?
4 what is the capacity of government to appoint outside of recommendations made?

Table 1.11: Assessing the impact of judicial selection commissions on the discretion of government in judicial selection

Country	Are all judicial appointments governed by the commission?	Output	Is the government bound to accept the recommended name(s)?	What is capacity of government to appoint outside of recommendations made?	Impact of commission on discretion of government score
England and Wales	Yes – a special selection commission is used for Supreme Court appointments.	Select 1 name per vacancy, which the government must accept.	Yes	None. Government can ask for another name but must say why and must appoint second recommendation.	4
Ireland	No	Recommend at least 7 names per vacancy from which government can choose.	No	Unlimited. Government can and has selected outside list provided.	0
Israel	Yes	Select judges.	Yes	None	4
Northern Ireland	Yes	Select 1 name per vacancy, which the government must accept.	Yes	None. Government can ask for another name but must say why and must appoint second recommendation.	4
Scotland	Yes	Select 1 name per vacancy, which the government must accept.	Yes	None. Government can ask for another name but must say why and must appoint second recommendation.	4

Sources: Constitutional Reform Act 2005; Courts and Court Officers Act 1995; Judges Act 1953; Justice (Northern Ireland) Acts 2002 & 2004; Judiciary and Courts (Scotland) Act 2008.

In each case, a positive response (one where the government's discretion is bound by the actions of the commission) is afforded a score of 1. We can then determine the relative impact of the judicial selection commission on the discretion of government in judicial selection. Table 1.11 summarizes the findings.

Systems in which the judicial appointment commission gives the executive a single recommendation result in the greatest restriction on government discretion. In these systems, the executive has the power to refuse that name with written reasons and request a second name. However, the second name may be the same as the first and the executive may not refuse the selection of the commission on that occasion. In this way, such a commission plays a much greater 'selection' role in the judicial selection process because its recommendations are limited and directly binding on the executive. Such systems received an 'Impact of commission on discretion of government score' of 4. This means that they scored positively on each of the four indicators of impact on the discretion of government in judicial selection. The institutional design of these systems was such that their operation resulted in the discretion of government in judicial selection being very low. This was 'successful' institutional reform having regard to the objectives of the establishment of the judicial selection commission in each case.

Conversely, Ireland received a score of 0. This shows that each indicator of the institutional design of the judicial selection commission in Ireland falls short as a measure to constrain the discretion of the Irish government in judicial selection.

Table 1.11 shows that of these systems, the government in Ireland has the fewest restrictions placed on its discretion in the judicial selection process by the judicial selection commission. This is due to:

1 The capacity of the government to decide whether to refer the vacancy to the JAAB at all,
2 The volume of recommended candidates given by the JAAB to government per vacancy,
3 The capacity of the government to appoint someone who has not been recommended by the JAAB – either through judicial promotion or by choosing someone who has not applied to the JAAB for consideration.[43]

Table 1.12 compiles the information set out in Tales 1.10 and 1.11 on levels of political commitment to institutional change and the test to determine the impact of the institutional change (the new judicial screening commissions) on the discretion of government.

43 The government in Ireland has not appointed people who have applied to the JAAB and been rejected by that body. The political norm for the Irish government has been to make appointments from the recommendations of the JAAB but it is not a statutory imperative.

Table 1.12: Political commitment to institutional change and impact of JSC on discretion of government

Country	Political commitment to institutional change score	Impact of JSC on discretion of government score
England and Wales	2	4
Israel	2	4
Ireland	0	0
Northern Ireland	2	4
Scotland	2	4

Ireland is clearly an outlier in both categories.

CONCLUSIONS

Politicians can introduce institutional change for a range of reasons. The purpose of this chapter was to understand where the pressures to introduce institutional change originate and gain strength and to know the reasons why governments either introduce or resist calls to change. This chapter shows that political commitment to institutional change that reduces the discretion of government is a critical component of effective institutional change. In these cases, the expressed political commitment was combined with tools to engender support and debate about change of judicial selection systems. It appears that the driver and end goal of politicians in these cases is to reduce government discretion in judicial selection. Where such political commitment occurred, it was shown that the ensuing institutional change bound the government to the recommendations of a delegated body. Political commitment, it is argued, matters to the impact of institutional change.

There is something interesting about the story of institutional change in Ireland. What was different about the motivations of politicians in introducing institutional change? How did politicians design the new institutional model and with what objectives? How did these objectives compare to the actual design of the new institutional model and how was it given effect in legislation? These questions are examined in detail in Chapter 2.

CHAPTER 2

Judicial selection reform in Ireland: the trigger for reform and the instrument of reform

This chapter examines the circumstances of the introduction of change of the judicial selection system in Ireland and the instrument of that change – the Courts and Court Officers Bill 1994 (which was replaced one year later by a new coalition government with the Courts and Court Officers Bill 1995, which ultimately became the Courts and Court Officers Act 1995). This chapter draws on forty, in-depth interviews with key political protagonists involved in these institutional processes (including six members of the coalition governments that introduced the actual reform). The analysis also relies on the parliamentary records of the debates on the Bills, as well as secondary sources such as memoirs written by members of government and advisers to the two coalition governments of 1994 and 1995.

This chapter is organized as follows. First, it sets the context in which a political contest about judicial selection could occur – the unregulated and largely informal political nature of the judicial selection process historically in Ireland. Second, it discusses the absence of external or political debate about alternative judicial selection mechanisms prior to the political crisis in 1994. Third, it presents the details of the political crisis between government coalition partners to show how the question of judicial selection processes came to political attention. Fourth, it demonstrates how the details of institutional change were agreed and how this process was so different to those institutional change processes experienced in the other countries presented in Chapter 1. Finally, it illustrates how, as a result of the institutional design, the change introduced in Ireland had a less meaningful impact on the discretion of politicians to choose their preferred candidate than in comparable countries.

CONTEXT OF POLITICAL CONFLICT – THE INFORMALITY OF THE JUDICIAL SELECTION PROCESS

In order to understand how such political conflict could take place, it is important to appreciate the historically unregulated nature of judicial selection in Ireland. Although there was provision in the Constitution for the role of the government in judicial selection and basic statutory eligibility criteria for judges of different courts, judicial selection in Ireland had previously been governed by unofficial political processes.[1]

1 See Chubb (1991), Casey (2000) and Byrne and McCutcheon (2014).

Historically, judicial appointments in Ireland were predominantly governed by the informal aspect of the appointments process – that of personal networks and political allegiances. This element of judicial appointments dates back to before the formation of the State as, during the nineteenth century, many of the barristers appointed to the Irish Bench had either been members of parliament in the Westminster parliament or had served as Attorney General or as some other law officer in Ireland (Byrne and McCutcheon, 2014). Delany observes that politics played a considerable part in the preferment of individuals to the Bench in Ireland prior to independence in 1922. Of those who were appointed to judgeships between 1801 and 1921, over half had sat in the House of Commons and nearly three-quarters had been law officers – either as Attorney General or Solicitor General. Given that the function of the law officer is to advise the government on legal matters, this put them at the forefront of political activity. This was an inherited process and no different to the system in England where 80 out of 139 appointments, made between 1832 and 1906, were members of parliament at the time of their appointment and, of these, 63 were appointed while their party was in office (Delany, 1975).

Article 68 of the Constitution of the Irish Free State, 1922, provided that all judges should be appointed by the Governor General on the advice of the Executive Council. The Constitution of Ireland 1937 took a similar line in relation to judicial appointments. Article 35.1 of the Constitution states that 'The judges of the Supreme Court, the High Court and all other Courts established in pursuance of Article 34 hereof shall be appointed by the President.'

The constitutional prerogative of the government to nominate a person for judicial appointment by the President is based on Article 13.9 of the Irish Constitution, which provides that the powers and functions of the President are exercisable by him or her only on the advice of the government, except where the Constitution expressly provides for the President to act with absolute discretion or on the advice of the Council of State. Judicial appointment is not a function in which the President enjoys such discretion. The appointment of a judge is an act 'requiring the President's intervention for its effectiveness in law, [but] in fact [it is] the decision and act of the Executive' (Finlay P in *The State (Walshe) v. Murphy* (1981) IR 275, cited in Hogan and Whyte, 2003, p. 998). This shows that, beyond the general requirement that judicial appointments be made by the President on the advice of the government, the Constitution is otherwise silent on the role of the government in judicial selection or how it should go about performing this advisory role under Article 13.9. There is no further guidance as to the conduct of judicial selection in Ireland, other than Article 36 of the Constitution, which provides that the number of judges and the terms of their appointment are to be regulated by statute. Governments were therefore free to adopt such procedures as they saw fit and no government saw fit to establish any more formalized processes between 1937 and 1994. The system in the Constitution of the Irish Free State 1922 and the Constitution of Ireland 1937 can be classified as the executive nomination and appointment model of judicial selection – discussed in Chapter 1. It was widely accepted that the influence of political allegiances on judicial appointments continued in post-1937 Ireland (Delany, 1975).[2]

The Courts (Supplemental Provisions) Act 1961 set out the formal qualifications required to be a judge of the Supreme Court, High Court, Circuit Court and District Courts. Barristers and solicitors were required to have ten to twelve years' experience practising as a lawyer before being eligible for appointment to these courts. The provisions of the 1961 Act replaced those of the Courts Act 1924. The 1961 Act repeated the terms of service specified in the 1924 Act, with the exception of those for the District Court where (until it was amended in the Courts of Justice Act 1953) only six years' service as a practising barrister or solicitor was the required. In the 1924 and 1961 Acts, judicial appointments to the Supreme Court, High Court and Circuit Court were restricted to practising barristers. However, appointments to all courts were opened up to both practising barristers and solicitors with appropriate periods of practice experience by the Courts and Court Officers Act 2002. Since then, six solicitors have been appointed directly to the High Court, although none yet to the Supreme Court. Additionally, two solicitors who had been judges of the Circuit Court were subsequently 'elevated' to the High Court.

Table 2.1 summarizes the legislation governing the formal qualifications and minimum experience for judges of each court. In addition to this, a person will be eligible for appointment to the High Court if they have served either as a judge of the Circuit Court for two years, or if they have, within the two years preceding their proposed appointment, served as a judge of certain international courts and had practiced as a barrister or solicitor prior to that appointment (section 4, Courts and Court Officers Act 2002).

Having met the basic statutory terms for qualification, a person was then eligible for the next stage of judicial recruitment. Prior to 1995, this was governed informally. Qualifications of a formal type were laid down, as shown, but nothing more was prescribed (Delany, 1975). The change introduced to the

2 A former Taoiseach wrote in 2003 that 'Because of the efforts of the first Cumann na nGaedheal government, most public appointments were excluded from political influence, but jobbery had become a feature of Irish politics in relation to the small range of posts that remained outside the purview of the Civil Service Commission and the Local Appointments Commission, posts such as local authority gangers, rate collectors, vocational teachers, government messengers, and – in a genteel way – judges' (FitzGerald, 2003).

judicial recruitment process through the Courts and Court Officers Act 1995 was the first formalized process for judicial selection, other than simply prescribing qualifications and minimum experience in statute.

Table 2.1: Minimum statutory qualification and years of professional experience for Irish judiciary (changes in each Act highlighted in bold)

	Courts Act 1924	Courts of Justice Act 1953	Courts (Supplemental Provisions) Act 1961	Courts and Court Officers Act 1995	Court and Court Officers Act 2002
Supreme Court	Barrister 12 years	Barrister 12 years	Barrister 12 years	Barrister 12 years	**Barrister or solicitor 12 years**
High Court	Barrister 12 years	Barrister 12 years	Barrister 12 years	Barrister 12 years	**Barrister or solicitor 12 years**
Circuit Court	Barrister 10 years	Barrister 10 years	Barrister 10 years	**Barrister or solicitor 10 years**	Barrister or solicitor 10 years
District Court	Barrister or solicitor 6 years	**Barrister or solicitor 10 years**	Barrister or solicitor 10 years	Barrister or solicitor 10 years	Barrister or solicitor 10 years

Source: Statutory references cited in the table.

Although the Constitution provides that judges are to be appointed by the President on the advice of the government, in practice only the Taoiseach and Minister for Justice (together with other party leaders in the case of a coalition) are involved in the selection. The rest of the government are simply informed of the name of the chosen person (Coakley and Gallagher, 2004). Coakley and Gallagher assert that the traditional process has been essentially informal but secret and political connections have played a major role.

The informality and lack of structure or regulation around the process of judicial appointments provided the space within which a political conflict could occur. One such feature was the 'constitutional convention' that the Attorney General would be appointed to a vacancy that arose on the High Court during his or her tenure. In the instance of a vacancy on the High Court or Supreme Court the Attorney General usually had the 'first right of refusal' as it was called (Bartholomew, 1971).

This 'first right of refusal' was at the heart of the political crisis that created the imperative to reform the judicial appointments process in Ireland. Judicial appointments in Ireland were in the control of the government of the day, with no restrictions other than the general prescription set out in the Constitution and the statutory minimum requirements. Beyond this, the government had complete discretion to appoint their preferred candidate. It is in this context that a political crisis between two coalition partners developed. The crisis centred on the appointment of the Attorney General, Mr Harry Whelehan SC, the legal adviser to the government who was a political appointment of the Taoiseach and leader of the Fianna Fáil party (Mr Albert Reynolds TD), to one of the most senior judicial posts in the legal system, President of the High Court.

The tradition of allowing the law officer the 'first right of refusal' was inherited from pre-independence Ireland. In the period 1874 to 1921, of the thirty-nine law officers, only five were not promoted to the Irish bench or appointed Lord Chancellor of Ireland. One was elevated directly to the House of Lords.[3]

> This uniformity of practice in the pre-independence period may have given rise to the view that a law officer had a claim to the first – or any – judicial vacancy that arose during his tenure of office. (Casey, 1996, p. 245)

Early post-independence political leaders did not stand over this as a principle, but operated it in practice. As Casey (1996) observes, the first President of the Executive Council, Mr W.T. Cosgrave, told the Dáil in 1924: 'I do not think it would be a good principle to adopt that because a man was Attorney General he naturally took any vacancy which might arise in the judiciary.'

Cosgrave's successor, Eamon de Valera, was of the same view and, in 1940, told his newly appointed Attorney General, Mr Kevin Haugh, that the appointment did not imply any commitment whatever on the government's part to subsequent appointment to the next, or any vacancy, on the judicial bench (Casey, 1996). Despite these words, Mr de Valera appointed Mr Haugh to the bench and indeed then appointed every Attorney General who served him to the bench (Casey, 1996).[4]

The practice of governments over time indicated the existence of the principle. The existence of the convention is also supported by leading Irish legal academics of the period:

> As a matter of tradition, it is said that the Attorney General has certain claims on the first refusal of every judgeship vacant during his or her period of office. (Delany, 1975, p. 76).

3 These were Edward Carson (SG for Ireland 1892); James Chambers (SG for Ireland 1917); David Plunkett (SG 1875–7); Hugh MacDermot (SG 1865; AG 1868–70); C.H. Hemphill (SG 1892–5). 4 These were Kevin Haugh, Kevin Dixon, Cearbhall O'Dálaigh and Thomas Teevan (Casey, 1996, Chapter 9, ref. 23).

This was the view of Professor Bartholomew who interviewed all living Taoisigh (or Prime Ministers). In the case of a vacancy on the High Court or Supreme Court the Attorney General usually has the 'first right of refusal' (Bartholomew 1971). It was also the view of the political decision-makers of the period between 1982 and 1995 who were interviewed in the course of this study:

> There was an unwritten rule that an Attorney General is entitled to a judicial appointment. You might check with an Attorney General did he want to be appointed before making the appointment, now, or in another five years or at all. Another precedent in the system is that the Chair of Bar Council is made a High Court Judge. (Pre-1995/MJ/1)[5]

> The AG was entitled to be a judge, it was his privilege as he was in and out of politics. (Pre-1995/TAO/2)

In defending the nomination of Mr Whelehan to the Office of the President of the High Court, the then-Taoiseach Albert Reynolds quoted Basil Chubb, whom he described as being 'one of the most eminent authorities on constitutional governance'. Reynolds commented that Chubb had written in 1992 that 'by custom the Attorney General, a political appointee, who is the government's legal adviser and state prosecutor, is always offered any vacancy to the High Court that occurs during his term of office' (Chubb, 1992, p. 295). Reynolds said: 'I underline the word "any", which clearly includes the Presidency'. (Reynolds, 15 Nov. 1994, Dáil Éireann debates, 447, c.26)

Another Attorney General was of a different view and said that, although there is a perceived tradition that the Attorney General has a right of first refusal to a High Court post, it did not extend to the position of President of the High Court.

> In the case of Harry Whelehan it was the justification used by Reynolds for the appointment, but I would query whether the convention ever ran to the President of the High Court or the Office of Chief Justice. There is no real precedent for that. (Pre-1995/AG/4).

The opinion of the Taoiseach on the constitutional convention was not based on advice from Mr Whelehan, who told a Dáil Committee he had not advised the Taoiseach about this (Casey, 1996). Rather the Taoiseach, Mr Reynolds, said that he drew on his own understanding of such practices from his prior experience in government, giving as a precedent the appointment of a former Attorney General, John Murray SC, to the European Court of Justice.

5 See Appendix 1 for interview schedule.

> It was certainly clear to me at the time that the practice was just implemented, that he had first refusal on any judicial function. He (Whelehan) made his call and it was granted. (Reynolds (1994) cited in Report of the Sub-Committee of the Select Committee on Legislation and Security, p. 92, c.396)

Indeed, Mr Whelehan was of the same view, when he told a Dáil Committee[6] that his authority for the precedent allowing the Attorney General to be appointed was based on a constitutional convention that he had learned as a law student from his lecturer in constitutional law.

Nothing in the Constitution or in statute references the preferment of the Attorney General in this way. It was not a formal rule. It was a norm that was simply 'understood' by the legal community and government. It is not surprising that Mr Whelehan would have felt comfortable relying on it or that Mr Reynolds would have felt justified in affording him its benefit. The 'convention' typifies the unregulated nature of judicial appointments in Ireland prior to 1995. This informality also made possible the type of political contest that occurred in 1994 between the members of the Labour Party and Fianna Fáil who served in government together. Informality made it a straightforward matter to change the practice after the crisis and since 1995, the rules have been formally established. The Attorney General is now informed, in writing, that he or she does not have an entitlement to any judicial office that may arise during or after his or her tenure (Post-1995/AG/2 and Post-1995/AG/8). However, one interviewee was of the view that such communication had been in place prior to 1995 (POL/6).

The informal nature of judicial selection processes in Ireland is important in understanding the nature of the political conflict that occurred in 1994. It provided both the space for a contest to occur between unhappy coalition partners and the space to introduce a structured system as a political solution to this contest. If there had been a more regulated system in place, the political contest could not have occurred in the same way.

THE ABSENCE OF DEBATE OR DEMANDS FOR CHANGE OF JUDICIAL SELECTION PROCESSES IN IRELAND

As described above, institutional change to the judicial selection process in Ireland occurred as a result of a political crisis between the coalition partners in the Irish government in 1994. Prior to 1994, there had been no substantive calls to reform the judicial selection process, no work by the Department of

6 Ireland. Houses of the Oireachtas (1994). *Report of the Sub-Committee of the Select Committee on Legislation and Security*. Dublin: Stationary Office.

Justice on alternative mechanisms of judicial selection and no evidence of sustained public or stakeholder concern either about the role of the courts or who was appointed to them. Bartholomew (1971) provided no evidence of discussion about alternative methods of judicial selection or sustained dissatisfaction with, or concern about, the extant system. Ireland inherited its system of judicial selection along with its legal system when it achieved independent statehood and no serious policy proposals had been mooted to change the judicial selection process in the intervening period.

Chapter 1 identified Ireland as an outlier from the other countries surveyed for this study for a variety of reasons. When the issue of possible changes to judicial selection structures became a topic of discussion in the other jurisdictions examined, there followed a period of debate and consultation that took place over a period of one to two years. The absence of debate about judicial selection in Ireland highlights the reality that institutional change was introduced as a result of political conflict and not the enactment of long-held policy preferences.

Of course, the political crisis could be regarded as having been a good opportunity to introduce long-standing policy preferences that would otherwise not have found expression in the programme of work of the coalition. But there is no evidence, either in documentary form or in interviews with leading members of the government of the day, that this was so. One contributor to this study, who was involved in the political events of 1994, commented that such institutional change would not have occurred in the absence of the crisis, 'unless or until something else drove it' (POL/6). Evidence gathered in interviews suggests that it would not have occurred unless there was some other driving factor, and that it was not part of the thinking of either of the coalition parties in 1994.

POLITICAL CRISIS BETWEEN COALITION PARTNERS IN 1994

This book argues that institutional change in Ireland arose as a result of political conflict. Understanding the political crisis in Ireland in 1994 is crucial to explaining the reasons for institutional change. It also helps us to understand the form of institutional change introduced. The dynamics of the political crisis help to inform the motivations of the decision-makers and their justification for institutional change. As will be seen, institutional change was ultimately introduced a year after the political crisis and the nature of this change was considerably weakened over the intervening period. This helps us to understand that the motivation for institutional change was the frustration felt by a party in the governing coalition.

This section explains the nature of the political crisis and its link to concerns over government discretion in judicial selection. This frames the context in which institutional change and the design of new institutional structures occurred. The Irish government in 1994 was made up of a coalition of members of the Labour Party and Fianna Fáil. It was the first coalition between these two parties.

> From the outset, there was a degree of nervousness in the Labour Party in relation to the coalition with Fianna Fáil. (POL/1).

The Labour Party had been in coalition government before, but always with the Fine Gael party. Fianna Fáil had only been in one coalition and it was a relatively new experience for them – historically, they had been used to governing on their own.

Tensions between the coalition partners were exacerbated by a change in leadership in Fianna Fáil shortly after the coalition was formed, from Charles Haughey TD to Albert Reynolds TD. It was widely believed that the new Fianna Fáil leader resented having to share power with Labour. The two parties had clashed repeatedly during the previous government's term of office (a coalition of Fianna Fáil and the Progressive Democrats). For example, Mr Reynolds, the then Minister for Industry and Commerce, had come under sharp attack from Labour over his possible implication in allegations of misconduct in the beef industry.[7]

There appears to have been two major precipitating factors that culminated in the political crisis between the coalition partners (POL/1): the first was the conclusion of a politically sensitive tribunal relating to allegedly corrupt payments in the beef industry and the second was the retirement of Chief Justice Finlay.

In 1992, the sitting President of the High Court, Mr Liam Hamilton, was the presiding judge in a politically sensitive Tribunal of Inquiry. The Tribunal of Inquiry produced a report with which the Labour Party was dissatisfied on a number of levels. At the same time the Chief Justice, Thomas Finlay, was about to retire. Mr Justice Liam Hamilton, who had delivered a conclusion in the Beef Tribunal report that was less damaging to the Fianna Fáil members of government than had been expected, was considered the front running candidate for the position of Chief Justice.

> Liam Hamilton was the President of the High Court and the holder of the 2nd highest office in the judiciary. It would have taken a big reason not to appoint him as Chief Justice when the position became vacant. (POL/1)

7 For more details on the Beef Tribunal and Irish politics see O'Toole, F. (1995) *Meanwhile back at the ranch*. London: Random House; and Cullen (2001) *With a little help from my friends: planning corruption in Ireland*. Dublin: Gill & MacMillan.

On this occasion, the traditional approach to judicial appointment – in which a judge who was believed to be politically well-disposed to a party would then gain preferment from that party – was unacceptable to the Labour Party because of their reticence about this individual appointment. The Labour Party preferred to keep Mr Justice Hamilton in his current job, where he was regarded as 'an excellent manager of the busiest court' (Finlay, 1998, p. 246). Instead, the party favoured appointing another jurist, Mr Justice Donal Barrington, as Chief Justice (POL/1). However, as Judge Barrington was then serving at the European Court of First Instance, he did not meet the statutory qualifications of the day, which required judges to be practising barristers at the time of their appointment. He was therefore ineligible for the appointment to the Supreme Court.[8]

Consequently, Labour was unable to have their preferred candidate appointed. There were significant Cabinet tensions around the appointment of Mr Justice Hamilton as Chief Justice. A Cabinet sub-committee comprising the Taoiseach, Tánaiste, Attorney General and Minister for Justice was set up following one Cabinet meeting at which the (Labour Party) Tánaiste had resisted the appointment of Mr Justice Hamilton as Chief Justice. Mr Justice Hamilton was subsequently appointed as Chief Justice, with the 'grudging assent' of the Labour Party (POL/6). Hamilton's appointment in turn left the Office of the President of the High Court vacant. This was the first act in the short sharp succession of contested senior judicial appointments that was to lead to institutional change.

The next act began when Harry Whelehan SC, the then Attorney General, expressed an interest to the Taoiseach, Albert Reynolds TD, in the vacancy in the Office of the President of the High Court. The Taoiseach responded favourably and accordingly Mr Whelehan was likely to be the appointee. The critical and inescapable point to note here is that the Taoiseach did not appear to be concerned about the views of his coalition partner, who had already expressed reservations about such an appointment. This was in large degree because the Taoiseach and Fianna Fáil were used to governing on their own without reference to coalition structures. The Labour Party, who were more used to the give and take of coalition government, were unhappy with these developments and determined to have their voice heard in the appointment. As will be seen in Chapter 3, judicial selection in coalition governments in the period 1982 to 1994 (with the exception of this case) was typified by the sharing of judicial appointments between coalition parties on roughly agreed ratios.

In relation to the proposed appointment of Mr Whelehan, the consensus within the Labour Party was that Mr Whelehan's views would be much closer

8 The Courts and Court Officers Act 1995 changed this and ensured that such a situation would not arise again, by ensuring that service as a judge of the European Court of Justice, the European Court of First Instance or Advocate General would constitute 'practice as a barrister' for the purpose of the Courts and Court Officers Act and appointment to the Irish judiciary.

to majority Fianna Fáil opinion than to Labour's. He was viewed as a 'Catholic conservative who, as Attorney General, had presided over the very politically difficult "X" case relating to the protection of the life of a pregnant 14-year-old girl' (POL/1).[9] Furthermore, he had produced what was seen as a conservative view of Cabinet confidentiality during the Beef Tribunal, which the Labour Party believed had unduly favoured Fianna Fáil. For these reasons, the Labour Party was not happy with Mr Whelehan as a candidate for the Office of President of the High Court. Moreover, if he was appointed, Labour was going to lose its influence for the second time in quick succession over the appointment of the two most senior judicial positions in the State – appointments that would not arise again within the lifetime of that government.

The Labour Party expressed their dissatisfaction within government.[10] There followed a high-level argument between senior members of the two parties. Central to this disagreement was the behaviour of the Taoiseach in relation to the appointment, in particular his move to progress the appointment when the leader of the Labour Party was out of the country on State business. The trouble that had been simmering internally between the two parties had now reached the point of no return and both parties faced the prospect of a general election (POL/1). To outside observers, the political tension arose from the single issue of the appointment, or otherwise, of Harry Whelehan to the Office of the President of the High Court. But mutual mistrust had been brewing for some time. One of the participants in this study who had been a Cabinet minister at the time in 1994 made the observation that no one really had an overwhelming problem with the appointment in itself – the issue had 'just got stuck in a political mess' (POL/4). Another observed that Mr Whelehan's ideology on social issues was 'just too far removed from that of the Labour Party'. The objection of the Labour Party was given an emotive edge by allegations that emerged that the Attorney General's office had dealt inadequately with issues arising from a child abuse case.

The decision to reform the judicial selection process arose directly from the political difficulty presented by the attempted appointment of the Attorney General to the Office of the President of the High Court. In fact, the appointment of Mr Whelehan itself was not the sole point of contention. The Whelehan controversy may be seen as the nadir of on-going political tension between the then government coalition partners (POL/1). But it threw light on an underlying institutional weakness of the Irish system, whereby the

9 *A.G. v. X* [1992] IESC 1; [1992] 1 IR 1 (5 Mar. 1992). **10** For more on this see Kelly, D., O'Regan, M. and O'Halloran, M. (1994) 'Reynolds accepts "wider" responsibilities'. *Irish Times*, 16 Nov.; Kennedy, G. (1994) 'Taoiseach says Whelehan is "only nominee" for High Court post'. *Irish Times*, 5 Oct.; O'Toole, F. (1994) 'Labour's real beef against Harry Whelehan'. *Irish Times*, 7 Oct.; Browne, V. (1994) 'Spring's opposition made Whelehan all the more determined'. *Irish Times,* 18 Nov.; Carroll, J. (1994) 'FF strongly opposes attempts to block Whelehan as next High Court President'. *Irish Times*, 20 Sept.

government could nominate and appoint a senior member of the judiciary and could do so on grounds that, while not overtly party political, would be widely understood as having been enabled through the individual's close links to a political network. The event that precipitated the crisis was the Fianna Fáil Taoiseach's appointment of the Attorney General to a senior judicial vacancy in a manner that had long-standing precedent and that would, in other circumstances, have been unexceptional.

The Labour Party took exception to this appointment for a number of reasons. It held that the constitutional convention by which a serving Attorney General could put themselves forward for a High Court vacancy could not continue. A political solution was necessary to enable the coalition to continue. The Labour Party held that the appointment could proceed, but only on the condition that a new judicial selection model would be established for the future and that the legislation to give effect to this change must be published before the appointment could proceed.

DEVELOPMENT OF INSTITUTIONAL CHANGE OF JUDICIAL SELECTION PROCESSES IN IRELAND

The political crisis described above reveals the context in which institutional change of judicial selection processes in Ireland arose. What is also of interest is the way in which institutional change was developed and shaped until it was finally enacted in law. Chapter 1 showed that, where institutional change had been introduced in other comparable countries, it typically followed a period of policy deliberation and stakeholder consultation. It has been shown that this occurred, usually, over a two-year process, following on discussion and debate about the merits of change and/or political statements (including, for example, in election manifestos and programmes for government) about the desirability of institutional change of judicial selection processes. In this Irish case, institutional design processes were different. This section shows how institutional design of the new system developed between the time of the political crisis in November 1994 and the enactment of the new institutional model in the Courts and Court Officers Act 1995 in November 1995.

POLITICAL IMPETUS BEHIND THE COURTS AND COURT OFFICERS BILL 1994

Interviews with senior political and legal figures in the 1994 government in 1994 reveal that the political purpose of the Courts and Court Officers Bill 1994 was twofold (POL/1, POL/5 and POL/7):

1 To provide an agreement that would enable the Labour Party to stay in government, and

2 To provide that, in future, some measure of political security would be available in making judicial appointments by ensuring that the government of the day must receive recommendations from an independent board, while ensuring that the decision-making power stayed firmly with the government.

Institutional design of this new model occurred without reference to external stakeholders or any policy deliberative process such as consultation exercises or policy papers. Instead, emergency talks were arranged between high level delegations from each coalition party in October 1994 to try to reach a solution which would allow them stay in government together. The major coalition partner, Fianna Fáil, was represented by Brian Cowen TD and Noel Dempsey TD; the minority coalition party, Labour, by Brendan Howlin TD and Ruairi Quinn TD.[11] The negotiators reached an agreement that provided that, before he took up his position as President of the High Court, Mr Whelehan would draft a Bill to introduce a new system for judicial appointments. They developed a document containing the proposed new structure for judicial appointments. The document was given to Mr Whelehan for him to begin to draft the heads of the Bill based on the political agreement.

The political direction he received was that, whatever the form of the system that would emerge, it must include the Presidents of the different courts, the Presidents of the different legal professional representative bodies – the Law Society and the Bar Council – and some lay people. The direction also specified that whatever was produced must not be binding on the government because, as discussed earlier, the Constitution gives the government the right to advise the President on the appointment of judges. The draft legislation was produced in a matter of weeks. In an interview for this study Mr Whelehan commented that:

> It was a kind of unreal scenario because my appointment would be made on the condition that Fianna Fáil and Labour would propose legislation to change the system and that legislation was available in outline. I was given a framework of what was needed, as part of the political agreement, and I put shape on that before I left office. It was a matter of weeks.

The government agreed the legislative changes proposed by the sub-committee at a Cabinet meeting on 15 October 1994, less than a week after the sub-committee met. Fianna Fáil would not agree to a new system of judicial appointments without the vacancy in the presidency of the High Court being

11 The meeting between the two party leaders, Albert Reynolds TD and Dick Spring TD took place on 9 October 1994 – Kelly, D., O'Regan, M. and O'Halloran, M. (1994) 'Reynolds accepts "wider" responsibilities'. *Irish Times*, 16 Nov.

filled and that the new system would not apply in relation to the filling of that vacancy. It was a political exchange that was not rooted in policy-based concerns for the judicial selection processes.

The Courts and Court Officers Bill 1994 was published within two weeks of the urgent weekend meeting of senior ministers to develop the legislative framework. It was the intention of the Labour Party that this legislation would be enacted as a matter of priority, thereby preventing any further judicial appointments being made that would not follow the new regulated process. The legislative process proceeded quickly; the Courts and Court Officers Bill went to a second stage hearing in the parliament on 2 November 1994.

One of the negotiators, Deputy Brian Cowen, later spoke in Dáil Éireann (parliament) at length (Dáil Éireann, 29 November 1995, lines 235–43) on the genesis of the proposed Judicial Appointments Advisory Board (when similar institutional change to that agreed by the coalition parties was introduced one year later by the successor government in the Courts and Court Officers Bill 1995). Deputy Cowen explicitly stated in Dáil Éireann that the reform was a 'charade', that it had nothing to do with judicial reform or the efficacy of the courts system and that the '*raison d'être* for setting up that Cabinet sub-committee was simply to try to break the impasse on filling the position of President of the High Court'. Deputy Cowen also commented in the Dáil that other political actors had later sought to justify what had happened as part of a programme of judicial reform. He claimed that the purpose of the committee, the deliberations of which were confidential at the time, was to get the Tánaiste 'off the hook' during three days of intense political negotiations. He commented that this was 'solely a political response to a temporary political problem that had nothing to do with the proper administration of the courts'. He also stated that such reform was never part of the thinking of the Department of Justice, nor was it ever part of the thinking of the Fianna Fáil party, 'It is a misnomer in terms of judicial reform' (Cowen, Dáil Éireann, 29 November 1995, lines 243). The introduction of the legislation to change the judicial selection system did not, in the end, save the coalition. As events would have it, the tension between the coalition partners was so great that relationships broke down irrevocably and the coalition broke up. Within one week of being appointed, Mr Whelehan resigned as President of the High Court because of the continued political scrutiny both of his handling of issues in the Attorney General's office and the questions that had surrounded the circumstances of his appointment.

For the first time in Ireland a new government was formed without recourse to a general election – this time with Labour forming a coalition government with Fine Gael and the Democratic Left party. As the Labour Party remained in government, the question of judicial appointment reform inevitably and inescapably remained on the political agenda (whether it was wanted or not) although with a good deal less urgency than it had during the period of extraordinary tensions that characterized the weeks preceding the breakdown of the earlier coalition.[12]

POLITICAL IMPETUS BEHIND THE COURTS AND COURT OFFICERS BILL 1995

Once the new government was formed, the issue was not progressed with any haste. Most parties in the new government were neither publicly committed to, or privately interested in, institutional change of the judicial selection system in a way that reduced the discretion of government to choose judges (POL/1; POL/6). Rather than move to enact the Courts and Court Officers Bill 1994 with the speed that had characterized its introduction and progress through second stage in November 1994, the Bill languished on the order paper for nearly a year when, in November 1995, it was withdrawn by the government and replaced with a revised bill, the Courts and Court Officers Bill 1995 – a year after the political crisis and a year after the calls for 'urgent' reform of the judicial selection process. Considering the need to bed down the new coalition successfully, it is understandable how time could pass. But the delay, nevertheless, impacts on implementing institutional change and presents an important puzzle in our analysis.

The reason for the delay between the formation of the new government and the publication and enactment of the 1995 Bill could be that the new government took the opportunity to include broader court reform in the 1995 Bill and this required time for policy development and legislative drafting. The programme for government agreed by the incoming government in December 1994 provided for a review of the Courts and Court Officers Bill 1994 with a view to determining the adequacy of the staffing levels of the courts having regard to the backlog of cases and significant delays in the court system.[13] This does not explain, however, the failure to enact the provisions of the Courts and Court Officers Bill 1994.

Crucially, the reform ultimately enacted had to be agreed with new coalition partners, Fine Gael and Democratic Left, both of whom had criticized the 1994 Bill for being a political ruse to overcome a political crisis. Opposition spokespeople in 1994 had been uncompromising in their criticism of the manner in which the Bill had been introduced as a response to the political crisis. It was called 'the most extensive smoke screen ever to billow out of Government Buildings' (Dáil Debate, 2 November 1994, line 1409) and 'what Labour gets in return for Fianna Fáil making Harry Whelehan President of the High Court' (Dáil Debate, 2 November 1994, line 1420).

12 DeBreadun, D., 1994, 18 Nov. 'Legacy of the programme for government may still be passed on'. *Irish Times (1921–Current File)*, 6. 13 Parliamentary questions show that this

The 1995 Bill was similarly derided by opposition parties, who focused on two aspects: that the Bill was a 'watered down' version of the same proposals published a year earlier, and the length of time this 'urgent' Bill took to be published by the new coalition. Both of these criticisms are important for this analysis of institutional change because they speak to the core issues in this story of institutional change. This is not a criticism of the institutional change produced, just a reflection of the reality that this institutional change was borne of political necessity rather than long-standing policy preferment by any political party at the time. It is important to appreciate this in order to better understand institutional change processes of politically sensitive matters that are important to politicians in government, such as the selection of judges.

The 1994 Bill was produced in a short period of time and, because of the political necessity of enacting it quickly, was unlikely to have been amended significantly to increase the discretion of government in judicial selection in the remaining stages of the legislative process. To have done so would have been a shift in policy for the Labour Party that would have been damaging to their credibility on the issue and, on this basis, it is likely that they would not have agreed to any such proposals at Cabinet had they been mooted.

The period between the formation of the new government in late 1994 and the publication of the 1995 Bill is critical. The programme for government provided for a review[14] of the 1994 Bill to be conducted. In doing so, the question of a new system for judicial selection was put on hold for the period of that review. The 1995 Bill could not differ too greatly from its 1994 progenitor, however, because of the presence of the same Labour personnel in government for whom it had been an issue of vital (political) importance just twelve months previously.

The Labour Party was a member of both governments and agreed to the terms of both the 1994 Bill and the 1995 Bill. The two Bills represented different levels of constraint placed on the government in the exercise of their constitutional function to advise the President on judicial appointments. What is uncertain is whether any differences between the Bills emerged as a result of a change of position within the Labour Party, or as a result of negotiations with their new coalition partners, or as a result of lobbying from interested parties in the intervening period, or some combination of these.

It is clear that with the passage of time from the political tensions of 1994, the urgency on the need for reform of the judicial selection process receded. It was not the judicial selection system in general that was problematic for the Labour Party, but rather the behaviour of their coalition partners between 1992 and 1994 in respect of judicial appointments and senior judicial

review was completed in June 1995 (Parliamentary Question 16507/95). However, no such review was ever published. 14 This was not published.

appointments in particular. It is suggested that the conflict over this issue reflected the unease and the tension between those particular coalition partners, rather than a problem with the selection of judges by partners to a coalition government in Ireland generally. Evidence gathered in the course of this study from interviews with political leaders and legal officers involved in judicial selection in coalition governments of the 1980s does not reveal similar tension over the issue of judicial appointments but rather a political agreement that such appointments would be 'shared' between the coalition partners, in varying ways.

The outcome of the 1994 political crisis was that the issue of judicial appointments was forced to the centre of the Irish political stage unexpectedly. Institutional change of the judicial selection system arose because judicial selection processes became the fulcrum of a major political storm that eventually resulted in the coalition government breaking up after only two years in office. The incoming government pledged to enact the reforms that had been mooted. But because of the circumstances, there was no consensus and, in truth, no widely shared clear views at all, about what really was at issue.

This is the context in which reform proposals were developed.

THE INSTRUMENT OF INSTITUTIONAL CHANGE: THE COURTS AND COURT OFFICERS BILLS

In Chapter 1 it was shown that the introduction of judicial screening models has been the common way to give effect to the policy objective of reducing governments' discretion in judicial selection. It was also shown that judicial screening models can be designed in different ways, with different effects on the reduction of government discretion.

In that analysis, Ireland was presented as an outlier. The new institutional model in Ireland had less impact on government discretion in judicial selection than in comparable models. In contrast to the comparable countries, there was little political commitment in Ireland to institutional change and this is evidenced by the circumstances in which the issue arose and was developed. We now turn to assess the impact of institutional change through an analysis of the design of the new model of judicial selection.

The implementation of the reform of the judicial selection process in Ireland occurred over two pieces of legislation: the Courts and Court Officers Bill 1994 (the 1994 Bill) and the Courts and Court Officers Bill 1995 (the 1995 Bill).

Of particular interest is that there are three institutional models to be considered – the one originally introduced in 1994 immediately after the political crisis (the 1994 Bill), the one introduced one year later (the 1995 Bill) and the one that was ultimately enacted (the 1995 Act). Each has different implications for the reduction of government discretion in judicial selection. The model that was ultimately enacted had much less impact on government discretion than the model introduced immediately following the political crisis. The passage of time between the political crisis and the enactment of the model enabled two things:

1 a diminution in the political urgency to introduce changed judicial selection processes, and
2 the opportunity to reflect on the consequences of reducing government discretion in judicial selection to the levels proposed by the 1994 Bill.

The Bills set out the model to be used for the new judicial selection system. Both Bills established a new model for judicial selection involving:

1 a requirement that people interested in judicial appointment apply for consideration for judicial appointment;
2 the establishment of a new independent board to participate in the judicial selection process, which was to be comprised of judicial officers, representatives of the legal professions and other, non-legal people, and whose purpose was to screen applicants for judicial office and to make recommendations to government of suitable people from which the government was to choose their preferred candidate and nominate that person for judicial appointment by the President.

The two Bills proposed essentially the same model of establishing an independent judicial screening board to recommend names of suitable judicial candidates to government. However, the Bills were different in the extent to which they would each bind a government in making a decision about a judicial appointment because they provide for different numbers of candidates to be recommended to government from which the government could choose a person for nomination for judicial appointment by the President. The institutional changes introduced in Ireland did not restrict the discretion of governments to choose their preferred candidates for appointment in the same way as comparable institutional change in jurisdictions such as England and Wales, Scotland, Northern Ireland and Israel.

Two things are important: the two Bills had different impacts on the level of discretion that would be enjoyed by future governments in judicial selection and both Bills reduced the discretion of government in judicial selection less than similar reforms introduced in other jurisdictions.

There are several analytical questions to consider. Would the provisions of the 1994 Bill and the 1995 Bill have addressed the issues that existed in the political crisis caused by the Harry Whelehan appointment? What did the 1994

Bill and the 1995 Bill contain and how did they impact on the discretion of politicians in selecting judges? What are the differences between the 1994 Bill and the 1995 Bill and what are the implications of these differences for the discretion of politicians in selecting judges? Why did the new government not progress the 1994 Bill as a matter of urgency when one of the partners to the coalition had been instrumental in its design and the other parties to the coalition had been vociferous in their support for judicial selection reform from the opposition benches?

The issues in the appointment of Mr Whelehan were the decision of the Taoiseach to push ahead an appointment in the full knowledge that his coalition partners were unhappy, and the informality of the unregulated judicial selection process that enabled the development of the constitutional convention on which Mr Whelehan sought to rely. There was also the question as to whether the Office of President of the High Court (or other courts) would be covered by the new legislative provisions.

On the first issue, neither this legislation nor any other legislation could account for the conduct of individuals in coalitions. A lack of trust had developed between the coalition partners over a period of time and relations between the two political parties were poor. This manifested itself in a failure by the Taoiseach to sufficiently acknowledge the perspective and wishes of his coalition partners and this was the principal reason for conflict over judicial appointments.

On the second issue, the establishment of a regulated system of judicial selection that required judicial aspirants to formally apply for appointment implicitly enabled the abolition of the disputed constitutional convention. However, this was not made explicit in the legislation. In any event, the convention was abolished by a later statement in the terms of the appointment of subsequent Attorneys General that there was no entitlement by virtue of their office to any special preferment in relation to judicial vacancies. If the government of the day wanted to appoint the Attorney General to a judicial office, though, they could do so – even without having to refer the vacancy to the new Board.

Significantly, the 1994 Bill did not cover the Office of Court Presidents despite the fact that the 1994 Bill emerged from a crisis over the appointment of a Court President. It did not provide for the new process to apply to future appointments to the Office of Court Presidents or to the Office of the Chief Justice.[15] In 1994, the then Minister for Justice, Máire Geoghegan-Quinn, stated that this exception was desirable because the government, in considering appointments to these top judicial offices, would want, among other things, to ensure continuity and consistency in the running and operation of various

15 Section 22 defines judicial offices that will be subject to the proposed Judicial Appointments Advisory Board but omits the President of each Court.

courts and that, in order to do so, the government would first have regard to the suitability of serving judges when appointing persons to fill these offices. This was an extraordinary political statement to make at the same time as having appointed the serving Attorney General directly to the position of President of the High Court. It concedes that having done precisely that, the government did not have a higher regard for the sitting judges of the High Court than they did their own Attorney General who had no experience as a High Court judge.

The decision to omit Court Presidents from the remit of the JAAB predictably caused a strong political reaction from the opposition benches during the debate on the 1994 Bill. The opposition commented that the Bill was a trade-off in the 'rather inelegant squabble' between the government parties over the appointment of the then current Attorney General to the Presidency of the High Court (Dáil Debate, 2 November 1994, line 1410) and that his appointment would be contrary to the spirit of the Bill being debated by the Oireachtas at the time of his appointment. He would be the last Attorney General to have availed of the 'first right of refusal' to a position on the High Court and certainly the last person appointed to the Office of the President of a Court without having first been a sitting judge. It was argued that his appointment would be a 'stark exception to the rule' that would be put into law when the Bill was enacted because, under the Bill, sitting High Court judges will have to be considered first for appointment to the Presidency of the High Court (Dáil Debate, 2 November 1994, line 1410). The tradition of giving the Attorney General the first offer of a judicial appointment during his term of office would no longer continue. It was argued that although the Bill's ostensible purpose was to provide for new procedures for judicial appointments, it expressly excluded from its terms of reference the High Court Presidency, despite the fact that it was the political crisis arising from an appointment to that very office that caused the publication of the Bill in the first place (Dáil Debate, 2 November 1994, 1422). It was further argued that, as the matter was effectively a live one before the Oireachtas, the government could not act on the appointment of any judges (including that of Mr Whelehan), while the manner of appointment was being debated by the Oireachtas.

The 1995 Bill addressed the issue of appointments of court Presidents by requiring the government to have regard to the suitability of serving judges when nominating someone to fill such an office (section 23). This resolved the matter and placed some regulation on such appointments and, since then, Court Presidents have been appointed from the ranks of sitting judges of that or another court.

The Courts and Court Officers Bill 1994 provided for the establishment of a judicial screening commission. This was effected by the establishment of an independent advisory board (the Judicial Appointments Advisory Board) that would receive applications for judicial positions and conduct a screening for suitability. It would then recommend a number of names to the Minister for Justice, from which the government would choose its preferred candidate for judicial appointment.

Under the 1994 Bill, the Judicial Appointments Advisory Board (JAAB) was to consist of senior members of the judiciary, the Chairman of the Bar Council and the President of the Law Society. Its function was to advise the Minister and the government, through its committees, of the names of persons suitable for appointment as judges.[16]

The 1994 Bill[17] provided that the JAAB would perform its functions through a series of committees. For the consideration of persons suitable for appointment to the Supreme Court, the High Court and the newly constituted Appeal Court, there was to be a committee consisting of all the members of the Board, except the Presidents of the Circuit and District Courts. For considering persons suitable for appointment to the Circuit Court, there was to be a committee consisting of the President of the High Court, the President of the Circuit Court, the Chairman of the Bar Council and the President of the Law Society. In the case of appointments to the District Court, the committee would consist of the President of the District Court, the Chairman of the Bar Council and the President of the Law Society.

The 1994 Bill also provided that a committee could consult the Attorney General of the day on the suitability of a person for judicial office. The 1994 Bill placed a requirement on the various committees only to submit the names of people whom that committee was satisfied fulfilled the relevant statutory requirements and had displayed in his or her practice a degree of competence and probity consistent with the proposed appointment and was suitable on grounds of character and temperament.

The Bill required that, where a judicial office was vacant, the Minister for Justice would formally request the relevant committee to submit the names of at least three and not more than five persons whom the committee believed were suitable for appointment and to give reasons for their suitability.[18] The names would be submitted to the Minister by the JAAB. In making the appointment, the government was required by the Bill to first have regard to the names of those persons that had been submitted by the JAAB to the Minister for Justice in making a decision on advising the President on the appointment of a judge. As we have stated, the JAAB was to recommend not less than three and not more than five names. This was done within the constitutional parameters that required the ultimate decision about judicial appointments to rest with the executive. Article 35.1 of the Constitution provides that the government has the responsibility for nominating a person

16 Section 23, Courts and Court Officers Bill 1994. 17 Section 24, Courts and Court Officers Bill 1994. 18 Section 25, Courts and Court Officers Bill 1994.

for appointment to the judiciary by the President. Provided the ultimate decision on the appointment was made by the government, the process leading up to that decision could be reformed. However, quite what level of discretion must, constitutionally, be retained by government is not defined and has been interpreted differently by different governments and their Attorneys General.

The system created under the 1994 Bill would not be binding on the government because of the constitutional requirements. The government could appoint someone who had not been recommended by a committee of the JAAB. However, it was intended to substantially reduce the discretion of the government in its decision-making by limiting its choice to no more than five nominees. In introducing the Bill, the Minister made the point that the Bill expressly requires the government to first have regard to the three to five names recommended by the JAAB in advising the President on the appointment of a judge.

> That is a significant direction to Government and highlights the pivotal role that I expect the new board and its committees to play. No Government could lightly ignore a recommendation made to it by a committee of the board. (Geoghegan-Quinn, Dáil Éireann, 2 November 1994, line 1386)

The Courts and Court Officers Bill 1995 (the 1995 Bill) was published in November 1995 by the new Minister for Justice, Nora Owens TD. The new government committed in the programme for government, 'A Government of Renewal', to review the provisions of the Courts and Court Officers Bill 1994 to ensure that measures will adequately address the need to tackle the backlog of cases to be heard in all courts.[19]

The Courts and Court Officers Bill 1994 was withdrawn from the order paper of the new Dáil. The new government had, at least theoretically, a clean sheet from which to start reform of the judicial selection process. However, the political circumstances required the enactment of legislation to change the judicial selection process in a way that reflected the Labour Party demands in the previous coalition government in 1994 – that government discretion in judicial selection be curtailed. The presence of Labour as a minor coalition partner in both the outgoing government and the new government meant some consistency was required between the approaches taken in the 1994 and 1995 Bills on the structure of a preferred process for judicial appointments. One member of the government in 1995 commented in an interview conducted for this study on the development of the 1995 Bill as follows:

19 That review was completed in June 1995 (Parliamentary Question 16507/95).

> Labour had been talking about it from about the previous August. It was being done at the time to save the government and the structures were already pretty well in place, the heads of Bill were in place. It went through fairly fast; nobody wanted to argue against it. It was one of those things that was accepted as being 'good'. People thought would be 'good' for the system. Saying you didn't want it meant saying you wanted the nepotism and all that and in fairness it wasn't. I mean the number of bad judges was very limited and I mean who's to say – a very good barrister can turn out to be a mediocre judge and a very mediocre barrister can do very well on the bench. (POL/4)

Part IV of the 1995 Bill provided for the establishment of the JAAB. The Bill provided that the membership of the JAAB would consist of the Chief Justice, the Presidents of the High, Circuit and District Courts, the Attorney General, a practising barrister nominated by the Chairman of the Bar Council, a practising solicitor nominated by the President of the Law Society and up to three people to be appointed by the Minister for Justice

The government's discretion to make the appointment was to be constrained by the Bill in two ways. First, the government was required to have regard to the names sent by the JAAB before advising the President of the person who was to be appointed to the judicial office. Second, if a person was appointed to the judiciary in circumstances where that person had not been recommended by the JAAB, notice of this would be made in the state official notices bulletin, *Iris Oifigiúil*.

The Board was given general powers under the Bill to advertise for judicial appointments, require applicants to fill in application forms, consult people concerning the suitability of applicants for judicial office, invite people to submit their names for consideration, arrange for the interviewing of applicants and such other things as the Board considers necessary to discharge its functions.[20]

The Bill also provided that a person who wished to be considered for appointment to judicial office should inform the JAAB and provide the JAAB with any information which they require for considering the application.[21] It provided that, where the Minister made a request to the Board for names in respect of a judicial vacancy, the Board would 'submit to the Minister the name of each person who has informed the Board of his or her wish to be considered for appointment to that judicial office' and the Board shall 'recommend to the Minister the names of at least ten persons for appointment to that judicial office'. Where fewer than ten people had applied, or where the Board found itself unable to recommend ten people, the Board was permitted to submit fewer than ten names. Where there was more than one vacancy at any given

20 Section 14, Courts and Court Officers Bill 1995. 21 Section 16, Courts and Court Officers Bill 1995.

time, the Board was required to submit ten names in respect of *each* vacancy, but it was not specified whether these should be the same ten names, or ten additional names.

DIFFERENCES BETWEEN THE COURTS AND COURT OFFICERS BILLS 1994 AND 1995

There are important differences between the two Bills produced in 1994 and 1995, the chief one being the impact that the different proposals would have on the discretion of government in choosing judges. It is important to understand what changes occurred, why they occurred and the impact on the effectiveness of the institutional change in achieving its purported purpose.

The 1995 Bill and 1995 Act differ from the 1994 Bill in two key respects (see Table 2.2 for a summary):

1 the number of names to be recommended to government.
2 the composition of the Judicial Appointments Advisory Board, including the presence of the Attorney General on the Board.

The 1995 Bill repeated the provision in the 1994 Bill that where the government was making an appointment to the Office of Chief Justice or to President of the High, Circuit or District Courts, it must first have regard to the currently serving judges on each court. This generated criticism from the opposition who argued that the apparent unanimity of the opposition on the second stage debate on the 1994 Bill that the Office of President of the High Court ought to be subject to the new appointments procedure had been quickly forgotten by those who crossed the Dáil floor into Cabinet.

The 1995 Bill provided that there would be representation of lay people on the Board, in addition to representatives of the judiciary and the legal profession. The 1995 Bill provides in section 13 that the Minister would have the right to nominate three persons to the board for three-year renewable terms of appointment. The Minister argued that this would allow her to introduce a wide range of experience and voices into the process – such as commercial experience or representatives of victims of crime or women's groups. This was criticized by the opposition as being designed to ensure the government would have a 40 per cent representation on the Board (with the presence of the Attorney General). Opposition members tabled amendments to delete the appointment of the Attorney General to the JAAB and to appoint the Chairman of the Law Reform Commission to the JAAB, which had been a provision in the 1994 Bill.

As mentioned, in the 1995 Bill, a further change in the composition of the board is that the Attorney General of the day was to be a member. The

Minister, Nora Owens TD, argued that the Attorney General of the day is uniquely suitable to be a member of the Board, because of his or her knowledge of the legal profession. The 1995 Bill provided that the Board could recommend the Attorney General for a judicial appointment, but if the Board is considering the Attorney General for appointment, he or she would be required to withdraw from the deliberations of the Board. This is quite different from the 1994 Bill that envisaged the Chairman of the Law Reform Commission having a seat at the JAAB.

The opposition also criticized the decision to include the Attorney General on the Board, arguing that Attorneys General, by virtue of the political manner of their appointment to the Office of Attorney General, are inextricably linked with the politics of government and that their presence on the Board and in the decision-making process could diminish the impartiality of the JAAB.

However, the Minister countered that the Attorney General played a key role in advising the government on all matters relating to law and the only reason the Attorney General was not included in the structure under the 1994 Bill was for political expediency reasons due to the tension that existed with regard to the then Attorney General and his relationship with the government. The outcome in the 1995 Act was that the Attorney General is a member of the Board.

The Courts and Court Officers Bill 1995 replicated the 1994 Bill's regulated system for judicial selection by government, but did so in a way that provided much greater discretion to future governments than that provided by the earlier Bill. Although it replicated the 1994 Bill in creating a new independent board that would screen applicants for judicial office and recommend names of suitable persons for judicial appointment to government, the 1995 Bill created much greater discretion for future governments in choosing their preferred candidate from those recommended by the independent board simply by extending the number of recommended candidates from which the government could select its preferred candidate. However, the essential element of the Bills – the extent to which government discretion would be constrained by the independent board – can be summarized by showing the variance between the Bills in the number of names to be sent to government from the board for consideration for judicial office (see Table 3.2).

The principal difference between the 1994 Bill and the 1995 Bill is the varying number of candidates they require the independent Board to recommend. This is important for our analysis of the impact of institutional change on the discretion of government in future judicial appointments. The 1994 Bill provided that the JAAB would recommend not fewer than three people and not more than five – a system which provided the government with the requisite choice as required by the Constitution, but limiting its selection (within what is a small pool of suitably qualified lawyers) to a maximum of five persons.

Table 2.2: Differences between 1994 Bill and 1995 Bill and 1995 Act

	1994 Bill	1995 Bill	1995 Act
Number of names to be recommended to government	Not fewer than three and not more than five in respect of each vacancy.	At least ten names in respect of each vacancy.	At least seven names in respect of each vacancy.
Composition of JAAB	Chief Justice, President of the High Court, President of the Circuit Court, President of the District Court, President of the Law Society of Ireland, President of the Bar Council of Ireland, Chairperson Law Reform Commission.	Chief Justice, President of the High Court, President of the Circuit Court, President of the District Court, President of the Law Society of Ireland, President of the Bar Council of Ireland, Attorney General, three individuals nominated by the Minister for Justice. All members to be involved in all deliberations (except the Attorney General if discussing his or her candidacy for judicial office).	Chief Justice, President of the High Court, President of the Circuit Court, President of the District Court, President of the Law Society of Ireland, President of the Bar Council of Ireland, Attorney General, three individuals nominated by the Minister for Justice. All members to be involved in all deliberations (except the Attorney General if discussing his or her candidacy for judicial office).
Role of the Attorney General on the JAAB and judicial selection process	To be consulted by JAAB.	Member of JAAB who participates in JAAB discussions and in government discussions on judicial selection.	Member of JAAB who participates in JAAB discussions and in government discussions on judicial selection.

Source: Courts and Court Officers Bill 1994 and 1995 and Courts and Court Officers Act 1995.

The 1995 Bill, as it was first published, removed this restriction and provided that the board would recommend at least ten names in respect of each vacancy. During committee and report stage of the legislative process the Minister came under political pressure on this point and she moved to amend the Bill to provide that it would recommend at least seven names in respect of each vacancy. This is what is ultimately contained in the Courts and Court Officers Act 1995. The intention of the Minister initially was clearly to give the government maximum flexibility in their decision. She argued that requiring the Board to recommend only three to five names as was proposed in the 1994 Bill would restrict unduly the government's discretion in the matter of judicial appointments which it has by virtue of the constitutional arrangements relating to this matter and for this reason she contended that the Board should be required to recommend a reasonable number of names. However, there is no explanation as to why a 'reasonable' number should be 'at least ten names' in the Bill as initiated and then reduced to 'at least seven names' by the time the Bill was enacted.

This new element in the Bill was clearly a marked departure from the provision in the 1994 Bill. Opposition spokespeople were heavily critical of this decision to increase the number of candidates to be recommended by the JAAB to the government. Deputy Geoghegan-Quinn, the Minister for Justice who introduced the 1994 Bill, was unforgiving in her interpretation of the reason for the increased number of recommendations to ten from the maximum of five in her own bill, the Court and Court Officers Bill 1994:

> I laughed when I read the Minister's statement that: 'Requiring the appointments board to recommend only three to five names as proposed in the 1994 Bill would restrict unduly the government's discretion in the matter of judicial appointments'. I presume this refers to political discretion and that she and the Government felt there was a great political restriction on them in that they were not allowed to have more than five nominees recommended to them. (Geoghegan-Quinn, Dáil Éireann, 29 November 1995, line 31)

What was perceived to compound matters further was that the greater discretion given to the government coincided with the expansion of the courts by a total of ten judges, as provided by the 1995 Act (which provided for three additional High Court judges and seven additional Circuit Court judges). The number of judges was increased as a result of significant historic and problematic delays in the courts and as an alternative to introducing a Court of Appeal (as had been provided in the 1994 Bill). The opposition argued that with the creation of these new positions, the JAAB would have to recommend so many people as to deliberately undermine the purpose of the Bill. The proposal to create an additional three High Court judges and seven Circuit Court judges combined with the requirement of the 1995 Act that the Board recommend seven names in respect of each vacancy, would mean that the board may shortly have to recommend the names of at least seventy members of the Bar, which was slightly less than 10 per cent of the profession at the time.

> By widening the net the Minister is deliberately undermining the more considered recommendation in the original Bill where the board was given an option of recommending three, but not more than five, persons for a vacancy. There can only be one conclusion, the Minister will decide who the judges are. (O'Donoghue, Dáil Éireann, 28 November 1995, line 1777)

The opposition tabled a series of amendments to reduce the number of candidates recommended by the JAAB from ten per vacancy, to the position that had been taken in the 1994 Bill, 'not less than three persons and not more than five'. The Bill as amended by the Select Committee on Legislation and Scrutiny provided at section 16 (2) that 'the Board shall recommend at least seven persons for appointment' to judicial office. This was an important decision as it considerably changes the role of the JAAB in recommending candidates to the government.[22]

Members of the government from this period commented that the justification for the increased number arose from a concern not to unduly exclude people who would otherwise be recommended.

> The structures of the JAAB, they were difficult to come up with. You had difficulty with the judges, you had difficulty because these were qualified people and you were demanding of them to more or less have their qualifications questioned by saying they had to apply and they would be looked at by their peers to see if they were good, bad or indifferent. And that was something the lawyers didn't like. There was a certain amount of resistance to the system put in place and therefore that's why it was so broad and that's why I think the numbers were put in. The big number seven. For one vacancy you could nominate up to seven rather than making specific recommendations. If you got twenty-five applications and you were only putting in two people, you were kind of saying that the other twenty-three weren't really good enough. We were trying to get over a situation where you were making judgments. (POL/2)

Different approaches were taken by the different Bills on the level of political discretion to be retained by government in judicial selection. These Bills, the instruments of reform, were introduced within one year of one another. The passage of time following the political crisis in 1994 combined with political discussion between the new coalition partners resulted in a changed approach

22 'Under the original November 1994 Bill when the Labour Party was in Government with Fianna Fáil and following the famous meeting at Baldonnel it was proposed that the judicial appointments advisory board would recommend not fewer than three persons and not more than five persons. The idea at that time was to give some autonomy, limited though it had to be by the Constitution, to the appointments board in making recommendations to the Minister. It must have been perfectly clear to the Tánaiste and the Labour Party that if one extended the number of names which could be submitted to the Government then one would negate to a large extent the effectiveness and autonomy of the board … I do not know what changed between November last year and December this year but we now have the extraordinary situation where the judicial appointments advisory board must submit at least seven names. I stress that the board is not being asked to submit for recommendation not more than seven names, but rather is being told to submit at least seven names' (O'Donoghue, Dáil Éireann, 28 November 1995).

to the placing of constraints on the discretion of politicians in government with respect to judicial selection processes.

This provides further support to the contention that the impetus for this reform of the judicial selection process in Ireland was political necessity alone and not a policy-based concern of politicians. As observed in Chapter 1, the purpose of such institutional change in other countries was to create a separation between politics and the selection of judges and to provide measures by which the diversity of the judiciary could be enhanced to be more reflective of the communities they served.

As we have seen the most significant point of difference between the institutional design of the 1994 Bill and its 1995 successor was the output of the newly created judicial selection commission. The question is, within the Irish constitutional parameters, how far can the discretion of the government be constrained and how does this translate, in practical terms, to choosing a numerical output that would be both constitutionally permissible and place strong constraints on the discretion of government?

The 1994 government took the view that three was a constitutionally acceptable number. The 1995 government took a different view. This could be because of different legal advice (from a new Attorney General) in relation to the constitutionally permissible boundaries of the legislation. Interview evidence shows that it was because of a shift in political preference on how far the government was willing to be constrained in choosing judges. But the argument is important in considering the shape and parameters of any future reform.

The argument here is a matter of degree. How much the government's prerogative could be constrained by the new statutory provisions? Arguments can be advanced that range from the government having unfettered discretion in selecting judicial candidates, to being required to choose one of two names to nominate to the President for appointment.

At the broadest end of the spectrum is the argument that the only way in which the government's decision-making authority would have been unconstitutionally threatened was if the government had no decision to make, for instance if the JAAB had only recommended one name *and* there was no provision for the government to appoint someone that had not been recommended by the JAAB. In every other circumstance, the government would have had a choice of sorts. At the other end of the spectrum is the argument that anybody that performs more than a screening function and purports to choose candidates for judicial office is unconstitutionally usurping the function of government in relation to judicial appointment, as prescribed by Articles 35.1 and 13.9.

The system envisaged in the 1994 Bill would have acted as a strong constraint on a government exercising its function under Article 13.9 to advise the President of Ireland in relation to judicial appointments. In particular, the provision for a maximum number of recommendations from the JAAB was a much greater restriction than that which was ultimately enacted in the 1995 Act, which placed no upper limit on the number of recommended candidates. Clearly, the calculation in 1994 was that the constraints placed on the government by the Bill remained in the realm of the constitutional, as determined by the then Attorney General and his office. The restrictions on the discretion of the government provided by the 1994 Bill represent the greatest constraints envisaged on the discretion of government in performing their constitutional function under Article 13.9 in all of the proposed instruments of institutional change to the judicial selection system in Ireland.

The restrictions envisaged in the 1994 Bill still fall short of constraints on executive discretion in judicial appointments introduced in other countries. At the time of its introduction, however, the government had little international basis for comparison as, at that time, only Israel had such a system for appointing judges and in that system the judicial selection commission selects the judge (which would almost certainly be unconstitutional in Ireland). The introduction of the more tightly binding systems in the UK jurisdictions would not begin until 2002 with Scotland.

There is an important element of the 1995 Act in relation to government discretion which is that the government can nominate an individual for judicial appointment without any reference to the JAAB. This has been done extremely sparingly by government (in the case of appointments of senior lawyers) and so has not had the impact that, used differently by government, it could have on the operation of the new judicial selection process. There is, however, evidence of an increased reliance by governments on the 'promotion' of a judge from one court to another in order to fill a vacancy – historically, this had been limited to the appointment of High Court judges to fill vacancies on the Supreme Court but has, since the establishment of the JAAB, been increasingly used to fill High Court vacancies with sitting judges of the Circuit Court. Filling a vacancy on a court in this way is outside the statutory remit of the JAAB. This will be discussed in more detail in Chapter 3.

The important element of institutional design has been the output of the JAAB – the number it recommends. This is critical to the effect of any reform of the judicial selection process on government discretion in making judicial appointments. As we will see in Chapter 3, this element of institutional design has important consequences for institutional functioning. The model in the 1994 Bill would not have provided the discretion to members of the JAAB to adopt different practices based on varying interpretations of the Act as it clearly states that the JAAB should recommend no more than five names.

CONCLUSIONS: HYBRID MODEL OF JUDICIAL SELECTION

The implications of the changes between the 1994 and 1995 Bills are significant in the following way: the 1995 Bill widened the pool of candidates that would be recommended to government by the JAAB and therefore enhanced the discretion of the government in making individual judicial appointments. The original Bill was initiated because of a political crisis occasioned by a series of contentious senior judicial appointments, but the passage of time reduced the tensions and made the perceived need for reform less pressing for the Labour Party. The other parties to the coalition had never publicly expressed interest in changes to the judicial selection process. It is possible that the changes evident in the 1995 Bill are also the product of reflection on the new model, or the result of negotiations among new Cabinet partners. What is most likely, and has been confirmed by interview data, is that the relative political importance of the issue simply waned and the new government sought to introduce fewer restrictions on government discretion in judicial selection.

A major contention of this book is that reform of the Irish judicial selection system was not a product of policy preferences or political commitment, but rather a reaction to a political crisis. The political salience of the issue diminished with time, though, and thus, while still committed to introducing new and more formal procedures governing judicial appointments, the government became less committed to introducing the kind of self-denying ordinance that would voluntarily distance them from the capacity to influence the process. At some point between the introductions of the two Bills a political decision was taken to use a different model, with different consequences for the discretion of the government. This bears out the contention that, in the absence of a well-prepared reform programme, set out in formal proposals and backed by extensive public discussion, the impetus for substantive reform is likely to be too weak to be carried through.

The Irish model that was agreed and implemented in 1995 can best be described as a hybrid model of judicial selection, combining elements of other models of judicial selection discussed in detail in Chapter 1: the executive nomination and appointment system and the judicial selection commission nomination system. The Irish hybrid model includes a non-political body of delegated governance, the JAAB, to remove full control of judicial selection from the government. Its particular institutional design resulted in a situation where it was to recommend a sufficiently large amount of candidates to enable the government to retain comparable levels of discretion (particularly in regard to the High Court and Supreme Court) as it held before the institutional change. The decision to allow the JAAB to recommend 'at least seven names in respect of each vacancy' provided the space for institutional drift in the JAAB.

As will be shown in Chapter 3, this had important effects on the institutional functioning of the JAAB.

Institutional change in Ireland, at least on this occasion, was introduced in a hurried and urgent way as a solution to a political crisis that threatened to end the life of the government unless a resolution was reached. The issue that generated the political crisis was judicial selection, but it was not the subject of judicial selection itself that was problematic between the coalition partners, but rather the controversy caused by two successive senior judicial appointments, which represented the tipping point of on-going tensions between the coalition parties.

Ireland also differed from the other countries reviewed in this book in terms of the impact of the change. The change introduced in Ireland was less effective in reducing political discretion in judicial selection because it provides for a greater number of names to be recommended from which politicians may choose their preferred candidate than in other comparable systems that put greater restraints on government discretion. Political commitment is necessary for the introduction of institutional change that reduces the power or discretion of government, especially in areas that are of particular interest to politicians. The legislation that was introduced immediately after the political crisis in 1994 would have placed greater constraints on the discretion of government in relation to judicial selection than the legislation that was ultimately enacted.

The conclusion to be drawn from this is straightforward – political commitment to institutional change of the judicial selection system diminished between the political crisis of 1994 and the enactment of the ultimate instrument of change. As a result, the judicial selection commission that was established by the Courts and Court Officers Act 1995 was a hybrid model that combined elements of judicial selection commissions, but retained crucial elements of the executive nomination and appointment model of judicial selection. This permitted institutional drift within the JAAB, and chapter 3 will examine this in detail.

CHAPTER 3

The operation and impact of the new judicial selection model in Ireland

The year 1995 marks a watershed in the system of judicial appointments in Ireland with the creation of the JAAB. This was the first time that the process of judicial appointment had been formally codified and it was given statutory underpinning in the Courts and Court Officers Act 1995. Before the JAAB was introduced, judicial appointments were held in the hands of three key decision-makers within government. In contrast this new process provided a role in judicial selection for members of the judiciary, the legal professions and certain lay people appointed by the Minister. The new process required judicial aspirants to formally identify their interest in judicial appointment, to formally apply for such a position and be considered by a body external to politics and political influence. This was a significantly altered institutional process for judical selection from the perspective of the judicial aspirant but what impact did it have on the discretion of Irish governments in choosing judges for appointment?

More specifically, and the central question for this chapter, is whether and how the scope and discretion of the government to appoint its preferred candidate was significantly changed by the introduction of the new delegated institution, the JAAB. This requires us to understand not only the ways in which the procedures governing the judicial appointments process were structurally changed but also how the members of the JAAB understood their role, how they interpreted their remit and whether this may have changed over time. How did the interpretation of the 1995 Act and its implementation by the JAAB impact on the role of the Irish government in choosing judges? Who controlled this interpretation in the JAAB and did this interpretation vary over time? What were the internal rules and governance processes that can enable us to understand the institutional functioning of this key body in judicial selection in Ireland? How did the operation of the JAAB impact on the discretion of government in judicial selection and was this a uniform impact or did it too contain variances? How robust was the institutional model created in the 1995 Act?

This chapter provides an account of the inner workings of the JAAB and Cabinet in relation to judicial selection in the period 1982–2007. This period enables us to examine the twelve years prior to 1995 and twelve years following the introduction of the Courts and Court Officers Act in 1995. We examine the judicial selection process in Ireland from the perspective of the 'key decision-makers'. The term 'key decision-makers' is used here to describe the principal actors in the political process who make the decision on who is to be appointed. In his 1969 study, Bartholomew identified these individuals as the Taoiseach and the Attorney General, with some role for the Minister for Justice. A similar pattern emerged in the course of this research as was noted by Bartholomew. When posed the question, 'Who are the principal decision-makers?', extensive overlapping agreement among all participants confirmed that the Taoiseach, Attorney General and Minister for Justice (to a greater or lesser extent depending on the individuals and the political circumstances of the day) were the key decision-makers. One emerging trend is that in coalition government, the leader of the minor coalition political party also plays a strong role, since judicial appointments can reflect the balance of power shared between coalition partners or are made with the explicit agreement of the coalition partners.

The elements of the judicial selection process that were examined include:

- the JAAB operations and processes,
- the Cabinet process for judicial selection, and
- the role of the Attorney General, Taoiseach and Minister for Justice in judicial selection in Cabinet.

Other issues connected to judicial selection include interviewees' perspectives on the role of gender, minority representation, network effects, political party affiliation and the role of lobbying for judicial appointment.

The results of these interviews are presented by examining the responses of the participants on each of the elements of the judicial selection process. The responses of the key decision-makers in office in the period 1982 to 1994 and 1995 to 2007 are considered separately, with a view to assessing what changes, if any, occurred between these two periods and whether or to what extent such changes can be attributed to the institutional change introduced in 1995.

Relatively little has been written about the politics of judicial appointment in Ireland, whether on the politics of government, party politics and judicial appointment, or the more subtle politics of preferment and position and the nature of experience and exposure that might place one legal practitioner in a more prominent or favourable position relative to another in the eyes of the government of the day. Only two previous studies provide data on the Irish judiciary and examine the process of judicial selection, including from the perspective of those judges appointed through that system. Bartholomew (1971) provides an overview of the judicial selection process in Ireland in 1969 and the profile of the Irish judge at that period. A study by this author, conducted in 2004 (Carroll, 2005), provides an analysis of the typical Irish judge of the High Court and Supreme Court and their experience of the judicial selection system. This included judges who had been appointed both prior to the institutional changes of 1995 and after its commencement.

The data source for this study is a set of forty interviews drawn from serving and former government ministers, other senior politicians, Attorneys General and senior political advisers in government and senior members of the judiciary and the legal profession and other members of the Judicial Appointments Advisory Board presented anonymously. In some cases, interviewees may have held more than one office. For example, each Attorney General after 1995 was also a member of the JAAB, some individuals held multiple positions in government and the judiciary and some office-holders held multiple positions of relevance in the government. Details of interviews are included in Appendix 1.

Between 1982 and 2007, there were five Taoisigh, eleven Ministers for Justice, nine Attorneys General and two coalition leaders. Of this total number five were unable to participate in this study due to death or serious illness. In total, seventeen of the remaining twenty-two participated in the research, giving a response rate for the available key decision-makers of seventy-seven per cent. Each interviewee was asked the same series of questions, adapted to reflect their position in the government and the respective role of the office-holder of that position in the Cabinet or the JAAB. As the formal process for judicial selection is the same for all courts in Ireland the interviewees were first asked about judicial selection processes in general and then they were also asked whether there were informal differences between judicial selection processes for different courts in Ireland.

This chapter sets out how the process and politics of judicial appointments in Ireland really worked. This is the first time these data have been collected and presented and they represent the first detailed examination of the judicial selection system in Ireland over a period of a quarter of a century.[1]

1 The period 1982 to 1994 was marked by a series of coalition governments in Ireland. Between February 1982 and November 1982, there was a short-lived single-party minority Fianna Fáil government. From November 1982 to 1987, a Fine Gael–Labour coalition held power. The period between 1987 and 1989 saw another single-party minority Fianna Fáil government, which was followed in 1989 by a Fianna Fáil–Progressive Democrat coalition that lasted until 1992. Finally, from 1992 to 1994, a Fianna Fáil-Labour coalition held power and this was the government that experienced the political crisis that triggered the perceived need for institutional change. This government was followed by a coalition government of Fine Gael, Labour and Democratic Left which was in office from 1994 to 1997. This was the government that ultimately enacted the legislation to give effect to institutional change in the judicial selection process in Ireland.

The period 1995 to 2007 saw some important changes in government. Until 1997, the government was formed by a coalition of three parties, Fine Gael, Labour and Democratic Left. In 1997 this coalition lost power and Fianna Fáil returned to government once again in coalition with the Progressive Democrats. This coalition won power again in 2002, resulting in its continuous period in office from 1997 until 2007 and the same person – Bertie Ahern

We begin with an overview of the instrument of institutional reform, the text of the Courts and Court Officers Act 1995 itself. This provides a benchmark against which the implementation of the Act and operation of the judicial selection process in the post-1995 period can be assessed using evidence from interviews with the participants. In order to provide a wider context for this analysis, this chapter then presents the views of legal practitioners and judges (who have experienced the judicial selection process) regarding the way judicial selection in Ireland operates and how much difference the institutional changes made in practice. The purpose of this is to provide a cross-reference of the views of political decision-makers with those in the JAAB in order to provide a complete perspective on the judicial selection system in Ireland from all its users.

This chapter then goes on to examine the operation and processes of the JAAB over time. The purpose of this is to determine how the institutional change was implemented by the JAAB. The 1995 legislation set out the parameters for its activities. Once the JAAB was set up, its members had to work out a modus operandi to implement the legislation and establish its institutional processes. As shall be seen, the JAAB made some important decisions since its establishment that have, in effect, narrowed its own discretion and autonomy and expanded the scope of discretion available to the government.

JUDICIAL SELECTION PROCESSES IN IRELAND – FORMAL INSTITUTIONAL CHANGES INTRODUCED IN 1995

As shown in Chapter 2, a new and more formalized judicial selection system was established by legislation as a response to a political crisis involving the appointment of judges. The new structure was established by Part IV of the Courts and Court Officers Act 1995 (the 1995 Act) and amended slightly in Part III of the Courts and Court Officers Act 2002 (the 2002 Act). This section examines the statutory provisions for the new regulated judicial selection system and the statutory powers and functions provided to the Judicial Appointments Advisory Board (JAAB).

Section 13(1) of the 1995 Act provides for the establishment of the Board for the purposes of 'identifying persons and informing the Government of the suitability of those persons for appointment to judicial office'.

This is core to this study. The purpose of the establishment of the JAAB is crucial to the analysis of the motivation and intent of the policy makers introducing the institutional change in 1995. It informs any analysis of how

– was Taoiseach throughout this period. The present study ends in 2007: therefore the post-1995 period was dominated by Fianna Fáil-Progressive Democrat coalitions.

that purpose and function has been exercised over time. The statutory function of the Board is to both identify individuals for judicial office and to inform the government as to their suitability for judicial office. The performance by the Board of this function is considered in detail later in this chapter by examining the operation of the judicial selection process both from the perspective of the members of the JAAB and the perspective of the Cabinet members involved in judicial selection.

Section 13(2) provides that the Board is to be composed of the Chief Justice, the Presidents of the High Court, Circuit Court and District Court, the Attorney General, a representative of both of the legal professional representative groups (the Law Society of Ireland and the Bar Council of Ireland) and three persons appointed by the Minister 'who shall be persons engaged in, or having knowledge or experience (being knowledge or experience that the Minister considers appropriate) of commerce, finance, administration or persons who have experience as consumers of the services provided by the courts that the Minister considers appropriate'. This stipulation is broad ranging and, effectively, allows the Minister complete discretion to appoint any persons he or she prefers. Furthermore, although these persons are widely perceived to be 'lay persons', there is no statutory barrier to the Minister appointing a practising lawyer to this position. Section 13(3) provides that the legal profession representatives and the ministerial appointees are appointed for 'a period not exceeding three years' but can be reappointed and there is no statutory barrier to the number of times they can be reappointed. In 2015 the Minister for Justice and Equality sought, for the first time, public expressions of interest to fill a vacancy that had arisen among the lay members of the Board.[2]

Section 14 gives the power to the Board to 'adopt such procedures as it thinks fit to carry out its functions'. This important section gives broad ranging powers to the Board in the operation of its statutory function. It provides a statutory basis from which the JAAB can establish institutional processes that it deems suitable and necessary for the performance of its functions. The drafting of this provision enables substantial institutional varation which may have an impact on institutional functioning. Notwithstanding the generality of the powers given to the Board by the 1995 Act, section 14 identifies a subset of specific powers the JAAB may wish to use, such as advertising for applications for judicial appointment, requiring applicants to compete application forms, consulting persons concerning the suitability of applicants, inviting persons (identified by the Board) to submit their names for consideration by the Board and arranging for the interviewing

2 However, this changed process is not specific to the Judicial Appointments Advisory Board or the Department of Justice generally, rather it is reflective of a broader government programme of seeking public expressions of interest for state board appointments following a political controversy over such an appointment in another government department in 2014.

of applicants. The manner and extent to which these powers have been used from 1995 to 2007 is considered in detail later in this chapter in the section analysing the operation of the Board using interview data with JAAB members.

Section 15 is a technical provision that provides for the membership of the board in the event of the death or retirement of a member of the Board.

Section 16 is core to the analysis of the institutional design of institutional change and its impact on the discretion of government in future judicial appointments. Section 16(1) provides that 'A person who wishes to be considered for appointment to judicial office shall so inform the Board in writing and shall provide the Board with such information as it may require enabling it to consider the suitability of that person for judicial office, including information relating to education, professional qualifications, experience and character'. This is a broad provision enabling substantial institutional varation in the manner in which it is implemented by the Board with important implications for the nature and quality of the information held by the Board about the judicial aspirant, its capacity to make an assessment about the suitability of the applicant for judicial office and the nature and quality of the information it may then provide to the Minister in making its recommendations. Variation in the implementation of this provision will also have an impact on the experience of the judicial aspirant of the statutory judicial appointments application process.

Section 16(2) provides that 'on the request of the Minister', the Board shall, either where a judicial office is vacant or before a vacancy arises, 'submit to the Minister the names of each person who has informed the Board of his or her wish to be considered for appointment to that judicial office and the Board shall recommend to the Minister at least seven persons for appointment to that judicial office'. This gives power to the Minister to make a decision about whether or not to refer a judicial vacancy to the Board at all. While there is no statutory obligation on the Minister for Justice to request the JAAB to make a recommendation in relation to a particular judicial vacancy, the evidence from 1995–2014 suggests that Ministers overwhelmingly use this provision as judicial vacancies arise. In 2002, the JAAB commented in its Annual Report that, since the establishment of the Board, the Minister had requested the Board to make a recommendation in respect of every judicial vacancy that had arisen:

> since the Board was established, the Minister has, in the case of every judicial vacancy, requested the Board to make recommendations in accordance with section 16, including cases in which the government ultimately availed of its power to advise the President to appoint a judge already in office to a particular vacancy which had arisen or would arise (Judicial Appointments Advisory Board, 2002, p. 23).

Table 3.1 summarizes information about the number of court vacancies and the number of requests by the Minister to the JAAB for nominations. It shows that, of the 116 vacancies on the courts, the Minister sought recommendations in 107 of vacancies.

Table 3.1: Court vacancies and Ministers' requests for nominations from the JAAB, 1996–2014

Year	District Court vacancies	Minister requests	Circuit Court vacancies	Minister requests	High Court vacancies	Minister requests	Supreme Court vacancies	Minister requests
1996	3	3	11	11	4	4	3	3
1997	2	2	2	2	3	3	0	0
1998	4	4	3	3	2	2	0	0
1999	2	2	2	2	3	3	1	1
2000	1	1	0	0	4	4	0	0
2001	3	3	4	4	0	0	0	0
2002	5	5	3	3	5	1	1	1
2003	1	1	0	0	3	1	0	0
2004	4	4	5	5	5	3	1	1
2005	0	0	1	1	3	2	1	0
2006	3	3	0	0	1	1	1	1
2007	6	6	6	6	6	6	0	0
2008	6	6	0	0	1	1	0	0
2009	4	4	2	2	0	0	1	1
2010	1	1	0	0	1	1	1	1
2011	4	4	6	5	2	2	0	0
2012	8	8	7	7	4	3	2	0
2013	5	5	1	1	5	5	2	0
2014	2	2	8	8	16	16[3]	1	1
Total	64	64	61	60	68	58	15	10

Source: Judicial Appointments Advisory Board Annual Reports, 2002–14.

Section 16(3) provides that the Board will 'provide the Minister with particulars of the education, professional qualifications, experience and character of the persons whom it recommends under this section'. In practice this has meant that the Board has forwarded the Curriculum Vitaes of the

3 On one occasion in 2014 the Minister for Justice and Equality communicated with the Board in general terms, rather than in response to a specific vacancy, concerning the filling of vacancies, 'which would arise in the event that serving judges of the High Court were appointed to the new Court of Appeal' (JAAB Annual Report 2014, p. 9).

candidate to the Minister. This could be viewed by some as a minimalist interpretation of the section. A more broad interpretation might include, for example, choosing to send psychometric test results of an applicant, interview analysis of the applicant, publications by the applicant, written reports of soundings and consultations in relation to an applicant, the detailed analysis of the Board about the applicant or such other things as may help the Minister make a decision about a preferred candidate. The point is that the Board has discretion in establishing its own processes and the way in which that is done has an impact on how JAAB performs its statutory function.

Section 16(4) provides that where there are fewer than seven persons who inform the Board of their wish to be appointed to judicial office or where the Board is unable to recommend at least seven persons, the Board shall 'submit to the Minister the names of each person who has informed the Board of his or her wish to be considered for appointment to that judicial office and the Board shall recommend to the Minister for appointment to that office such of those persons as it considers suitable for appointment.' This provision enables the Board to recommend fewer than seven persons to the Minister for a vacancy – either because it has no choice and there have been fewer than seven applicants, or because it has decided that there are fewer than seven suitable applicants. This subsection should be an important part of any debate about statutory change to reduce the names to be recommended by the Board – it already has this power. Yet, as we will see, there seems to remain a persistent institutional difficulty in relation to this element of the 1995 Act.

Section 16(5) provides that where there is more than one vacancy on the same court the Board shall 'submit to the Minister the names of each person who has informed the Board of his or her wish to be considered for appointment to that judicial office and the Board shall recommend to the Minister the names of at least seven persons in respect of each vacancy or such lesser number as the Minister shall specify following consultation with the Board.' This subsection is very important where there are multiple vacancies on a court. It has been treated in different ways by the Board over time. It is clearly open to multiple interpretations – let's say there are five vacancies on one court at about the same time and the Minister refers all five vacancies to the Board for recommendations *without* making any further direction to the Board that it should recommend a specified number of candidates. Let's say that there are one hundred applicants for the five vacancies. What is the correct number to be recommended by the Board in this instance? Is it thirty-five? Is it more than thirty-five? Is it everyone who is suitable? Is it seven? Should the Board treat each vacancy completely separately and recommend the same seven names for each vacancy? If the Board interprets this section as requiring at least thirty-five recommendations to the Minister for the five vacancies, it gives a large degree of discretion to the Minister to identify preferred candidates. If the Board interprets the section to mean seven recommendations for the five vacancies, the Board has reduced the discretion of the Minister and government to a level that may not have been intended by the Act and may indeed be an unconstitutional usurpation of the government's selection function. The Board adopted a restrictive approach in its early years, but subsequently has tended to recommend all those who are suitable. There is some recent evidence of a more restrictive approach being adopted by the Board, but not one approaching the statutory number seven. There is no evidence in this study of Ministers making a specification under section 16(5) for a 'lesser number of recommendations'.

Section 16(6) provides that when advising the President in relation to an appointment to a judicial office, the government 'shall firstly consider for appointment those persons whose names have been recommended to the Minister pursuant to this section.'

In summary, the 1995 Act provides that the Board, when asked by the Minister, will send to him or her three things:

1. a list of all of the people who *applied* for consideration for judicial office;
2. a list of at least seven persons whom the Board *recommends* for appointment to that office; and
3. the *particulars* of those persons whom the Board is recommending for appointment.

The institutional design of the JAAB in the legislation is that it will receive applications and then make some assessment that includes making a judgment that prefers, or chooses, one candidate over another. That is not to say the Board chooses the candidate that will be appointed, rather it prefers or chooses *some* of the applicants from *all* of the applicants for a given vacancy and then recommends those people to government as being suitable for appointment. Its function is to inform the government on the people who are suitable for appointment, but the legislation clearly envisages a form of selection among the applicants to be performed, in the first instance, by the JAAB, prior to a second selection among the recommended candidates being performed by government.

Where there are fewer than seven applicants, the Board is obliged to send forward all the names of the applicants and the names of those whom it recommends with the relevant particulars. Where there is more than one vacancy, the Board is obliged to send forward the names of all of the applicants and either seven names in respect of each vacancy or such other number as the Minister shall specify following consultation with the Board. It is implied in the latter two instances that the Board should operate in the same way and send the particulars of those whom it recommends to the Minister.

Section 16 of the 1995 Act clearly envisages the JAAB performing a selection between applicants function. The provisions envisage a 'long' list of names to be sent to the Minister – all those that applied for consideration for judicial office – and a 'short' list of at least seven names (or fewer in the cases specified) recommended by the Board for appointment to judicial office. The provisions clearly require the government to give first consideration to the names recommended by the JAAB before advising the President on an appointment.

This section of the Act creates a critical institutional role for the JAAB in judicial selection in Ireland. The Board is required to perform an analysis that

Table 3.2: Court vacancies and elevations of a sitting judge of another court 2002 to 2014[4]

Year	District Court vacancies	Elevations	Circuit Court vacancies	Elevations	High Court vacancies	Elevations	Supreme Court vacancies	Elevations
2002	5	0	3	0	5	0	1	1
2003	1	0	0	0	3	1[5]	0	0
2004	4	0	5	0	5[6]	2	1	1[7]
2005	0	0	1	0	3	1	1	1
2006	3	0	0	0	1	0	1	1
2007	6	0	6	0	6	1	0	0
2008	6	0	0	0	1	0	0	0
2009	4	0	2	0	0	0	1	0
2010	1	0	0	0	1	0	1	1
2011	4	0	6	1	2	1	0	0
2012	8	0	7	1	4	1	2	2
2013	5	0	1	1	5	0	2	2
2014	2	0	8	1	16	6	1	1
Total	43	0	39	4	50	13	11	10

Source: Judicial Appointments Advisory Board Annual Reports, 2002–14.

4 There were ten vacancies on the newly created Court of Appeal and all were filled by the elevation of a judge from another court. Nine judges were elevated from the High Court and one judge was elevated from the Circuit Court. 5 Of the three High Court vacancies in 2003, the government sought recommendations in respect of only one vacancy. One of the remaining vacancies was filled by the elevation of a judge of the Circuit Court and one was made by direct appointment by the government. 6 One of the five vacancies on the High Court in 2004 was filled by direct appointment by the government (Judicial Appointments Advisory Board Annual Report 2004, p. 14). 7 On this occasion the JAAB did not make any recommendations to the Minister having considered applications for the vacant Supreme Court position. The position was filled by the elevation of a judge of the High Court.

prefers one applicant to another and send recommendations to the Minister on foot of this analysis accompanied by the particulars of those who are so recommended. The legislation even provides for how this should be done in circumstances where there are either a small number of applicants or multiple concurrent vacancies on the same court. These points are important for our analysis of institutional design and functioning. The manner in which these functions are exercised by the Board are considered in greater detail later in this chapter in the analysis of the operation of these processes based on interview data with nineteen members of the JAAB and the relevant political actors in the post-1995 period.

Section 17 of the 1995 Act provides that the provisions of the Act do not apply where the government proposes to advise the President to appoint to a judicial office a person who is already a member of another court. The Minister is not obliged to make a request where he or she intends to appoint to the vacancy a sitting judge of another court. Table 3.2 details the number of 'elevations' that have been made in the period 2002–14.

One of the concerns about the elevation of judges is that it could threaten judicial independence because of a perception that judges might give rulings favourable to the state in order to curry favour in the hope of elevation. We can see from the table below that the use of elevations for judicial appointments is reasonably common; however, the overall picture is somewhat distorted by the high number of elevations to fill Supreme Court vacancies. On the basis that it is not possible to 'elevate' someone from another court to a District Court vacancy, appointments to the District Court must be excluded from the analysis. Excluding District Court vacancies, there have been 100 vacancies on the courts in the period 2002–14, of which 27 have been filled by an elevation. The use of elevations to fill vacancies varies substantially across the various courts, from being the overwhelming practice in the Supreme Court to a comparitve rarity on the Circuit Court, as shown in Table 3.3 below.

Table 3.3: Elevations as a percentage of court vacancies, 2002–14

Court	elevations
Circuit Court	10%
High Court	26%
Supreme Court	91%

One Minister for Justice commented on the use of 'elevations' to fill judicial vacancies as follows:

> The promoted judges were people who had substantially good reputations across the legal profession for the manner in which they were conducting their courts. On one occasion there was a particularly good judge on a given court, who had worked to an extraordinary degree in the

> court where he was appointed for many years and who had done an extraordinary job and we (myself and the Attorney General) recommended to government that this individual be promoted. There was another occasion when someone retired from one of the courts who had done a lot of criminal work and there was a gap in that court and there was a particular applicant on the list of approved applicants that had come from JAAB who was a women, who was well thought of and who was engaged in a substantial criminal law practice and the initiative to appoint her came from me I think and I discussed it with the Attorney and we recommended the appointment. (Post-1995/MJ/5)

What are the implications of this use of elevations for the role of the JAAB in judicial selection in Ireland? Obviously the JAAB has had a very limited role in the selection of judges for the Supreme Court, which has, in all but one case since 2002, been conducted entirely at the discretion of government. Since 2002, all of the appointments to the Supreme Court, bar one, have been made from serving High Court judges who have themselves, in nearly every case, been appointed to the High Court in the post-1995 JAAB era and so have been the subject of the JAAB process. Comparatively few Circuit Court vacancies have been filled by the elevation of a District Court judge and, interestingly, all such elevations occurred during the lifetime of the 31st Dáil. That the bulk of elevations, proportionally, has occurred in the case of High Court judges to the Supreme Court might give us pause for thought on the use of the JAAB for judicial elevations – what it implies in practice is that sitting High Court judges submit themselves to analysis by leading members of the legal profession, their own court president and court presidents of courts that are 'below' their jurisdiction and whose decisions they may have overturned by appeal or judicial review. This point will be considered in more detail in Chapter 5.

What this analysis of judicial elevations implies for the role of the JAAB in judicial selection in Ireland is that the JAAB has the greatest power in respect of District Court vacancies, a power which is slightly distilled at each stage in practice by the incremental use of elevations through the various courts, up to the Supreme Court where the JAAB has nearly no role. It is worth remembering that the practice in the pre-1995 JAAB era was to appoint Supreme Court judges from the ranks of serving High Court judges because of the view that Supreme Court judges should have trial experience. The use of elevations, therefore, does not 'take' any power from JAAB in respect of Supreme Court appointments – the practice of the government is the same before and after the introduction of the JAAB.

There is an important point emerging – the JAAB has the greatest power vis-à-vis the government in respect of District Court and Circuit Court vacancies because:

- those courts have the largest number of vacancies,
- with the largest number of applicants,
- and so the scope to recommend 'at least seven' of these applicants has the greatest proprtionate impact on the discretion of government to choose a preferred individual for a given vacancy,
- and the occasion on which it can exercise this restriction of government discretion is very often.

These factors, coupled with the fact that these are the courts where government members receive the greatest political lobbying for positions and where there is the greatest incentive to reward local political involvement with a judicial appointment, mean the power of the JAAB in District Court appointments is comparatively awesome. District Court appointments are also the set of appointments with the largest universe of potential applicants. So the proportionate impact of the JAAB reducing that universe to a shortlist, however long, has the greatest proportionate impact on government discretion. Obviously, the shorter the shortlist, the greater the impact. It is therefore even more difficult to understand the institutional decision of the JAAB to reduce its power vis-à-vis the government with a practice where it recommended a large number of candidates for vacancies on these courts.

Section 18 provides that the Board shall not recommend its own members, except in the case of the Attorney General who may apply for consideration but who must remove him or herself from the deliberations of the Board when it is discussing their suitability for judicial office. Section 19 provides that a person who wishes to be considered for appointment to the judiciary shall give a written undertaking that they agree, if appointed, to take such courses of education as may be required by the President of the Court to which they are appointed. Section 20 provides that all of the proceedings of the Board and its communications shall not be disclosed (except for the purposes of the Act). This is an important section guaranteeing the confidentiality of the judicial aspirant and the proceedings of the Board. Clearly, the only people who could disclose the proceedings of the Board are its members. There is some evidence of some judicial applicants having been told informally they did or did not make the list of recommended candidates sent to government. In circumstances where the Board does not communicate formally with applicants as to the outcome of their application, this might be a considerate act on the part of an individual Board member but it does not sit well with the obligation of confidentiality of proceedings. A more professional approach might be direct communication with judicial applicants as to the outcome of their application to the JAAB, obviating the perceived need for informal communications of this nature. Sections 21 and 22 are technical sections providing for financial and administrative support to the Board. The Minister for Justice, in conjunction with the Minister for Finance, is responsible for providing such resources as he or she determines.

Section 23 provides that where the government proposes to advise the President of an appointment to the Office of the Chief Justice or the Office of the President of the High Court, Circuit Court or District Court, the government shall 'first have regard to the qualifications and suitability of persons who are serving at that time as judges in courts established in pursuance of Article 34 of the Constitution'. This is an important provision because it ensures that in practice the government will always appoint a serving judge, of any court, to these offices. To appoint a non-judge to such office following the enactment of this provision risks being interpreted as the government rejecting all of the serving judiciary in favour of a non-judge for appointment to such an office.

Chapter 2 showed that this provision directly relates to the political issue that led to the introduction of this institutional change (the appointment of the serving Attorney General to the Office of the President of the High Court). Its omission from the 1994 Bill was a significant and obvious point of criticism from the opposition. This is an important provision for the purposes of this study because it is the only provision of the 1995 Act that places limits on the discretion of the government to appoint a preferred candidate to such an office. It should be said that this is not an absolute limit on the discretion of the government, which remains free to run the political risk of appointing a non-judge as President of a Court. However, this has never been done. In practice this provision means that a judge of one court can be appointed President of any other court. The new President of the new Court of Appeal appointed in 2014 was a serving judge of the High Court, the new President of the High Court appointed in 2016 was a judge of the Court of Appeal. Chief among the anomalies associated with the District Court[8] is that a serving judge of the District Court, but not its President who is an ex officio member of the Circurt Court,[9] cannot be appointed as an ordinary judge of the High Court but could be appointed President of the High Court.[10]

The Courts and Court Officers Act 2002 amended the 1995 Act relating to the JAAB by widening the pool of prospective judicial appointments to the High Court and Supreme Court. Section 16(7) of the 1995 Act was amended to provide that *both* solicitors and barristers can be appointed to the High Court and Supreme Court but only where they have an 'appropriate knowledge and appropriate experience of the practice and procedure of the Supreme Court and the High Court'. There is no further statutory guidance

8 Such as appointment to the District Court rendering the individual ineligible for appointment to the High Court despite that individual having the 'qualifications' necessary for appointment to the High Court before their appointment to the District Court, see Courts and Court Officers Act 1995, section 28(e). 9 Courts and Court Officers Act 1995, section 33. 10 Courts and Court Officers Act 2002, section 4.

on how this should be interpreted and it is up the JAAB and the government to interpret what constitutes such appropriate knowledge and experience of these courts. Clearly, the section envisages that there is a subset of solicitors and barristers who are eligible for appointment (by virtue of the number of years' practice experience among other things) and who have this knowledge; however, not every solicitor or barrister is so possessed of this knowledge and experience. How does the Board assess the applicant's personal conduct of proceedings in the Supreme Court and the High Court, whether as an advocate or as a solicitor instructing counsel[11] and how does this impact on the diversity of appointments to the High Court and Supreme Court as between solicitors and barristers?

The 2002 Act also establishes a requirement for the Board to prepare and publish Annual Reports to the Minister on its activities during the year. Section 11 of the 2002 Act creates a new section 20A of the 1995 Act that enables the Minister (after consultation with the Board) to specify the form and content of the Reports – the number of persons considered by the JAAB for appointment, the gender and professional background of applicants, the procedures of the Board and criteria used to select persons under section 16 of the 1995 Act. The provisions enable the Board to share whatever information about its processes and activities it chooses. There is no evidence of a Minister making a specification as to the form and content of the Annual Report.

It is important to reflect on the statutory provisions underpinning the establishment of the JAAB and its processes and powers because they tell us something about the intent of policy makers in establishing the Board through legislation. They also provide us with a benchmark against which the actual implementation of the institutional change can be assessed using interview data with members and the output of the Board, including the number of people recommended over time and its Annual Reports on its processes. This analysis of the legal structure underpinning the Board also assists in a comparative statutory analysis of comparable judicial selection institutions in other jurisdictions. Chapter 4 will consider how comparable institutional change was introduced in another jurisdiction (Scotland) and this statutory analysis is an important base for that exercise.

JUDICIAL SELECTION IN IRELAND: VIEWS FROM THE 'SELECTED' IN 1969 AND 2004

Before examining the implementation of the new judicial selection system, it is helpful to consider the views of judges and legal practitioners on judicial selection historically in Ireland and the effect of the new system. This helps

11 An analysis of the impact of this statutory change from 2002 to 2006 was conducted by this author: see Carroll (2007).

contextualize the evidence gathered in interviews with members of the JAAB and Cabinet.

Bartholomew (1971)[12] asked the judges in his study about their appointment by government to the judiciary. This was in the course of a study on the background information of the Irish judiciary in 1969 that included information on birthplace, ethnic background, education, religious commitment, political party affiliation, occupation before appointment, lawyers in their family relationship, socio-economic status before appointment, paternal occupation, age at time of appointment and other factors that

> might in some fashion be influential on the decisions handed down by a judge on the bench and that might indicate in general the type of person that a judge is – a composite picture of an Irish judge. (Bartholomew, 1971, p. 31)

Bartholomew conducted personal interviews in 1969 with all of the sitting and retired judges of the Supreme Court, High Court and Circuit Court, with two exceptions. Of the thirty-five judges of the District Court, seven judges were interviewed personally and ten returned a written questionnaire. In two instances, information was obtained by secondary sources. Bartholomew's study was therefore not only original in the Irish context, it was also comprehensive in it scope.

> This is strictly a pioneer study. Nothing of the sort has been done before in Ireland. Its purpose is to determine something not before known with any degree of accuracy – the characteristics of Irish judges, their social and political backgrounds, and something of how they came to be appointed. (Bartholomew, 1971, p. 32)

Bartholomew writes that, in the period prior to 1969, the judicial selection process was tightly controlled by three members of government – the Taoiseach, the Attorney General and the Minister for Justice. The formal system was simply that the Minister for Justice compiled a list of potential candidates and presented it at a Cabinet meeting, but that 'list' may have contained just a single name. Bartholomew argues that the negotiation in relation to judicial appointments did not at that time occur at the Cabinet

12 Byrne and McCutcheon (1996) stated that no new study of this form had been published since Bartholomew's, although studies of this kind are common in other jurisdictions. They also noted that there was very little accessible information on the social and political backgrounds of Irish judges, probably due to the conventional reticence attached to holders of judicial office. 'The result has been that judicial autobiographies are a rarity in Britain and Ireland and any biographies are likely to be of an earlier era. In their absence students of law have had to be content largely with collections of anecdotes' (Byrne and McCutcheon, 1996, p. 121).

table, but rather prior to the Cabinet meeting. The importance of this is that judicial selection was carried out by a kind of 'Cabinet within a Cabinet', rather than being the product of discussion by the full group of ministers with constitutional responsibility for advising the President on judicial selection.

In the case of High Court and Supreme Court appointments, the role of the Taoiseach and Attorney General was more pronounced than in the case of appointments to the Circuit Court and to the District Court. The relative power and influence tended to vary within the decision-making trio over time, but, certainly, they were the key players in Cabinet when it came to judicial appointments. The general process was that, in reality, although the Minister for Justice brought the nomination to Cabinet, the name had been agreed beforehand and there was virtually no discussion at Cabinet as to the merits or otherwise of the proposed appointee. Nobody was appointed against the wishes of the Taoiseach. Bartholomew made the point that a judicial aspirant might make his interest known discreetly, perhaps long before any vacancy has occurred, and that such suggestions were not classed as direct 'lobbying' of the members of the Cabinet (Bartholomew, 1971).

> No formal vote is taken at the Cabinet meeting; an informal agreement on a particular person evolves. If the Taoiseach … has a favourite, that man will get the job. Certainly no one has ever been named judge over the objections of the Taoiseach. The person chosen is then formally consulted and consent secured. Then the President, who has not been consulted on the appointment, is told the name of the appointee and the formal appointment is made by the President. (Bartholomew, 1971, p. 33)

In 2004, this author undertook a study to update the findings of Bartholomew's 1969 study. The purpose of the study was to develop a profile of a typical judge of the superior courts in 2004 and to compare the results of the 1969 and 2004 studies to determine what differences exist between the two profiles.[13] This study (Carroll, 2005a; 2005b) of the Irish senior judiciary also asked the then members of the Irish High Court and Supreme Court why, in their opinion, they had been appointed to the judiciary, their experience of the JAAB and the role, if any, of political connections in their appointment. The interviewees included judges who had been appointed between 1980 and 2004 so the data, therefore, reflect the experiences of judges of the judicial selection process both before and after the institutional change that is the subject of this study.

The perspectives of the successful appointees on their appointment are discussed below. Methodologically, I recognize that these interviewees, while representing the total universe of relevant actors, are likely to have a selective perspective on the process, since they have been its beneficiaries. As a counter-

13 This study did not include Circuit Court or District Court judges.

weight, some interviews were also undertaken with other senior members of the legal profession to check the degree to which their perspectives are shared with those of the judges. There was little fundamental disagreement about how the system has functioned.

What is remarkable is the strong convergence in views across all groups in their understanding of the essential features of the judicial appointments process – both prior to 1995 and also subsequently. The key finding from these interviews is that there was no fundamental change in the way the judicial appointments system worked or in the role of government in making judicial appointments as a consequence of the reforming legislation of 1995.

Overwhelmingly, and perhaps unsurprisingly, the members of the judiciary observed that they had been appointed first and foremost on merit. It is generally accepted (by the judiciary, by politicians and by the commentators to date) that the system of judicial selection did not, in general, promote the interests of the politically well-connected, but unskilled, lawyer over the meritorious candidate. The system, opaque as it may have been, ensured that, for the most part, those who were appointed to the judiciary were of a high calibre. Sixty per cent of the superior court judges interviewed in the 2004 study believed that the principal reason for their appointment was their professional status. Forty-one per cent of superior court judges in Bartholomew's 1969 study believed they had been appointed on the basis of their professional standing.

A note of caution must be sounded here. Judges' assessments of the reasons for their appointment must be read as human self-assessment. It seems reasonable that a judge might play down any political role in their appointment. The experience of the interviews, however, led me to believe that this may have been the case in very few instances. Judges were frank in their assessment that they were simply at the top of the game or top of their field or that they were politically friendly with the governing party. Other reasons they attributed for their appointment included good knowledge of the Irish language, having done a large amount of State work or run an inquiry or other investigation for the government. Some judges, who were perceived to be associated with a political party because of a previous involvement (often in college or in the early days of their career), found the ongoing political association frustrating, especially in circumstances where it no longer reflected their political preferences, which had changed over time. The other point to note is that this study did not include Circuit Court or District Court judges where, as will be shown when we examine the process from inside the Cabinet, there is greater evidence of political connection having been an important factor than was the case at High Court and Supreme Court level. This is especially so in relation to District Court appointments. The relative significance of a political factor in judicial appointments should also be read in the context of evidence of a general decline in the relationship between party political connection and such appointments over the period 1969–2004 and a greater fragmentation of political association generally in Ireland in the more recent decades. The judges of the 2004 study also offered other reasons (in addition to merit) why, in their opinion, they believed they had been appointed. All of the women who were interviewed observed that they believed they had been appointed because of their gender, 'because I was a woman. Absolutely no doubt about it.'

Other reasons that were cited included, for example, as a reward for service (acting for government in state cases or performing a sensitive inquiry for government), their relationship with the Attorney General, their experience of the European Court, having done a number of high profile public cases, and the modestly-put 'being in the right place at the right time'.

When asked about the role of politics in their appointment, 18 per cent of the Superior Court judges interviewed in 2004 were of the view that their party political connections had an influence on their appointment to the judiciary. One contributor commented that their political connections 'certainly didn't hinder their appointment'. A number of judges appointed in the mid-1990s felt they had been appointed precisely because they were not associated with any political party; this was at a time when party patronage in judicial appointments was viewed negatively in political circles. For example, immediately after the political controversy in 1994 regarding the appointment of Mr Harry Whelehan to the Office of the President of the High Court, it was felt that appointing senior lawyers who were well known to be apolitical, with no political party connections, was a better approach to judicial appointments. Some of the High Court judges appointed around this time made this observation – that they had been appointed because they were *not* political. Of course this approach is, itself, a political approach to judicial appointments.

Of those judges surveyed in 2004 that did have an affiliation with a political party at the time of their appointment, 17 per cent supported Fianna Fáil, 7 per cent supported Fine Gael and 7 per cent supported the Progressive Democrats (a political party formed since Bartholomew's study in 1969). These figures show that there have been substantial changes when compared to the results of the 1969 study.

In 1969, 65 per cent of superior court judges supported Fianna Fáil at the time of their appointment and 18 per cent supported Fine Gael. The high proportion of support by judges for Fianna Fáil at the time of their appointment may partly reflect the long period of power held by that party prior to Bartholomew's 1969 study.[14] From 1969 to 2004 there was a remarkable decrease in support among the judges for both parties, particularly Fianna Fáil. What is especially interesting is that the overall proportion of

14 Bartholomew (1971, p. 35) commented that the Fianna Fáil party had been in power for all but five of the thirty-eight years prior to his study in 1969.

judges that claimed not to have any political affiliation rose to 62 per cent of the respondents in 2004, as against 12 per cent in 1969.

Of the superior court judges in the 2004 study that did not profess their support for a political party prior to their appointment, some state that they had been involved as a student or while at the Bar. However, they observed that at the precise time of their appointment, they were no longer affiliated actively or socially with the political party. Other judges expressed the view that, although they were not affiliated with a political party at the time of their appointment, they might still be regarded by their colleagues or the media as a 'Fianna Fáil' or 'Fine Gael' appointee.

It is clear that the importance of political party connection in judicial appointments has always been well understood by the judiciary, as well as by the politicians. In 1971 Bartholomew commented that almost all judicial appointments are based on partisan political considerations and that all Irish governments have 'to a greater or lesser degree been politically motivated in the making of judicial appointments' (Bartholomew, 1971, pp 33–4).

Some of the judges in the 2004 study commented that it was hard to know what factors affected judicial appointments because it can depend on such things as whether the Taoiseach of the day takes an interest. Some Taoisigh have left it entirely to the Attorney General. Furthermore, it was said that, in the past, the Minister for Justice had relatively little influence in High Court and Supreme Court appointments. However, the 2004 study reveals that the judges believed that this had changed, and that (based on their experiences and the personalities of the Ministers for Justice at the time) the Minister for Justice was now thought to be generally more active in judicial selection. It was observed that, in a coalition, there is the possibility that appointments could be even more political because they may be used to appease a junior partner in the coalition. There are many different reasons why individuals are appointed but, other things being equal, the evidence in the 2004 study is that the appointment will reflect the party-political preferences of the government (Carroll, 2005b).

A number of judges commented that although there had been some dramatic instances of cross-party judicial appointments, there was simply no doubt but that the system prior to the establishment of the Judicial Appointments Advisory Board (JAAB) was entirely within the political gift – on a 'nod and a wink' (Carroll, 2005b). The general view of the judges[15] was that the new system was a good idea in theory but that in practice it had made very little change to the political patronage system of appointments that existed in Ireland even though there is now a public perception that all judges are appointed by an independent board.

15 Carroll (2005b). Twenty-two of the twenty-eight interviewed judges in that study had been appointed through the JAAB system.

> While that is theoretically true, in the sense that there is a Judicial Appointments Board to whom anybody that aspires to a judicial appointment has to apply and notionally they are appointed by that board or at least they're recommended by that Board for appointment by the government. But the reality is very different because the Board are required to recommend seven people in respect of each vacancy and inevitably the government of the day pick their own supporter. There are exceptions to that rule – but very very often the government pick their own supporters. (Carroll, 2005b)

Despite a legislative silence (prior to the 1995 Act) on how judges were to be chosen, other than a requirement as to length of practice as a lawyer, the rules of judicial selection were thought to be well understood by all involved. Effectively, there were 'no rules but everyone knew the rules'. The government had nearly complete discretion to appoint someone who met the minimum technical requirement and the only constraining factor was the need to ensure that parties involved in coalition governments believed they had their appropriate share of appointments. Yet that leaves us without any systemic information about whether this represented the reality of political decision-making or whether there was yet more to be understood. The following is an attempt to present such a systemic analysis, focusing on the decision-making and processes within the JAAB and within the Cabinet.

JUDICIAL SELECTION PROCESSES IN IRELAND: VIEWS FROM INSIDE THE JAAB

Having considered the perspectives of the legal profession and members of the judiciary, it now falls to consider the perspectives of those charged with implementing the new institutional process for judicial selection – the members of the Judicial Appointments Advisory Board. Interviews were conducted with seventeen members of the JAAB covering the period 1995–2007. Of those, eight were members of the judiciary. This analysis follows the structure of Part IV of the 1995 Act and sets out the purpose of the JAAB, its composition, its powers and its function to recommend applicants suitable for appointment to judicial office to the Minister.

Composition

The JAAB is composed of the Chief Justice, who is its Chairperson, and the Presidents of the High Court, Circuit Court and District Court. The other members are the Attorney General, three nominees of the Minister for Justice (appointed for three years) and a representative from each of the two legal profession bodies, the Law Society of Ireland and the Bar Council of Ireland.

In practice, the Bar Council generally picks the Chairperson of the Bar Council as their representative. Practice in the Law Society has varied over time. It has appointed both Presidents and former Presidents to represent the Law Society on the JAAB.

One member of the Board commented that the JAAB is almost universally Dublin dominated, as the members of the judiciary, the Attorney General and invariably the Bar Council Chairperson are all based in Dublin.

The role of the ministerial nominees to the JAAB was an important part of the political debate in 1995. The political instruction to the Attorney General in 1994 was to include 'some role for lay people' in the new framework. The 1995 Bill was criticized by the opposition for including 'ministerial stooges' but the Minister argued it was important to have people representing other interests such as victims' rights, women's groups or commercial interests on the Board. In practice, it is felt that the role of the lay people on the JAAB has been limited by the lack of familiarity by those appointees with the broad group of practitioners who apply to the JAAB for judicial appointment.

The consequence of this is that legal and judicial members can dominate the operation of judicial selection commissions. Interview evidence shows that it is certainly the case in Ireland. As Chapter 4 will show, the judicial selection commission in Scotland actively takes steps to protect the expression of the views of the lay person on the Board. Examples of these activities include allowing the lay people to give their views before the legal and judicial members of the commission. Also in Scotland, where the chairperson is a lay person, the judicial selection commission takes steps to ensure that the influence of 'being known' to the members of the commission is reduced by conducting the first screening of candidates on a 'blind' basis – with the names and photographs removed from the applications. Commission members therefore only see the qualifications and experience of the candidates on the first reading of the applications. In Ireland, the process on the JAAB is that judicial and legal members give their views first and applications are not anonymized at any stage of the process. Instead, applicants provide photographs with their applications.

The view of politicians has been mixed about the role of lay people – some commented that it is best to re-appoint lay people to have continuity and for them to get to know the legal system and candidates. Others were adamant that they should fill a serious representative role on the Board.

> It is very important that lay people should have good reason for being appointed; not just because they deserve it politically. (Post-1995/MJ/2)

One judicial member of the JAAB commented:

> I found it difficult with the lay members that I first had when I was on the Board – there was X, who was splendid but knew none of the people who were coming forward for appointment. There was Y, who was adamant that they be regarded as an equal member of this board, rather than being referred to as a lay member. Y fought like a tiger on the Board and made their impact. They knew a lot of the candidates and said their view. There was Z, who had very strong views about certain people and very much in favour about appointment of women to the extent of being a little bit unbalanced about it. It depends on the personality. The trouble with most lay people on a board like that is that they don't know the applicants. (JAAB/6)

The views of the other members of the Board of the lay people and their role has been mixed but, in general, many expressed frustration that knowing the candidates is such an important element of the work of the Board and that lay members are hampered in their capacity to contribute without this 'industry' knowledge.

> The lay members are representatives of interest groups and of society as a whole. They bring expertise from their particular backgrounds. The people who have been on the Board have done that well – made useful contributions. They are serious people, they are not there as window dressing. (JAAB/10)

One lay member of the JAAB commented that:

> Not much happens at these meetings – it is not a very complex area of responsibility. You go to the meetings and it's all done very quickly. (JAAB/14)

All these comments provide an important insight on the experience of lay people on the JAAB. On the one hand we can see a more limited involvement for the lay members in the decision-making of the Board because they simply do not know the candidates in the same way as the legal members of the Board. We can also see some frustration on the part of the legal members of the Board at the lack of knowledge of the lay members. The question of being known to the decision-makers is one that will arise again and again in this presentation of judicial selection processes. Not knowing the candidates offers the lay members an opportunity to give an assessment based purely on the education, qualifications and experience that has been presented by the judicial applicant in written form. When we think of 'knowing' a candidate, we can sometime associate it with cronyism. When this point was made to the legal members of the JAAB they commented, not unreasonably, that they were being asked to make an assessment for a serious position and the more they knew of the person, including their character and temperament (which is not something that could be presented in written form), the better they were able to competently make that assessment. The difficulty with this is that it may rule out those who might be ideal judicial candidates but are not, for one reason or another, well known to the members of the Board. In an effort to reduce the effects of political networks in judicial appointments, the new process risks replacing those political networks with some other geographic or professional network.

Opaque

There are two potential problems with the operation of the JAAB. Its processes are opaque (both for judicial applicants and for the government who receive the recommendations) and there is no opportunity for judicial aspirants to participate in, or contribute to, any element of the deliberations about their suitability for judicial office.

From the perspective of government, the JAAB removes the completely unsuitable from consideration. These people are probably unlikely to have been serious candidates for judicial appointment in any event. Government receives a longlist of 'suitable' people for appointment to vacancies as they arise. However, there is no further categorization provided to government to help guide their decision.

From the perspective of the judicial aspirant, the selection system is truly opaque. The applicant prepares and submits the application form and thereafter receives no communication (beyond an acknowledgment) from the JAAB on the outcome of his or her application. As we have seen, the Board has broad statutory powers to take soundings or conduct interviews. While the Board does take soundings, it has never conducted any interviews out of concerns for confidentiality and concerns about what could or should be asked in those interviews. The candidate has no capacity to contribute to the process of considering their application other than by the provision of references to support his or her application. In other forums, interviews generally provide an opportunity to clarify issues in CVs or application forms, and to correct any of the misunderstandings or misapprehensions that possibly arise. Judicial selection commissions in other jurisdictions employ a range of processes, including interviews and assessment centres, to assess the suitability of judicial candidates. However, the judicial applicant in Ireland has no such opportunity and receives no feedback from the JAAB – they are not told whether they have been successfully progressed through the JAAB process. The JAAB performs a role that has a direct bearing on the career prospects of an individual. It performs a decision-making function. Yet it provides little information on how those assessments are quantified or the outcome of those deliberations.

It is important to consider these issues because, in addition to our need to understand institutions, there is a public interest imperative in seeing how constitutional office-holders are appointed and whether there should be common features of their recruitment. If these processes were to be used in the appointment of other senior office-holders in the public service, the reaction would be of justifiable concern. But the judiciary cannot be compared to most other such positions. It is only possible to consider it against comparable appointment processes internationally or to other constitutional office-holders in Ireland. Chapter 4 will highlight the recruitment processes of another constitutional office-holder in Ireland – the Comptroller and Auditor General. These issues arise again in a more in-depth analysis of the processes and operation of the JAAB.

Operation

The basic operation of the judicial selection process under the JAAB is that any individual who wishes to be considered for a judicial posting must apply to the Board in writing, providing information as to their education, professional qualifications, experience and character. Candidates must seek an application form to be sent to them by post and completed applications must be submitted in hard copy – emailed application forms will not be accepted. As shown earlier in this chapter, section 14 of the 1995 Act provides the Board with specific powers to conduct its work and the power to adopt such other procedures as required to carry out its functions. Based on evidence from interviews with members of the JAAB, it can now be shown how the JAAB has operated in practice between 1995 and 2007.

The process is as follows: the Minister for Justice may inform the Board that a vacancy has arisen or is about to arise (there is no statutory requirement for the Minister to do so).[16] The Secretary of the JAAB contacts the Chairman of the JAAB to discuss the process of responding to the Minister's letter. The Secretary arranges for advertisements to be placed in the national press in response to the vacancy that is the subject of the Minster's letter.

The Judicial Appointments Advisory Board advertises annually in the national press to invite persons, who wish to be considered for judicial appointments that may arise, to submit their names to the Board. More recently, the Board has published advertisements on its website and the websites of profes-

16 The 2002 Annual Report of the JAAB states that there is no statutory obligation on the Minister for Justice to request the Board to make a recommendation as to the filling of a particular judicial vacancy (Judicial Appointments Advisory Board, 2002) and that since the establishment of the Board, the Minister has requested the Board to make such a recommendation in respect of every judicial vacancy that has arisen.

sional bodies inviting applicants to submit their names in respect of specific judicial vacancies. Applicants provide details of their education, professional qualifications and details of their practice, experience and character.[17]

Candidates are also entitled to submit an unsolicited application at any time during the year. The application forms, CVs and photographs are circulated to each member about ten days in advance of the Board meeting. Candidates are also required to provide a tax clearance certificate along with a statutory declaration that their tax affairs remain in order since the issuing of their tax clearance certificate. As the JAAB retains applications for a calendar year, it generally has a surplus of 'live' candidates at any time. The JAAB writes to all of the applicants on file at the end of the calendar year to inform them that their application will no longer be kept on file, but that they are welcome to resubmit it for the following calendar year.

Originally, the statutory declaration had to be made within four weeks of the meeting of the JAAB to consider applications, but that was an 'administrative nightmare so now it has to be made within three months of the meeting' (JAAB/7).

The volume of work associated with the process was the subject of repeated comment by JAAB members.

> In the District Court, there were about 150 applications at any one time, 100 for the Circuit Court, 40 for the High Court and 15 for the Supreme Court. When a vacancy arose a meeting would be convened by the Secretary, on instructions of the Chairman, and all of the Board members would get files of applications about 10 days in advance. But of course you had people who already had their applications there and you'd re-read the same applications all the time. You'd be reading all the applications each time and whatever new ones had come in. (JAAB/8)

The JAAB meets to consider the applications. In general, the practice has been that the Chief Justice may open discussions on a given candidate, followed in order of seniority by the other judges, with the President of the court to which the candidate has applied taking a stronger role in the discussion than their colleagues. The representative of the branch of the legal profession to which the candidate belongs will also feature strongly in the discussion. The assessment process is based on the candidate's application form, CV, this discussion and any 'soundings' taken by a member of the JAAB (usually, because of the high number of solicitors who may not be known to other members of the JAAB, by the representative of the Law Society). A decision is made on each candidate and the JAAB agrees its list of recommendations for each court where there are vacancies. The Secretary of the Board contacts the

17 Applicants must also provide a tax clearance certificate and a statutory declaration that their tax affairs are in order.

Law Society and the Bar Council to ensure the people on the recommended list are in good standing and have the requisite number of years' practice experience. On receipt of letters confirming same from the respective professional bodies, the Secretary prepares the letter for the Minister. The letter to the Minister contains the names of all those who have applied in addition to all those whom the Board are happy to recommend. In the case of those who are recommended, the JAAB forwards their application forms and CVs to the Minister. The Minister brings the recommended names to Cabinet.

The JAAB can establish sub-committees to assist it in carrying out its functions. It noted in its 2003 Annual Report that it had availed of its power to appoint a sub-committee to deal with the large volume of applications for Circuit and District Court vacancies and commented that this has greatly assisted them in the efficient conduct of their business but that the decision to recommend a particular candidate will always remain with the Board (Judicial Appointments Advisory Board, 2003). At the time that this occurred, the process was that, once an application had been made, it remained on the books of the JAAB indefinitely, unless the candidate specifically withdrew it. This meant that, each time there was a vacancy, the Board had to go through the process of looking at all of the applications again. Secondly, there were people on the list of applicants who had applied in the early years of the Board's existence who were clearly no longer eligible because they had either gone past an age where they were eligible for appointment[18] or for other reasons.

> In two cases, we'd found they had died and obviously hadn't withdrawn their application or there were other circumstances, such as people having gotten very ill. (JAAB/8)

Eventually, a sub-committee was set up to do two things: one was to look at the application form itself. The second was to try to cull the number of applicants on file. On the suggestion of the sub-committee, the Board agreed that an application would only be valid until the end of the calendar year. If a candidate applied, and was deemed suitable, their application remained valid and was held on the JAAB files for this period. If another vacancy arose during that year then the applicant would be considered without the need to reapply. At the end of the calendar year the application expired. Equally, the sub-committee suggested that all of the older applications would expire and that those people would be informed that they were being removed from the list

18 Courts (Supplemental Provisions) Act 1961, section 30 (1): 'The age of retirement of a justice of the District Court shall be sixty-five years.' 'There was also a rule of practice that anyone who was over 65 would not be appointed, the reason was that if you're a district judge you have to be re-appointed every year and for the High Court, you'd have five years into it before retirement and so it was felt there was not much point' (JAAB/8).

and invited to reapply if they wished. 'The result was that the number of applications in District Court fell to about 80.' (JAAB/8) This sub-committee, established in 2001, also examined the application form in response to some concerns within the Board about its structure and content. A consulting firm, Deloitte and Touche, was hired to advise on the considerations that should be taken into account in such a form.

Following the enactment of the Courts and Court Officers Act 2002, solicitors became eligible for direct appointment to the High Court and the Supreme Court. The application form was revised to make it easier to identify people and to make it more relevant for the breadth of people applying for positions on the different courts. The application form is available on the JAAB website.[19]

> We wanted to make the form more user-friendly for solicitors, because it was very orientated towards the Bar, there were questions which really pointed to experience as an advocate for example, whereas under 1995 Act solicitors were eligible for appointment to the Circuit Court. (JAAB/8)

The form was also redesigned to make it easier to identify the applicant, by the inclusion of photographs – one for everyone on the Board (JAAB/7). The old form was a single page form to which an applicant could attach their Curriculum Vitae. The new form was more comprehensive and allowed the applicant to submit as much about their practice and experience as they wished.

The form included a requirement to include a statement of earnings for the previous three years. Interviewees stated their view that this was important because it gave the Board an idea of the extent of the applicant's practice. Furthermore, it allowed the Board to see if a person's earnings had declined over a period of three years prior to their application or remained constant. It was thought that this would give an indication of other underlying factors in the person's decision to apply to the Board – ill health or a collapse in their practice perhaps. While it might be a concern that to measure success in this way might unwittingly diminish the prospects of a practitioner who spends a great deal of time on pro bono or other socially valuable but non-remunerative work, the members of the Board commented that, in such cases, they would already know a person did such work on a regular basis. They also said that those people would be known favourably and that earnings would not be as important a factor for such people. The fact of doing such work was regarded as a positive factor for the applicant.

The JAAB has the power to engage in soundings in relation to a particular candidate to assist in determining whether they are suitable for appointment to

19 www.jaab.ie.

judicial offices. The members of the JAAB who contributed to this study had mixed views on the role of soundings in the judicial selection process.

> Soundings is a bit like an applicant for a golf club, is he the right sort of person to admit into this club? It would be done on what is his background or her background and what are they like as a person. There is no formal process, someone would be saying do you know them, or do you know them or maybe we should check. But certainly in my time on the Board nobody said, ok we'll defer making a decision here until we do soundings on some of the applicants, if they were done they were done in advance, but the reality is that even though canvassing is not supposed to be done and I think even disqualifies you, but the reality is that most of the applicants would have been well known and I think that's why there's a balance on the Board. So soundings, yes if someone applied from Dingle, before I went into Board I would ring the President of the Kerry Law Society and say who's so and so a person or what are they like without disclosing why I was ringing. But it would be very informal, and certainly no decision was taken at Board that we'll take soundings on this person or that. (JAAB/8)

> We did use soundings to good effect with the Law Society representative, if he's good, he will be clever enough to take soundings about a practitioner without giving away that he has applied. And a lot of things will come out in the wash – you could have someone who appeared before you, was a good advocate with a good knowledge of law and was good on his feet but through soundings you might find out that he had trouble with his practising certificate and that put him out of consideration. I would oppose anyone who had been in trouble with the Law Society, however good he was. When a solicitor blots his copy book and loses face in the public eye, he will then be known as someone who was in difficulties with the Law Society. Part of the makeup of the judge should be that he is respected and how can he be respected if he in trouble with the Law Society? That put a lot of people out of court and so soundings that way were useful; with the Bar, soundings weren't necessary, the law library is an echo chamber – every whisper goes from ear to ear and they know everything about everybody. (JAAB/6)

> I didn't do it very much. You would need to ask somebody completely trustworthy, and in any event I knew the applicants well. The solicitor on the Board needed to do it more often, just because of the size of the profession and the geographic spread. I never had the experience that the soundings turned out to be wrong. They were always done discreetly and very well and there was never a leak either. (JAAB/10)

The Board also states that, to date, it has not availed of its power to engage in soundings with colleagues or experts in the area of law in which the potential interviewee has been practising but that it will do so where appropriate.

The Board has the power to invite persons identified by it to submit their names for consideration by the Board. However, as it states repeatedly in its Annual Reports, the Board has not availed of this power. 'There are clearly serious practical difficulties in exercising that power in the case of a body such as the Board whose role is to submit the names of persons who are suitable for appointment rather than decide who should be appointed' (Judicial Appointments Advisory Board Annual Reports 2002, 2003, 2004, 2010).

Section 20 of the 1995 Act provides that all proceedings of the Board and all communications to the Board shall be confidential and shall not be disclosed except for the purposes of this Act.

> Confidentiality is very important. If it is the ambition of a practitioner to be appointed to the bench then he must keep it to himself and the JAAB must not allow it to be known, he can't manage his practice if he is spoken of as a future judge. He may lose solicitors who won't brief him because he may go on the bench. (JAAB/6)

The Board has the power to conduct interviews under section 14(2) of the 1995 Act, but it has never used this power. In its Annual Reports the Board has repeatedly stated that it 'had not to date availed of its power either to arrange for the interviewing of applicants or to consult with other persons concerning the suitability of applicants' (Judicial Appointments Advisory Board, 2002).

An analysis of subsequent reports shows that the Board has never availed of its power to conduct interviews. Nevertheless, in all of its Reports, the Board noted its power to do so in the future. The question of whether to interview or not has been the subject of on-going debates within the JAAB and raises important questions about how potential judges are assessed and the role of the JAAB in determining the suitability of someone for judicial office.

> The issue arose also as to whether applicants should be interviewed and that is something that had been fudged quite considerably. There is I think an acceptance that in principle anyone who applies for a judicial vacancy should be interviewed to see if they're capable and to see how they present but there is a reluctance to do it, from the Bar particularly and to a lesser extent from the existing judiciary to go down the interview route. The reason for this is because the JAAB themselves think it would just take a lot of time and the other reason was the apparent superiority of the Bar, and I say that advisedly having close relations at the Bar, but there is this sort of 'how dare you even look at or question my competence, I'm making the application, is that not enough?' attitude

> sometimes. I don't think a solicitor would have the same reluctance to it as the Bar certainly at that time had, and I think probably would have now. The judiciary who are made up by and large of the Bar, certainly at superior court level, would have the same view: 'Well we know Joe Bloggs and he's an eminent senior counsel, we couldn't possibly ask him to come in and interview and have him open to the interview process because we know what his competency is already.' That is of course wrong in principle because not everyone who makes a good practitioner makes a good judge and equally the other way round. (JAAB/8)

> People are acutely conscious of opening Pandora's Box. You would run the risk of the consequences which can arise from interviews. You cannot ask the one question you might like to, what is your stance on this issue or that, as no potential judge could offer their position prior to hearing a case. So what then do you talk to them about? At the time I was on the Board I would have queried what value interviewing would have brought to the process. But no, there are such a large number of solicitors and barristers; perhaps some other process is necessary. But I would still have grave reservations about interviewing. (JAAB/10)

> I had said we should interview everybody. There are several problems with interviews, if it's a High Court vacancy and a barrister is seen going into the conference room then word will spread like wildfire around the library, that so and so is looking for an appointment to the High Court. And when it came to solicitors, there was a need for an interview. And I said when it came to Circuit Court I was prepared to go on a sub-committee to interview everyone. And yes it would take time but once we had done one or two the format would become more clear and it would be easier for next vacancy. But they all said, no it would be too unwieldy and they never did it. I think in truth, it's an important job and if you're going to recommend someone for it you should interview them beforehand. And an interview doesn't tell everything; you can be a very skilled interviewee and coached in the right tactics. But it would stir your memory, 'oh I remember that guy, I closed a sale with him in Cork once.' (JAAB/6)

The legislation gives the JAAB unconstrained powers to perform its function as it sees fit and refers to certain processes that it may wish to use in doing so. Of these expressed powers, the JAAB has used the power to advertise, require applicants to submit application forms and to engage in soundings in relation to applicants for judicial office. However, it has shown continual reluctance to engage in interviews for a variety of reasons. In particular, there is a reluctance to interview because of the amount of time it would take to interview all of the applicants, a perception that the members of the Board have insufficient expertise and experience of interview processes, a concern about the propriety of asking judicial applicants difficult questions, and a concern for the confidentiality of the applicants. Interviewing has been a concern the Board for some time – in its 2003 Annual Report, the Board noted that it had not conducted interviews but that it had agreed to 'obtain expert advice and the issue would be progressed in 2004' (2003, p. 20). In January 2014 the Chief Justice wrote to the Minister for Justice outlining the Board's intention to commence an interview process. There is no evidence that interviews have yet been conducted by the Board in respect of any vacancies.

The reluctance to interview is linked to elements of the institutional design of the JAAB. It is a body dominated by senior members of the judiciary who are unlikely to have enough time to give to interviewing judicial applicants each year. In order for interviews to be practical in terms of time, the JAAB would have to perform an exercise that identified a shortlist of candidates among the longer list of suitable people, whom the Board could then call for interview.

Interviews by the JAAB also raise the prospect of sitting judges interviewing potential judges which could have implications for the independence of the legal system and, indeed, for the broader independence of the judiciary. This is best illustrated by an example: a senior lawyer appearing in the High Court each day is considering submitting an application to the JAAB in the coming two or three years. A new President of the High Court is appointed who will be a member of the JAAB for the next seven years. The senior lawyer is the advocate in a series of very difficult and challenging cases that bring him or her into conflict with the President of the High Court. The independence of the individual lawyer is very important in making the argument on behalf of their client. But, for the lawyer who has decided to apply to the JAAB for consideration, there may be incentives to modify behaviour in such a way that avoids or minimizes any such conflict. This may happen consciously or unconsciously. It may be a result of the institutional design that enables a sitting judge to interview a practising lawyer, and take an adjudicative view that will have implications for the future career of the lawyer. While this scenario is possible under the current institutional arrangements, its influence is much more subtle than is likely to be the case in face to face interviews between the sitting judge and the prospective judge. It may be less likely to be a risk in a system that uses retired judges to interview judicial applicants.

On the other hand, a different President of the High Court might take the view that the robust and challenging lawyer was precisely the type of candidate that should be recommended to the Minister for judicial appointment. In either case, the question about the role of a sitting judge interviewing a potential judge is one that warrants further reflection, having regard to the independence of both the legal professionals and the judiciary in a constitutional democracy, but there is no need to run this risk.

Best practice for recruitment to the judiciary should include some element of interview. This would assist in providing government with the best available information about judicial candidates. The hesitancy of the JAAB to use its power to interview contrasts with the practice in judicial selection commissions in other jurisdictions that routinely interview potential judges and, in some cases, even use assessment centres to determine an individual's suitability for judicial office. It is also in marked contrast to the recruitment practices for other senior public jobs which can involve rigorous analysis of potential candidates. It is a matter for the Board that they did not use the statutory power given to them but it goes back to the heart of the question about optimum institutional functioning vis-à-vis the institutional design of a delegated body.

Recommendations

Having sought, received and considered the applications received, the next statutory function of the JAAB is to submit names to the Minister of those applicants whom it recommends for appointment to judicial office. This is a critical function – as per section 13 of the 1995 Act, which clearly states that the purpose of the board is 'identifying persons and informing the Government of the suitability of those persons for appointment to judicial office'. Evidence from interview data shows how the JAAB in the early 2000s made an important change to its processes for making recommendations to the Minister.

The 1995 Act does not oblige the government to select the appointee from the Board's list of recommended candidates; it may select some other individual on the condition that a notice is published to that effect. Therefore, the government is not, in law, constrained in its actions by the recommendations of the JAAB. There is only a remote risk of a political sanction if they do not use the JAAB process. However, now that the political norm is of governments using names from the JAAB list, the political risk inherent in going outside that list has increased considerably. In the cases where appointments were made on this basis, there was no political criticism of the government. The few appointments that were made in this way were, in any event, considered to be of individuals of a very high calibre. The government also has the discretion to fill a judicial vacancy by promoting a judge from a lower court. In practice, this usually happened only between the High Court and the Supreme Court but has recently been used more often between the Circuit Court and the High Court (with one such promotion occurring each year in 2003, 2004, 2005, 2011, 2012, and six such elevations in 2014).

Once the Minister requests recommendations from the Board, the JAAB becomes involved in the judicial selection process. Although the government remains free to appoint a preferred candidate, irrespective of the recommendations of JAAB, it would not appoint someone who had actually been declined by the JAAB. This is because it would undermine the system and also because it would create a negative aura around the judge in question after his or her appointment, especially as the members of the JAAB would know that the candidate had not been recommended by them. Morgan (2004) states that, notwithstanding this, the Board demonstrated its independence in 1998 when the government was about to appoint a candidate whom the Board did not consider suitable. Morgan (2004) comments that the Board 'confidentially threatened to resign and the Government climbed down'.

> The important point is that if someone applies to the JAAB and is not recommended, then they will not be appointed. This is because no-one will appoint someone whom the JAAB has decided not to recommend because no one needs a controversy over a judicial appointment, that's nothing but trouble. The JAAB's power is to produce a list from which the government appoints. (Post-1995/AG/2)

While the 1995 Act gives JAAB wide powers to establish its own processes in the performance of its function, it has been shown that it is quite prescriptive in relation to how recommendations are to be made to the Minister. Like many new institutions, the processes used over its lifetime were largely those that were introduced at its inception. Members of the JAAB set out the original procedures as follows: if there was vacancy, the JAAB nominated seven people from the panel of recommended people and if there were two vacancies they would generally nominate fourteen – if more than fourteen suitable candidates had applied.

> So if the vacancy was in the District Court, his agenda was 'Right, we'll consider all of the applications but we'll only send 7 people to the Cabinet, to the Minster of Justice for appointment.' He [the first chairperson, Chief Justice Liam Hamilton] took a particular interpretation of the Act, I thought it worked well and thought it was a good way of dealing with it. (JAAB/8)
>
> At the same time we would send up the complete list of applicants. So the Minister would get two lists – the list of those deemed suitable and then the longlist of everyone who had applied. (JAAB/8)

This reflects the process set out in section 16(2) of the 1995 Act – that 'on the request of the Minister', the Board shall, either where a judicial office is vacant or before a vacancy arises, 'submit to the Minister the names of each person who has informed the Board of his or her wish to be considered for appointment to that judicial office and the Board shall recommend to the Minister at least seven persons for appointment to that judicial office.'

> You just got the seven names but in reality it was fewer. I'm not sure I ever got as many as seven names for one vacancy. Usually there'd be two or three vacancies at a given time. I don't think I ever asked for seven names where there was only one vacancy, I always thought it was too many, because it did allow for the kind of cherry-picking, because they were never rated. You just got the seven names and you could pick who you wanted out of that. (Post-1995/MJ/2)

> I don't ever remember seeing the full list, because you see the freedom was there to ignore the whole seven. The freedom was there for the government to say well we don't want to appoint any of these but with the proviso that you publish that in Iris Oifigiúil. We didn't appoint anyone like that. (Post-1995/MJ/2)

> My recollection is that for the High Court I don't think we ever recommended seven. I felt that seven was too much for the High Court and Supreme Court, you'd *never* have seven people but you usually would be struggling to get two good candidates and you'd have four or five acceptable but unimpressive candidates, so why would you recommend them? You didn't want to knock them off because they weren't below the base standard so I would go with trying to recommend a small number. (Post-1995/AG/8)

It is clear from supporting interview evidence with government decision-makers that seven names was considered a large number of recommendations to have been included in the legislation.

> It's all done for political correctness. The only reason to have seven nominees is to give the appearance of an independent commission, but leave all the political latitude that was there before. The idea of an independent commission is corrupted by choosing seven as the number of nominees. Seven is a political get out clause. If only three were nominated, then there is a bigger selection function in the commission. How many times will they find more than seven who are suitable for senior posts? It's a get out clause, politically. If you take for example a Supreme Court vacancy, there will not be as many as seven suitable names and if there are not, then you're back to square one with the government making the completely unfettered decision anyway. Only the totally unsuitable are weeded out by this system, but they are unlikely to have made it anyway. (Pre-1995/MJ/3)

> Seven names is a mad system. What it does is ensures that there are no truly bad names. (Pre-1995/TAO/2)

These comments reflect the evidence in Chapter 2 that this system was established as a political necessity in response to a political concern about judicial selection. The legislation ultimately enacted in 1995 provided for much greater discretion for the government in choosing appointees because the legislation provided that JAAB would recommend at least seven names instead of three to five names (as provided by the Courts and Court Officers Bill 1994).

Several contributors have made the point that, particularly in the early days of the JAAB, there would never be seven names who could be recommended for the High Court or Supreme Court.

> At most you might have two or, in a particularly good vintage, three serious contenders for senior judicial posts. In fact there were really only one or two really good candidates at any one time. The Bar is bigger now of course but there is never a surfeit of candidates at that level. (Pre-1995/AG/4)

As shown in Chapter 2, the increased number of recommendations was included in the Courts and Court Officers Bill 1995 because of a concern by policy makers not to unduly tie the hand of government. It has to be remembered that the original proposal was that the JAAB would recommend between three and five candidates. The proposal in the 1995 Bill was that the JAAB would recommend at least ten names in respect of each vacancy and the final solution in the 1995 Act was that the JAAB would recommend seven names in respect of each vacancy. This is important when we consider how the implementation of the 1995 Act by the JAAB has evolved over time.

A key role played by the JAAB is their capacity to influence the government indirectly through the importance it may place on recruiting different types of lawyers to the bench. Filling vacancies with particular technical skill profiles is thought to be a priority of the JAAB, and can be an important consideration for government. A number of participants commented that the JAAB ensures that the preferred candidates on the list are made known to the government, usually through the Attorney General (who is a JAAB member).

> The JAAB in their discussions express views about who to appoint. For example, in the three-vacancy High Court situation, 21 names will be whittled down to three or four. Cabinet never gets 21 names, the Minister for Justice and the Attorney General tend to put forward names. If you're not on that 'love list' there's no chance really. The guys on the JAAB have egos and strong views, and the AG and justice officials pick that up and feed it back. (Post-1995/TAO/1)

> I understand the JAAB would look at this and have a discussion like 'they're all very well qualified but we're very short of experience in

> planning or family law etc.' This is what I would discuss with (the Attorney General) when he would come up with the list, or the list from the Chief Justice. They'd give us the names, but also that they'd had cognisance that the court was a bit light on this or that ... So I would get the names, but with a comment that one or two would be more suitable than the others on that basis. (Post-1995/MJ/2)

This was the core informal communication between the Board and the government. As time went on, with the increased number of recommendations coming to government, the JAAB performed less and less of a selection function, and more of a screening function: 'It is a screening mechanism, a quality filter'. (Post-1995/AG/2). This is important in considering how the implementation of the 1995 Act by JAAB evolved over time.

IMPLEMENTATION OF THE 1995 ACT BY THE JAAB, 1995–2007

The number of names proposed to government is a centrally important matter. It shapes the degree of discretion available to the government. As shown in Chapter 1, other judicial selection commissions recommend fewer names than in Ireland. Both Scotland and England recommend only one name to government. In Ireland, the constitutional prerogative of the government to advise the President on the appointment of judges may militate against such a restrictive system. As is clear from Chapter 2 though, the Irish government in 1994 agreed to a judicial selection commission model that would recommend as few as three names. Chapter 1 showed that seven names is a relatively large number by international comparison.

Over time, the JAAB came to prefer to recommend a larger rather than a smaller number of names to the government. This materially altered the institutional functioning of the JAAB and resulted in the government being required to exercise more discretion in the nomination of judges. How and why this happened is of considerable interest.

Interview data with JAAB members from 1995 shows that the approach adopted initially was to recommend seven names in respect of each vacancy. However, in the case of High Court or Supreme Court appointments, fewer might be recommended if the Board was of the view that fewer than seven were of a calibre that could be recommended, or in cases where the number of applications was extremely small. In its first Annual Report in 2002, the Board reflected some of the debate about the number of names that should be recommended. It made two points:

1 That the Board considered recommending to the government that they rank names in order of preference. It decided against this recommendation

as it was 'conscious, however, of the difficulties which might result from such a change, not least the question as to whether it would place unjustifiable constraints on the exercise by the Government of a function which is exclusively assigned to it under the Constitution' (Judicial Appointments Advisory Board Annual Report 2002, pp 23–4).

2 That the Board considered inviting the government to consider 'whether the present legislation should also be amended so as to reduce the minimum number of candidates whom the Board is required to recommend below the present figure of seven.' This was repeated in the 2003 Annual Report. The Board noted that in the case of vacancies in the Circuit Court and District Court, reducing the minimum number of recommendations below seven would result in the exclusion of a number of candidates 'whom the Board would otherwise have no difficulty in recommending' and so 'the Board has come to the conclusion that the present minimum number of seven is appropriate' (Judicial Appointments Advisory Board Annual Report 2002, pp 23–4).

The question of the number of recommendations was the subject of periodic internal debate on the Board. The Board referred to this debate in its Annual Reports but there is no evidence of it having taken any further action than this – for example, in having formal discussions with government. The Attorney General, who was both a member of the Board and legal adviser to the government, would have been privy to this debate and in a position to brief government as appropriate.

In the early 2000s the JAAB took a decision to change its practice and to increase the number of names it recommended to government. Certain members of the Board were concerned that the Board may, in its practice of recommending approximately seven names, be acting unconstitutionally by taking from the government its constitutional prerogative to select a judge for appointment. This was particularly so where there were more than seven persons whom the Board would have been happy to recommend. The Board took legal advice on this point.

> It should be noted in this connection, that the Board has received the benefit of legal opinion from senior counsel that, in arriving at a list of candidates whom it is prepared to recommend to the Minister as suitable for appointment, it is not confined simply to transmitting to the Minister the names of all those who meet the threshold requirements of eligibility and suitability and that its function is to select from the candidates so qualified (seven or more in number), those whom they are satisfied that they should recommend as suitable for appointment to the vacancy concerned, having regard to all the requirements laid down in the Act. (Judicial Appointments Advisory Board Annual Report 2002, pp 23–4)

However, interview data shows that the Board changed its practice following consideration of this legal advice and the Board made a decision that it would recommend a larger number of candidates to government. Thereafter, the Board would take the general approach of recommending all those who were 'not unsuitable' for appointment to judicial office, rather than the seven most suitable. Evidence from interviews with members of the JAAB from this time shows that some were unhappy with the decision and the new application of section 16 of the 1995 Act. It should be noted that this was a general approach, rather than a fixed rule, and that the practice on this issue ebbed and flowed over time but never reverted to the more restrictive approach taken in the early years of the operation of the JAAB. Nevertheless, it is understood that this general practice continues to varying degrees, including into the lifetime of the 31st Dáil (2011–16), and that the Board remains conscious of what it perceives to be legal uncertainty in this area.

It is clear that the number of recommended candidates increased substantially:

> All of a sudden we were recommending huge numbers of people to government. I mean that wasn't the point of the Board at all. I questionned it, I didn't agree with it, but there was a very strong view taken. (JAAB/4)

> I was under the illusion before I was Minister that, at most, JAAB recommended seven names to government in respect of the different levels of the judiciary but of course when you look carefully at the legislation, that's not what it says, the legislation says 'at least seven'. So when it came to appointments for the District Court you have in excess of 100 approved names, when it came to the Circuit Court you could have between 40 to 75 approved names. And the quality of the information was substantially confined to that contained in the CVs. There were also occasions that you would have a lawyer on the unapproved list, which you also got, and then on a later occasion, they would suddenly migrate to the approved list. It wasn't clear to me on some occasions why some people were on the unapproved list, who in my experience were extremely competent, and then migrated to the approved list. I won't comment on some of the names who from time to time were on the approved list. It was something of a mystery on occasion as to how a candidate ended up on one or other list – was it because of how they had filled out their CV or was it because some member of the Committee had a perspective on that individual. We needed some more clarity on the basis on which people were approved or not approved. Getting over 100 names and 100 CVs to read isn't an appropriate way to conduct judicial appointments and if it has been

> pulled back [since then] by the JAAB, it didn't happen while I was Minister for Justice. (Post-1995/MJ/5)

This new practice was in marked contrast with the operation of the Board from 1996 to the time of the decision where a tighter interpretation of the 1995 Act was taken by the then members of the Board. This discretion to interpret the Act in different ways is facilitated by the institutional design in the legislation, which provides that the JAAB shall recommend at least seven names in respect of each vacancy. It would not have been possible under the institutional design of the 1994 Bill, which explicitly provided that the JAAB would recommend not less than three and not more than five names per vacancy.

This change in process increased the government's discretion in choosing judicial candidates. The decision fundamentally changed the role of the JAAB from being a quasi-selection body to being a purely screening body. This change occurred in the early 2000s and has remained in operation for approximately fifteen years. This institutional change was made without any reference to the law-making institution that created the JAAB and devised its institutional structure and processes in the Court and Court Officers Act 1995. No account of this change in policy has ever been provided, except in the form of the Annual Reports of the JAAB, but even these have not described the scale of the institutional change. The Joint Oireachtas Committee on Justice and Equality were first briefed on this change in institutional practice in November 2014.[20] It should be a matter of concern to policy makers and legislators in Ireland that such a fundamental change could occur, largely unnoticed by the body politic, to the institutional functioning of a statutory body performing a delegated role on behalf of government. If it can occur in the JAAB, what other stautory bodies in Ireland are operating at such a remove from their institutional design and what are the implications of that? The experience of the institutional functioning of the JAAB truly makes the case for periodic review by parliamentary committees of the operation of the legislation

20 Joint Oireachtas Committee on Justice, Defence and Equality, Discussion on Judicial Appointments, 26 November 2014 – http://oireachtasdebates.oireachtas.ie/Debates%20Authoring/DebatesWebPack.nsf/committeetakes/JUJ2014112600002?opendocument#A00100 (accessed 31 Jan. 2016). Dr Carroll MacNeill: 'This change dramatically widened the scope for Government discretion in judicial selection, if it wished to choose a preferred candidate from the list. It is counter-intuitive for the Judicial Appointments Advisory Board, which – by statute – had been given an extraordinary new role in judicial selection and had the capacity to make a selection decision, for example to choose seven or fewer applicants out of 90 or 100 for the District Court, and send that selection to government. It is difficult, because there is an independent board, and as long as the government makes selection decisions from the recommendations of that board, the government cannot be accused of acting politically in its appointments. What is extraordinary is that the JAAB would have widened the discretion of government in this way, essentially relinquishing the selection role it had been given without reference to this committee or the Oireachtas generally or to the government.'

governing statutory bodies and delegated authorities. The case of the JAAB, dominated as it is by senior judges and senior legal professionals, might lead some observers to conclude that such an interaction with the law-making authority (the Oireachtas) would be problematic in terms of the proper separation of powers between judiciary and legislature. Such a view mistakes the position of the JAAB – it is not a constitutional body, it performs no role in relation to the adjudication of legal matters, it is a legislative creation only and, while not accountable to the legislature as such, is not immune from providing a periodic account of its operations to the Joint Oireachtas Committee on Justice. No individual applicant's confidentiality could be threatened by that, no individual judge could feel threatened in the performance of their judicial function. The JAAB has a secretary, who for the full period of the operation of the Board has been an employee of an agency of the Department of Justice, who could liase with the legislature on behalf of the Committee along with or instead of the lay members of the Committee.

The decision of the JAAB to recommend more candidates had different implications for judicial selection in different courts. The number of applicants for positions on the High Court or Supreme Court was generally considerably less than the number of applicants for District and Circuit Court appointments. Analysis of the Annual Reports since 2002 shows that, in general, there are about 20 applicants for a High Court position, but up to 100 for a District Court position. If an average of 10 per cent of applicants is unsuitable, the JAAB would then recommend about 18 people from whom the government could choose their preferred candidate for a High Court position and about 90 people from whom the government could choose their preferred candidate for a District Court position.

One consequence of this decision is that the number of candidates recommended is now so large that there could be no incentive for the government to appoint someone who had not been approved by the JAAB. The only exception to this is where such a person had not actually applied to the JAAB for consideration but this has only very occasionally happened since the establishment of the JAAB. The number of candidates now being recommended for appointment by the JAAB means the government has a wide choice in making its decision and a wide choice from what is, due to the size of the legal profession in Ireland, a small pool of serious contenders for the positions.

It is clear from this analysis that the JAAB plays an important role in judicial selection in Ireland but its relative importance has diminished over time, at its own hands. The JAAB is given broad statutory powers to perform its function. How the Board chooses to use these powers has important implications both for the nature of the information on which it can base its assessments and its ability to influence government in the final selection of judges. The statutory function given to the JAAB was to perform a process of selection between applicants for judicial office and to inform the government which persons were suitable – and, indeed, most suitable of all the applicants. The government was then statutorily bound to first consider these names in making its decision. However, by changing its practice in relation to the making of recommendations to government, the JAAB may be seen to have fundamentally changed its own role in the judicial selection process.

JUDICIAL SELECTION PROCESSES IN IRELAND: VIEWS FROM INSIDE THE CABINET

Cabinet process

As has been shown, the process for judicial selection in pre-1995 Ireland was straightforward. It was the choice of the Taoiseach, on the advice of the Attorney General, with input from the Minister for Justice and/or the leader of the minor coalition political party (if there was one). Interviews with the decision-makers from 1982 to 1995 in the course of this study confirmed that nothing had fundamentally changed since the time of Bartholomew's work in 1969. Participants were asked the details of how the process of judicial selection worked in their respective government administrations from the time the vacancy arose until the announcement of the appointment.

> The Attorney General would have been made aware of the vacancy arising in advance. At the time the superior courts were exclusively barristers and invariably Senior Counsel. The AG would go through the list of senior counsel, see who stood out, who might be willing, as the more junior senior counsels may not be willing anyway. Then I would raise the matter with the Taoiseach and would discuss possible persons whom I thought could be considered. (Pre-1995/AG/4)

> The Attorney General would be asked by the Taoiseach or the Minister for Justice: 'we have a vacancy, who should we appoint?' The Minister for Justice would bring the name to Cabinet, but never without consulting the Taoiseach, Tánaiste and Attorney General. (Pre-1995/AG/1)

What is interesting is whether the introduction of the JAAB had any impact on the Cabinet process for judicial selection. The new regulated process for judicial selection under the Courts and Court Officers Act 1995 provided that, when a judicial vacancy arises, the Minister for Justice may choose to write to the JAAB to inform them and to request that they submit names to the Minister that are suitable for appointment. Once the JAAB process had been completed, the names of the recommended candidates are formally sent to the Minister for Justice by the JAAB. Having received the names from the JAAB, the Minister for Justice brings a memorandum to Cabinet that simply recommends the name of an individual for appointment to the relevant court. Once this name is approved by Cabinet the Minister contacts the individual to inform them that the government wishes to nominate them for judicial appointment by the President of Ireland. Decision-making in the judicial appointments process after 1995 continued to be vested in the Taoiseach, the Minister for Justice and the Attorney General:

> There was informal discussion; the Attorney General would talk to the Minister for Justice and the Taoiseach, probably the other way round, when the names would emerge. There might even be some informal discussion before the JAAB met at all. (Post-1995/MJ/2)
>
> The practicality of making appointments was that, on all occasions, the Attorney General and myself would consult on that aspect of matters and in practical terms make recommendations to the Taoiseach and Tánaiste. In practice, I won't say every time the recommendations were agreed, but quite frequently they were and on that basis the system worked. There wasn't an appointment made that I can recall that wasn't made on merit, there wasn't an appointment made that didn't derive from a recommendation of JAAB on the recommended list save where we were promoting someone from a lower court and I hope the promotions we made were appropriate. (Post-1995/MJ/5)

All of the participants acknowledged that the Cabinet process itself is a formality and that the decision has been effectively made before Cabinet – especially in the case of senior appointments. However, one Taoiseach (Post-1995/TAO/1) commented that the Cabinet always discussed an appointment to the Supreme Court or the position of Chief Justice, especially as some members were concerned about a liberal/conservative element. The introduction of the new system had little impact on the Cabinet process for judicial selection and it remained substantially the same as the pre-1995 period.

Role of the Attorney General

Historically, there was a strong role for the Attorney General in judicial selection, particularly in respect of senior judicial appointments. Connected to this is the capacity of the Attorney General to brief barristers on behalf of the state and provide them high profile work that assists in building their practice and their profile.

The degree to which the advice of the Attorney General was sought and relied upon or the extent of the consultation with other government partners was not the product of any formalized government process. It was simply dependent on the personalities and relationships between the members of the decision-makers of the day.

> Traditionally, the Minister brought the names to Cabinet and ultimately has to fill the vacancy. But the Minister didn't propose the names. It was usually the Taoiseach who opened the matter for discussion and will mention the name or names under consideration. The primary interlocutor in the process is the Attorney General, to a lesser extent the Minster for Justice, but this might vary according to personality. There is no formal structure to it. (Pre-1995/AG/4)

> When it came to judicial appointments, the initiative moved to the Attorney General. The Attorney General was able and well known and the Ministers had not much experience of the judicial system from their own backgrounds. The suggestions of names for judicial appointment came from the Attorney General as opposed to the Ministers. (Pre-1995/TAO/2)

> I would exercise great caution in my recommendations, every Attorney General is conscious of the capacity of the Supreme Court to strike down legislation. (Pre-1995/AG/5)

> There was a big political influence in appointments; the Attorney General had no veto. My nominations were for the assistance of government in their decision. There were two cases where someone was appointed that I hadn't recommended; one where the proposal came from within government and I didn't approve. But the politicians' right to make the decision is very carefully guarded. (Pre-1995/AG/1)

The Attorney General can act as a powerful voice at the JAAB meetings reflecting the concerns of the government in relation to judicial appointments – either in respect of individuals or in respect of the sorts of legal experience perceived to be necessary in the courts at a given time. The Attorney General can also have an influence over the processes of the JAAB and its recommendations to government as will be seen in detail later in this chapter.

The role of the Attorney General remains important in political deliberations about judicial selection, with one Taoiseach commenting that he listened to the Attorney General a lot in making appointments. (Post-1995/TAO/1)

> The Attorney General has a special relationship with the Taoiseach; he could act as an effective veto on a judicial appointment. (Post-1995/AG/8)

The Attorney General is extremely important in the period following receipt of the recommendations of the JAAB. The Attorney General can relay to government any particular points made by the JAAB or any of the nuances of the discussion at the JAAB meeting.

> The Attorney General is the heavyweight at that stage. If his judgment were not trusted at that point, there would be something seriously wrong [in government]. (Post-1995/AG/7)
>
> It was commented that in purely practical terms, the role of the Attorney General was always very strong in judicial selection as the Attorney General would know the gaps on the bench and know the people involved as individuals. (Post-1995/AG/7)

The role of the Attorney General has been formalized by the introduction of the JAAB. The Attorney General is a member of the JAAB, attends the meetings of the Board and considers the applications for all of the courts. This has increased the workload of the Attorney General in relation to judicial appointments – as they are obliged to consider applicants who may be manifestly unsuitable and would not have been considered for judicial appointment in the era prior to the setting up of the JAAB. It has also enhanced the influence of the Attorney General – he or she retains the traditional influence with government in respect to judicial selection, but can now also influence the discussions of the JAAB and act as a conduit between the JAAB and government.

Role of the Taoiseach and the Minister for Justice

The role of the Taoiseach in judicial appointments was core to the process in the pre-1995 period. The Taoiseach had a role to play in managing coalition agreement on candidates, consulting with the Attorney General in relation to their suggestions and hearing the views of other Cabinet members on appointments to the Circuit and District Courts.

> The Taoiseach might come to me and say what about so and so? And it might have been a suggestion from the Tánaiste. (Pre-1995/AG/1)

The influence of the minor partner in a coalition government was often important with regard to judicial appointments. Coalition partners might have an informal arrangement that judicial appointments would be shared between them on some pro rata basis or that each partner might contribute to the debate on each appointment.

> I don't recall the coalition question was an issue except in the appointment of X. That was a political appointment; (the other party) felt they were owed something. (Pre-1995/TAO/2)
>
> It was a political arrangement. The Tánaiste always wanted a say in things and there was an unwritten agreement that, as far as I remember, every third appointment was to be a Labour appointment. (Pre-1995/AG/1)

Although the formal Cabinet process prior to 1995 required the Minister for Justice to present the names to Cabinet for consideration, the reality was that the Taoiseach, heavily influenced by the Attorney General, had already made the decision. The Minister for Justice, despite his or her formal role, had relatively little influence over judicial appointments – particularly senior judicial appointments. According to one Minister from the pre-1995 period, the process was that the government appointed judges on the nomination of the Minister for Justice. However, this Minister felt he was insufficiently familiar with the relevant personalities at the top of the legal world and could not know about their relative competences and skills. As a consequence, he stated that he largely relied on the Attorney General.

> Our in-house arrangement was that he came up with the names and did an assessment of them. It was an informal arrangement I had with him to give me guidance. The Department of Justice did have some input too – they wouldn't actually recommend anyone but might make a comment like 'Be careful there, we know he was pulled for drink driving'. But basically, it was all very informal and very political in terms of connections. It was the decision of the Cabinet on the nomination of Taoiseach rather than on the nomination of the Minister. There was no legislative rule governing it. But the Attorney General is the head of the Bar, and a good AG of long standing and experience will have a huge influence over judicial appointments even though he has no formal role in the process. (Pre-1995/MJ/1)

Although the subtleties of each administration differed slightly, the overwhelming consensus was that the decision was made by the Taoiseach and Attorney General in respect of senior judicial appointments. There was a slightly reduced role for the Attorney General in respect of District Court appointments where other members of Cabinet could be more influential than in the case of senior judicial appointments. Both in the pre-1995 and post-1995 periods, the Minister for Justice had a more significant role in appointments to the District Court. The Cabinet tended to rely on the recommendation of the Minister for Justice for District Court appointments.

> The Minister for Justice never had to consult me regarding District Court appointments. Frequently the Minister for Justice is a solicitor themselves, and it was regarded as different territory. (Pre-1995/AG/1)

In both pre-1995 and post-1995 periods, the role of inter-Cabinet canvassing was found to be more important and more effective in relation to appointments to the District Court. Cabinet members were more likely to make suggestions to the Minister for Justice in relation to such appointments than they were likely to make in relation to more senior judicial appointments. One post-1995 Attorney General commented that the role of the Attorney General is extremely important in relation to High Court and Supreme Court appointments but significantly less in District Court appointments.

> The selection of Supreme Court judges is terribly important in the context of judicial activism … but I don't remember District Court appointments. (Pre-1995/AG/5)
>
> It was not unusual for proposals to come from politicians for the Circuit Court and District Court. (Pre-1995/AG/1)
>
> This was because it was generally solicitors that were appointed to the District Court bench, and the Attorney General mightn't know their strengths in the same way, and also because, very often, District Court appointments are more geographically based so local political interest is more strongly manifest. (Post-1995/AG/7)

This shows that political connection and influence is stronger in District Court appointments than in any other judicial appointments in Ireland. We will see this again in assessing the role of political party connections in judicial selection.

The decision-making process in the post-1995 period still rests with the Taoiseach, Attorney General and Minister for Justice. The Minister for Justice is required to consult with the Attorney General on judicial nominations prior to bringing them to Cabinet (Post-1995/AG/8; Post-1995/AG/7; Post-1995/MJ/4). The consensus among the key government decision-makers is that only the nominated candidate's name will go to Cabinet but that both the Minister for Justice and the Attorney General (who is a member of the JAAB) will see the full list of those who are sent forward by the JAAB to the Minister for Justice.

> The full list can't be available to Cabinet. It is a very confidential process. It is inevitable that it would leak (that so and so had applied) and that could have an effect on someone's [legal] practice. (Post-1995/MJ/4)

Occasionally, there may be some comments from other Cabinet members at the Cabinet meeting about the nominated person but these observations do not get anywhere near the level of discussion or debate about the relative merits of the candidate or possible alternatives. The name brought to Cabinet has been agreed in advance between the key decision-makers and is then approved, rather than agreed, by the Cabinet.

The impact of the institutional change in the Courts and Court Officers Act 1995 on the role of the Taoiseach and the Minister for Justice is quite small.

Functionally, the Minister for Justice has more tasks to complete: he or she may write to the JAAB looking for recommendations, may give directions to the JAAB on how to structure their Annual Reports and may consult with the JAAB on the number of recommendations to send where there are multiple concurrent vacancies on the same court. Beyond these matters the role of the Minister is the same, and the weight of influence they have in judicial selection has varied in the same way as in the pre-1995 period – it depends on the personality of the Minister, their relationship with the Attorney General and Taoiseach and how well they know the candidates for judicial office.

The role of the Taoiseach is unchanged in judicial selection by the 1995 Act. The Taoiseach still takes the advice of the Attorney General and Minister for Justice, still manages the expectations and requirements of coalition partners and still has, as in most things, enormous influence in the Cabinet process.

Role of political connections

Political connections are undoubtedly one element of the politics and process of judicial selection in Cabinet in the period of this study, as they were historically and as they remain today. All contributors agreed that while the primary consideration in making judicial appointments was the merit of the candidate for appointment, especially at the senior level, where there were a number of candidates of equal stature and one of them was politically sympathetic to the party in power, that person would get the nomination. What emerges from the research is:

- government parties tend to favour individuals that they know personally and professionally when making judicial appointments.
- this knowledge is often, but not always, based on political connection.
- personal knowledge of a candidate will supersede the importance of party political connection because members of government feel they can stand over appointments where they personally know the character and temperament of the individual to be appointed.
- coalition governments tend to make a general arrangement about the distribution of judicial vacancies; it is not always based on a strict ratio and can be influenced by the relative seniority of the positions: for example, one Chief Justice appointment equals two High Court appointments.
- certain appointments conspicuously transcended party politics.
- party political connections are much more important at District Court level than at High and Supreme Court level.

21 See Tóibín, C. (1985) 'Inside the Supreme Court', *Magill*, 8:7 on the selection of the Chief Justice, and on same political party and cross political party appointments: 'O'Dalaigh believed that Walsh would be made Chief Justice. Walsh was the most eminent judge of the court; his contribution to the court had been the most far-reaching and significant in the history of the state; he had an international reputation. There were factors against Walsh,

Politics matters in judicial selection, but it is not the full story.[21] It is neither necessary nor sufficient for judicial appointment in Ireland. For those candidates who are eligible and suitable for appointment (and who in the post-1995 period have been recommended by the JAAB), being politically sympathetic to the government of the day is helpful in securing a judicial appointment, but being personally known to the decision-makers of the day is crucial.

> Generally, government appointments were made on observed merit. But if there were two equally meritorious candidates then Fianna Fáil will appoint Fianna Fáil, Fine Gael will appoint Fine Gael and so one. The truth is, if you know the people, you are generally more comfortable about appointing them. (Pre-1995/MJ/3)

> Good strong Fine Gael people made judges when they were there and good strong Fianna Fáil people made judges when they were there. To take the look off it every so often you'd appoint a decent one from the other side but it wouldn't be 50:50 or anything like it and that tradition stems up to the present day. Labour would get their nominees as well; barristers closely associated with Labour would get their nomination too. The way I'm describing it might sound like its all jobs for the boys but its jobs for the boys once you've defined competence. The higher you get the more competence comes into it and you certainly wouldn't get any duffers in the High Court and Supreme Court. (Pre-1995/MJ/1)

however. The most important was his friendship with Charles Haughey, then in the wilderness after the Arms Trial. The court had ruled in favour of Haughey's brother who had refused to give evidence to the Public Account Committee of the Dáil after the Arms Trial. The North was causing a serious security crisis. Walsh and O'Dalaigh had done nothing to help the state in its struggle against crime and terrorism. The government had no intention of making Walsh Chief Justice. Walsh knew this, as is clear from his letter to O'Dalaigh on the latter's resignation. No one, however, expected Jack Lynch's government to make Billy Fitzgerald Chief Justice.' (p. 20)

'On 17 October 1974 just ten months after the McGee decision Billy FitzGerald died. By this time the Fianna Fáil government of Jack Lynch had gone out of office and been replaced by a Coalition with Liam Cosgrave as Taoiseach. Less than a week after FitzGerald's death the government announced that Tom O'Higgins, a former Fine Gael Minister for Health, the most junior judge in the High Court, would be the new Chief Justice.' (p. 21)

'In December 1984 Tom O'Higgins decided to go to the European Court in Luxembourg and retired from the Supreme Court … There was intense speculation over who would take the job. Those who proposed McCarthy forgot that McCarthy had spoken at election platforms for Fianna Fáil and had been appointed to the court by Charles Haughey … Those who still believed in the liberalism of Garret FitzGerald thought he would appoint the most liberal judge possible. But he didn't do this. He appointed Tom Finlay, formerly a Fine Gael TD, formerly President of the High Court, one of the majority in the Norris judgment'. (p. 35)

> It's definitely political. But then you get completely cross-political appointments. (Pre-1995/AG/5)

> There were some spectacularly cross-party political appointments, beginning with the appointment of Tom Finlay in 1971. The Lynch government appointed Billy Fitzgerald and Tom Finlay. Lynch broke precedent of political appointments. (Pre-1995/TAO/2)

As noted earlier, party politics tends to be more important at District Court level than with senior judicial appointments. It was commented that politicians are more likely to get involved in respect of District Court appointments because there is a better chance of influencing the process. There are a greater number of District Court appointments and a much wider pool from which to select a nominee than the smaller number of high performers that might be considered for the High Court. There is also a more direct connection with the constituency issues of the ministers. The decisions of the District Court judge are more likely to affect their constituents directly and be reported in the local press than the decisions of High Court judges.

> The District Court is dealt with at a more political level. (Post-1995/AG/2)

> At that [High and Supreme Court] level, politics doesn't matter. The people tend to pick themselves. (Post-1995/TAO/1)

However, it can be a more difficult system for an Attorney General to monitor.

> With appointments to the District Court, it's much harder because I wouldn't really know any of them so you're trying to get a fix on them and a reference for them – and really any fella who hasn't been in jail can get a good reference. I think the JAAB should check the health of the individuals ... They do check their financial health, as to whether the guy owes money to the revenue, and check with the law society to see that they weren't a danger to society or anything. District judges are just harder because it's harder to get a fix on them, they're known to a small community and the politicians are simply much more interested in them. You can bring names of High Court judges to Cabinet and they're not interested – but [aspirant] District judges are much more likely to try to canvass them. (Post-1995/AG/3)

The issue of political connections in judicial appointments in Ireland should not overshadow the importance of personal or professional connection. The importance for a judicial aspirant to be personally or professionally known to the key decision-makers cannot be overstated. As many interviewees observed, at a senior level in the legal profession, there is a small group of suitable people for appointment to the High Court and the Supreme Court and, because of their professional status, these people would generally be well known to the senior political office-holders of the day through personal and professional networks. There are also occasions (for example in 1995/6 following the political controversy over the Whelehan appointment) where the most politically astute course of action for the government was to make a series of judicial appointments of people with no political connections.

The key government decision-makers were universally concerned that in appointing someone who was not known to them, they may risk making a bad appointment of someone who was not personally, temperamentally or professionally suited to the position. Arguably, the concern might have been greater with District Court appointments considering that the District and Circuit Courts are the largest courts and the courts where the general public are most likely to interact with the civil and criminal justice system. However, through judicial review, senior judicial office-holders have greater capacity to impact on the constitutional politics of the day with potentially significant and lasting effects for society. For this reason, greater attention was given to the technical and professional merits of nominations to senior judicial vacancies. From a purely practical perspective, there were fewer vacancies of this kind and a smaller pool from which to select possible candidates.

> Political partisanship disappeared in judicial appointments at a senior level. And yes, that may be because one party is in power for a long period, but I think it will have to persist because an orgy of jobbery would reflect very badly on a new government. (Post-1995/AG/8)

In any event, the role played by party politics in judicial appointments is believed to have no impact on the conduct of a judge once appointed.

> Once someone is on the bench, they can show no favouritism to their old political party, they are completely independent. Politics is not the factor that people think it is. (Post-1995/AG/2)

Identifying potential judges, canvassing and lobbying for appointment

One of the major changes introduced by the 1995 Act is a system by which legal practitioners can signal their interest in becoming a judge by applying to the JAAB for consideration. Prior to 1995 there was no such formalized system and judicial aspirants were required either to sit and hope or to signal their interest to key decision-makers in other ways. Unfortunately for the judicial aspirant who favoured the latter, the key decision-makers generally regarded this form of 'canvassing' for judicial appointment with marked distaste.

The advantage of the new system for legal practitioners is that they can clearly and transparently signal an interest in appointment to judicial office. The government can clearly see who is interested as the legislation provides that the Minister for Justice should receive the complete list of persons who applied to the JAAB for consideration.

Canvassing could take a variety of forms ranging from a judicial aspirant discreetly relaying their own views or the views of their friends or family that they 'really would make an excellent judge' or that they acknowledged that the 'time had now come for public service and they were willing to take that challenge'.[22] It could also take an indirect form with friends of the judicial aspirant making the appropriate murmur in the ear of the key decision-makers of the day. The key decision-makers were generally critical of this practice.

> When I was becoming Attorney General, people began to inform me that they would like to be appointed. It was said casually, informally. A lot of them would be solicitors who wanted to be appointed to the District Court and a large proportion were those whose practice might be in difficulties – either for financial or disciplinary reasons; or barristers in practice, who were just not getting there. (Pre-1995/AG/1)

> There was this narrative running about people being appointed because of their political colours which was substantially untrue but one of the things that did disturb me was some of the unofficial lobbying that took place around judicial appointments. This was where particular applicants would feel the need to lobby and it was surprising how few people did this, but there were some who did lobby Deputies in the house, lobby other ministers or lobby the Taoiseach to be appointed and I was concerned about the fact that that happened. I was concerned that there was the odd occasion when that created pressures to appoint a particular individual. (Post-1995/MJ/5)

> I noticed from your 2004 study that judges tend now to deny political connections once on the bench. In the 1980s there was a very strong political lobby for appointment at District Court and Circuit Court level – and a kind of lobbying for the High Court. It was more discreet, but no less effective. (Pre-1995/MJ/3)

A former Attorney General commented that he occasionally 'got a letter asking me to please consider so and so'.

22 See also Irish Council for Civil Liberties (2007) *Justice matters*, p. 49, and *Dáil Éireann* – vol. 523 – 5 October 2000, at 24 – Minister John O'Donoghue 'Since I took office, I have received over 40 representations from members of the Oireachtas in respect of judicial appointments. Eight persons, on whose behalf representations were made, were subsequently appointed, all to the District Court bench.'

> It was preferable that it didn't happen and I may have received only 5 or 6 such letters in my time as AG – very few. (Pre-1995/AG/4)

> I never experienced any pressure from anyone. It would have been known that it was very poorly regarded. So our process was uncanvassable. (Pre-1995/AG/5)

In general, there was never any pressure or heavy canvassing within the Cabinet – with one exception. One former Minister for Justice remembered the circumstances of one occasion of overt lobbying clearly – and unfavourably.

> Often the strongest lobbying is done for the least meritorious candidate. I remember one in particular for the District Court, who was brought in to the Dáil and brought to visit the different ministers' offices – I recall it was very unfavourably commented on in government. (Pre-1995/MJ/3)

The Courts and Court Officers Act 1995 prohibits canvassing of the JAAB or its members. However, the traditional practice of canvassing members of government (usually on behalf of a judicial aspirant) remained and continued to be viewed negatively by key decision-makers in government. One Taoiseach (Post-1995/TAO/1) commented that he was approached a few times regarding some 'more junior' appointments but that 'there was no way you could get involved in that'. Of the key decision-makers, it was most likely that the Attorney General would be canvassed.

> I was certainly approached, by barristers. 'Have you given any thought to so and so?', or 'You know so and so, his time may have come', and 'What about so and so, his wife has a health thing you know, I think he's keen to leave the rough and tumble behind'. (Post-1995/AG/7)

> I didn't get much political stuff, and when I did I resented it. In terms of a minister saying, look I'm constantly getting letters on behalf so and so, I would say sure, I know what you're saying but I would mentally count it against the candidate. I thought it was insulting to me, because I knew them all intimately and the idea that I should be in my recommendation to government influenced by someone writing to a minister. And even the ministers weren't that interested and they would say it in a way that would let them say 'yeh I mentioned it'. (Post-1995/AG/3)

> It can be counterproductive. (Post-1995/AG/2)

> Just tell them that the JAAB sends a list and that additional representations are not necessary. (Post-1995/MJ/5)

> You wouldn't believe it. Letters. Discreet words. And from sitting judges too. Terribly inappropriate. (Post-1995/MJ/6)

Others took a different view.

> It can have advantages and disadvantages. Frequently, with the senior jobs, someone might say 'look, is there any point in me applying?' And I might say I think it's a good idea or that I couldn't speak for the government but that if you got past the JAAB you could have a good chance. (Post-1995/MJ/4)

Another aspect of canvassing in the pre-1995 period was 'reverse' canvassing where the Attorney General might enquire of a prospective candidate as to whether they would be amenable to being appointed at that time. One former Minister for Justice pointed out that there are many whom you would wish to appoint, but who are not at a stage in their career where they are happy to leave practice for the 'rather different life as a judge' (Pre-1995/MJ/2). Reverse canvassing operated to try to establish this before the political agreement to appoint them was sought. As one Attorney General points out below, how else could it be done in the absence of any formalized system?

> It would be politically unthinkable to allow a situation where the Cabinet approved an appointment and the appointee is found unwilling. I did approach candidates to see if they would be interested, with the informal approval of the Taoiseach. It would be along the lines of 'if your appointment were to find political favour, and I cannot assure you of that, but it is reasonably likely, would you be interested'. Absolutely I did approach candidates; I loved giving the good news to people. And how else would you have done it anyway? (Pre-1995/AG/5)
>
> The Attorney General would approach people in the (Law) Library who would be good or acceptable to his political masters, and keep a list of two to three people in his head at any one time. I wanted the best person, I went to the people I felt good about. (Pre-1995/AG/1)
>
> Sometime the Attorney would approach the person to see if they were willing, it might be that they're in the full flight of a successful practice and may not have thought of it – but if asked, might think about it. Some were willing, some were not. (Pre-1995/AG/4)

Advance notice and reverse canvassing on the part of the Attorney General still seems to be an important feature of the system following the introduction of institutional change. If a judicial aspirant gets a suggestion from the Attorney General that it would be worth their time applying to the JAAB, it is all the better for the candidate as the Attorney General is likely to have consulted politically before making the informal approach.

> Certainly I would go to certain candidates and say 'if I could get political signals that you would be appointed if you were to get past the Board, would you apply?' In other words I would come to someone and say I think you'd be a great judge, would you think of applying. These would be candidates who would not otherwise apply, either for reasons of diffidence or because they think the whole thing is too political or wouldn't want to go into some competitive slot. But asked and assured that they would get the job; you would get some really good candidates to apply. And increasingly my impression over the last 15 years is that some of the good candidates have been procured in that way. (Post-1995/AG/3)

> I would never offer a judicial appointment, but maybe encourage someone to apply. The typically outstanding candidates. (Post-1995/AG/2)

> The Attorney General would hunt – you know, go to the Law Library and suggest that someone apply. (Post-1995/AG/7)

> The new system is better than the old because it stops people lobbying for positions. Now in exceptional cases the government would suggest that certain people should apply: 'Mick would you ever go for the job, you'd get a lot of support, we'd all like to see you there'. Some would, some would say no thanks, some would say they'd like it another time; that they wanted to work a few years more before taking a pay cut etc. It was always the Attorney General or the Minister for Justice that would do that – no way ever would a Minister of any other department get involved in that. (Post-1995/TAO/1)

Where a vacancy has been referred to the JAAB, is it appropriate for the Attorney General – who is a member of both the JAAB and a key government decision-maker – to approach an individual and suggest they apply to the JAAB? (The JAAB has the power to make such approaches but has never, so far, done so.) One JAAB member commented that the practice was not inconsistent with the principles of the JAAB, because of the manner in which it was done by the Attorney General.

> The Attorney General might approach a candidate, very gently and with no commitment. The Attorney General has always been very respectful of the appropriate role of the JAAB. But he might have gently suggested to a practitioner that he should apply, that his application might find favour politically if it got past the JAAB, which invariably it would because the Attorney General simply would not, in practice, approach anyone who was not of a sufficiently high calibre. (JAAB/10)

This is an important point. It shows that the role of the Attorney General remains central to judicial selection in Ireland (particularly for senior judicial appointments). The Attorney General has the same freedoms now in relation to approaching potential judges as they had before the institutional change. In fact, the Attorney General has an enhanced role because, even though an advisory board has been established, the Attorney General is a member of that Board and can therefore influence every stage of the judicial selection process. This is not to make any comment about the relative merits of this system; there are strong advantages to having this person – the link person between the political and legal worlds – perform such a role. There are also risks in enabling one individual to influence the process at each stage.

Network effects and 'being known'

One of the most important elements of the judicial selection process in Ireland in both periods is simply 'being known' to the relevant decision-makers. In the period 1982 to 1994, a senior legal practitioner had to be known to the Attorney General as someone 'solid' before they would be suitable for recommendation to the Taoiseach. The Attorney General might recommend or discuss a shortlist of names with the Taoiseach, who typically made the ultimate choice for senior judicial appointments.

One of the recurring observations from the contributors was that the size of the legal system was an important factor in the operation of the judicial selection process. It was argued that the small political and legal communities were heavily interlinked and that the decision-makers on judicial appointments tended to rely on the information they had from those networks that enabled them to know, with reasonable intimacy, the capacity and temperament of prospective judicial candidates. This was especially the case in relation to High Court and Supreme Court appointments where it would be simply impossible for the people involved in selection for judicial office *not* to know the candidates involved.

> The thing about being known, it is a small country; in the 60s and 70s everyone was known to each other, that is the case for the inner Bar certainly. Everyone who was a good senior counsel was known to everybody and the element of personal qualities in an appointment can only be determined by knowing someone – that they are able, intelligent and, crucially, of the right temperament. (Pre-1995/AG/4)

> The truth is it's a small community in Ireland – professional groups even smaller and you don't have to go very far before you meet someone you know. Human nature being what it is, you are more comfortable appointing someone that you know than that you don't know. (Pre-1995/MJ/3)

> You never know how someone will turn out as a Judge. I was always conscious of temperament, or brutality [in personality]. You couldn't put people like that on the Bench. There is a balance between knowing their skills and knowing the person. The other worry is the unpredictability of judicial review. (Pre-1995/AG/5)

One former Minister for Justice commented on how the value of knowing people transcended political party connections.

> X took a hard line on cross-party appointments, and he appointed people that he knew. He appointed a number of Fine Gael people and a number of Fianna Fáil people, and they were all people of quality and of high competence and would be recognized as such in the Bar, but it was [able to be] done because he knew the people. (Pre-1995/MJ/1)

One former Attorney General commented that he felt he only made one poor appointment and that he believed that one of the factors in that was that he didn't know enough about the person at the time of their appointment. He said that there is an important balance between the person's skills and their temperament, and that knowing them – especially through common practice – is a good way to see both their professional and personal skills, and their reactions under pressure. He continued that while this was possible in the small world of the law library in the 1970s and 1980s, it may be different today in the context of much larger numbers in the legal profession.

The importance of being known to the key decision-makers remained constant in the post-1995 institutional period – particularly for senior judicial vacancies.

> You would always know them – either through state cases, big cases but big profile generally, always well known. And they would make themselves known – broadly. (Post-1995/TAO/1)

> You get in big boxes with extensive details about applicants. It's seldom you come across someone who someone [on the Board] doesn't know. And you have the power to interview them [on the JAAB], but it's never been used. In a small society and legal community you'll tend to know them all. And you will know the completely unsuitable. (Post-1995/AG/2)

Almost all of the key government decision-makers made the point that there was an ever-present risk of the great unknown in appointing someone to the bench. This reflects the importance they placed on the candidate being well known to them or at least to their Attorney General.

> Our Attorney General used to say to me that you just never know what you're going to get – you have the most eminent solicitors and barristers and they turn out to be the most dreadful judges once they're appointed, and then the more moderate lawyers can turn out to be simply brilliant judges. (Pre-1995/MJ/1)

This sentiment was reflected time and time again in interviews with political contributors. Their universal concern was that, in exercising an executive function, they would appoint someone to the judiciary who could not be removed and would be found over time to be technically or temperamentally problematic as a judge.

Being known to a Cabinet member, either through party political connections or other personal connections, played a strong role in appointments to the Circuit and District Courts. However, what is crucially different about the post-1995 period is that, at least in theory, this could only become a consideration for government decision-makers among those people who had been recommended by the JAAB. The increasing number of recommendations made by the JAAB over time made it more likely that key decision-makers would know – personally, professionally or politically – candidates recommended by the JAAB.

However, what is truly different about this period is that while it is important to be known to the key decision-makers in government it is also, as we have seen from the interview data with JAAB members, important to be known to members of the JAAB itself. The network effects in a small political and legal community is now important at two stages of the judicial selection process – both in government and in the JAAB.

In Chapter 4, we will see how other judicial selection commissions have consciously attempted to reduce the impact of 'being known' to members of the commission by adopting processes that require screenings of anonymous applications. Specifically, we will see that the practices of the Scottish system provide an interesting counterpoint to the Irish system. We will also see that the number of judicial appointments in other, larger, countries militates against the likelihood of direct personal, professional or political connection being a factor in the bulk of judicial appointments. In Ireland, it is a core element of all stages of the judicial selection process. Whether it is simply impossible to avoid given the size of the political and legal community or whether policy makers would want to avoid it given what the contributors have said about needing to feel comfortable that they knew an individual's temperament and suitability for judicial office, is open to debate. Any further policy consideration of judicial selection in Ireland should reflect the impact of personal knowledge of judicial candidates in a comparatively compact legal and political community.

Diversity in the judiciary

Some of the other questions that political decision-makers faced were issues relating to gender balance on the courts and the peculiar situation in relation to religion on the courts, stemming from a long-standing concern to ensure representation for the Protestant minority since the foundation of the State. The question of gender balance in the judiciary had begun to be a concern of the government by the 1980s. One Minister recalls being conscious of the need to appoint more women:

> There is a value in a quota system on gender balance; it exists in public service boards but was never applied to judicial appointments. But there was an awareness of it; it was there in the back of your head when you were making the appointment, because there were a lot of women active in politics and so you were conscious of it. The appointment of women became much stronger in the District Court and now I say that appointments to the District Court are gender blind, there's so many of them. (Pre-1995/MJ/1)

> There was great anxiety to appoint the first female [senior] Judge. (Pre-1995/AG/1)

> If there were three men and a woman on the list, they do make an effort to pick the woman. (Post-1995/TAO/1).

In the post-1995 period, the urgency of appointing a female judge to the senior courts had abated somewhat and the question began to shift to the proportion of female judges on the courts and the representation of other minorities on the bench. One Taoiseach (Post-1995/TAO/1) commented that he thought there would probably be a growing number of women on the bench and in senior appointments in the future, but what would be almost more important in the years to come would be racial diversity, as Irish society became more racially diverse.

This view of inevitable gender equality was disputed by a post-1995 Minister for Justice who argued that the ever increasing numbers of women in the professions were not being reflected among senior judicial appointments and that a deliberate strategy of appointing women was necessary to rebalance this.

> I was concerned that men were unduly represented on the courts having regard to the substantial number of women in the professions, in both solicitors and barristers' professions. When it came to applications, one of the things I discovered was that, in some areas, proportionately, a good deal more men applied to be High Court judges than women, which was interesting. When you got into the District Court appointments, there wasn't a huge discrepancy between male and female applicants, in the

> Circuit Court there were still more male than female applicants. There was a very substantial number of recommended names, particularly at District and Circuit levels, quite a broad range of different areas of expertise, that came through and if it got to the point where there was a gap to be filled and there were both male and female applicants of a similar or equal standing quite clearly, I think if you look at the appointments made in the first two and half years or so when I was Minister, out of every three appointments, two were women and one was a man to try and redress that balance. I was concerned that in the past, perhaps not deliberately, but perhaps instinctively, male ministers may have favoured male appointments without really realizing they were doing this, or government may have favoured male appointments; I don't believe there was any ill intent in that or maybe it was just that by the time I was Minister the profession had reached a point where there was so many senior women in the profession that it would have been an issue. But it was quite interesting how few women applied or came through as recommended candidates at the High Court level, and that isn't a criticism of JAAB, it's just the numbers proportionately were affecting that. I was also concerned that proportionately there were too few women on the Supreme Court. I thought that was quite extraordinary. So again, consciously, there was some excellent women on the High Court and when it came to promoting people, their expertise on the High Court was taken into account and the need also to provide a greater gender balance would have featured in my thinking. (Post-1995/MJ/5)

Table 3.2 below shows the percentage of applications made by women for judicial vacancies between 2002–14.[23] There is a marked increase in applications by women to the High Court in 2012, which is repeated in 2013 and 2014. This contrasts strongly with 2008 and 2011 where only 4 per cent and 13 per cent respectively of the applications for High Court vacancies came from women.

One contributor argued that the value of a political appointments system was that politicians had the freedom to choose whomever they wanted and could respond directly to concerns about the need for appointments of minorities.

> If the judges are to be selected by majoritarian groups, would you get clones of those groups? Would you have had women appointed to the superior courts as comparatively early as we had? The fact that it was government making the appointment has a lot to do with that. (Pre-1995/AG/4)

23 This does not include Supreme Court vacancies because of the overwhelming tendency of the government to fill such vacancies by the elevation of a High Court judge.

Table 3.2: Applications by women for High Court, Circuit Court and District Court vacancies

Year	2002	2003	2004	2005	2006	2007	2008	2009	2010	2011	2012	2013	2014
High Court applications by women (%)	11	No vacancy	5	6	5	15	4	No vacancy	15	13	30	36	34
Circuit Court applications by women (%)	23	19	22	25	No vacancy	27	20	54	No vacancy	36	39	45	41
District Court applications by women (%)	75	29	26	26	29	27	32	33	36	38	39	43	44

Source: Judicial Appointments Advisory Board Annual Reports, 2002–14.

The representation of minority religions in the courts was a constant concern of the decision-makers in judicial appointments. Traditionally, there was always a seat on the Supreme Court for a member of a Protestant denomination and there were also concerted efforts to ensure representation of the Irish Jewish community in the High and Supreme Courts.

> You were always careful to have minority interest represented, always a consciousness that you needed a woman or two women. If you had a suitable Church of Ireland person you'd make sure they were in there. (Pre-1995/MJ/1)

One interviewee made the point that appointments were often based on a perceived service to the state:

> Another quirk of the system that you mightn't be aware of from outside was that people who acted for the state in tribunals or inquires, and had put in a lot of time over two or three years, we made them all judges when we got the chance. It was an acknowledgment of their service to the state. (Pre-1995/MJ/1)

CONCLUSIONS: CONSEQUENCES OF INSTITUTIONAL REFORM

The provisions of the Courts and Court Officers Act 1995 gave mixed powers to the JAAB to constrain political discretion in judicial selection:

1 There is no requirement for the government to refer a judicial vacancy to the JAAB; nevertheless, this has been the overwhelming practice.

2 There is no requirement for the government to accept a recommendation from the JAAB. It can appoint someone who has not applied to the JAAB or it can appoint someone who has applied to the JAAB and has not been recommended to the government as suitable for appointment (although there is no evidence to show that this has ever happened and the evidence is that government does select from the JAAB recommendations).
3 The government has the power to appoint a member of another court to fill a judicial vacancy without reference to the JAAB.
4 The JAAB is required by statute to recommend at least seven names in respect of each vacancy where there are at least seven applicants or unless there are fewer than seven applicants whom the JAAB is happy to recommend.

This chapter has examined the legislation establishing the Judicial Appointments Advisory Board, provided information on how JAAB works in practice based on interview evidence with its members over time and assessed, using this interview evidence, how the role of key government decision-makers in judicial selection in Ireland has changed in the period 1982 to 2007 as a result of the introduction of JAAB.

This analysis of the evidence from interviews with the key decision-makers sheds light on the politics of judicial selection in Ireland. It shows that, from the perspective of government actors, the judicial selection process is quite similar in the two periods. We have seen that the process within Cabinet is unchanged, that the role of the Attorney General has been enhanced and that the role of the Minister for Justice has been expanded but remains the same in terms of influence over appointments. We have seen how the role of the Minister can be stronger in relation to more junior judicial positions but that this factor depends (as it did in the pre-1995 period) on the experience and personality of the Minister for Justice. Similarly, we see that the overarching role of the Taoiseach and the need for co-operation between coalition partners in relation to judicial appointments is generally unchanged by the introduction of institutional change.

In both periods, it is clear that, for various reasons, being known personally or professionally to the key decision-makers is critical in judicial selection; decision-makers are more reluctant to appoint someone with whom they are not personally or professionally familiar. This is understandable when the importance of the role is considered. Human nature may dictate that a decision-maker in such a scenario might, from two identical candidates, appoint the person whom they know.

Table 3.3 provides an overview of the institutional changes introduced by the Irish government in 1995 to judicial selection processes and summarizes the key differences between the judicial selection system in Ireland before and after the change.

Table 3.3: Key differences between the judicial selection system in Ireland before and after the change

Element of Judicial Selection Process	1982–94	1995–2007
Cabinet process for judicial selection to all courts	Attorney General prepares list of suitable people, perhaps in consultation with other key decision-makers. Role of Attorney General is critical in preparing shortlist of candidates. Decision is agreed among key decision-makers in advance. Decision of Taoiseach is critical. Name is presented to Cabinet. No Cabinet discussion, formal approval only. Attorney General (usually) contacts candidate to say they have been approved by Cabinet for appointment.	Minister for Justice receives list of names from JAAB. Minister for Justice consults with Attorney General and Taoiseach in relation to proposed candidates. Decision is agreed among key decision-makers in advance. Decision of Taoiseach is critical. Name is presented to Cabinet. No Cabinet discussion, formal approval only. Minister for Justice contacts candidate to say they have been approved by Cabinet for appointment.[24]
Role of Attorney General in judicial selection and relative weight of views of Attorney General	Attorney General prepares list of suitable people, perhaps in consultation with other key decision-makers. Role of Attorney General is critical in preparing shortlist of candidates. Attorney General may engage in reverse canvassing to determine if candidate is interested in appointment.	Attorney General attends meetings of the JAAB. Attorney General may engage in reverse canvassing to determine if candidate is interested in appointment. Attorney General remains one of the core decision-makers in Cabinet in judicial appointments.
Role of Taoiseach	Critical. Involved at all stages of Cabinet decision in relation to judicial appointment, which could not proceed without agreement of Taoiseach.	Critical. Involved in all stages of Cabinet decision in relation to judicial appointment, which could not proceed without agreement of Taoiseach.
Role of Minister for Justice	Minister for Justice has strong role in relation to District and Circuit Court appointments. Minister for Justice brings name of nominated candidate to Cabinet.	Minister for Justice nominates three lay people for membership of the JAAB. Minister for Justice asks JAAB to consider candidates for a specified vacancy. Minister for Justice receives list of recommended names from JAAB. Minister for Justice has strong role in relation to District and Circuit Court appointments. Minister for Justice brings name of nominated candidate to Cabinet. Minister for Justice contacts candidate to say that he or she has been approved by the Cabinet for nomination for appointment to judicial office by the President.

24 There is an informal view that in some District Court appointments this can happen contemporaneously with the local government TD contacting the candidate to inform them of the appointment and that this had also been the case prior to 1995.

Table 3.3: Key differences between the judicial selection system in Ireland before and after the change *(contd)*

Element of Judicial Selection Process	1982–94	1995–2007
Role of minor coalition partner (if relevant)	Coalition partners may want a role in judicial appointments. Coalition governments may distribute decision-making in relation to judicial appointment according to an agreed ratio.	Coalition partners may want a role in judicial appointments. Coalition governments may distribute decision-making in relation to judicial appointment according to an agreed ratio.
Role of political party affiliation in judicial selection	Important. More important for Circuit and District Court appointments.	Important. More important for Circuit and District Court appointments.
Canvassing of politicians by judicial aspirants	Unsolicited canvassing frowned upon by key decision-makers, but occurs with some frequency, especially in relation to District Court appointments. Attorney General may engage in reverse canvassing to determine if candidate is interested in appointment.	Unsolicited canvassing frowned upon, but occurs with some frequency, especially in relation to District Court appointments. Attorney General may engage in reverse canvassing to determine if candidate is interested in appointment if they applied and were recommended by the JAAB. Attorney General may still approach candidate directly for appointment but this is less prevalent than before 1995.
The importance of being known to key decision-makers	Critical.	Critical.
Gender and minorities	'Anxiety' to appoint first senior female judge. Conscious effort to ensure balance of religious minorities at High Court and Supreme Court level.	Gender perceived to be less of an issue at Circuit Court and District Court level but always an issue at High Court and Supreme Court level. Religious balance less important than in pre-1995 era.
Role of the Judicial Appointments Advisory Board in judicial selection (only discussed with post-1995 decision-makers in terms of judicial selection process in their experience)		Significant role in formal process in managing applications from judicial aspirants and assessing general suitability of candidates. Initially, the JAAB recommended seven names in respect of each judicial vacancy, but then decided to henceforth recommend all of those applicants who were deemed not unsuitable for judicial appointment. Indirect influence on government, through discussion in front of the Attorney general in relation to 'gaps' of experience on the courts at a given time but no formal communication with government on ensuring a range of legal specialities on the courts.

Source: Interview data and Courts and Court Officers Act 1995 and 2002.

Based on an analysis of the legislation and data from interviews, it is evident that the introduction of the JAAB resulted in a very different experience of judicial selection from the perspective of judicial aspirants, the judiciary and the legal professions. This is because each of these groups had a different experience of judicial selection in Ireland following the introduction of the JAAB, whether because they were required to formally apply to the JAAB, or because they, or their colleagues, were members of the JAAB and had a formal statutory role in judicial selection for the first time.

From the perspective of the key decision-makers in judicial selection, however, the introduction of the JAAB had little impact. The conduct of the key decision-makers has not been changed in any significant way, with the following exceptions for the roles of the Minister for Justice and the Attorney General: the Minister for Justice receives the list of names from the JAAB for appointments to all courts. This is in contrast to the old system where the Attorney General created a shortlist of names for senior judicial appointments. The complete discretion with which the Attorney General had operated in the old system in devising this shortlist is now restrained in two ways: the list of applicants is limited, in practice, to those who apply to the JAAB for consideration and those who are deemed by the JAAB as suitable for appointment. This is not to say the role of the Attorney General is diminished in the new regulated system of judicial selection; on the contrary, although changed, the role of the Attorney General is just as important in this new process.

Although the government set up an arm's-length body to advise on judicial appointment, the design of the institutional change rendered it possible for government to retain political discretion in the new judicial selection arrangements. Strong scope for political discretion was built into the Courts and Court Officers Act 1995. Furthermore, the JAAB's implementation of the legislation gave rise, over time, to a practice whereby the JAAB appeared to resile from the discretion available to it under the legislation. The decision by the JAAB to change their processes for recommending names to the Minister for appointment fundamentally weakened an already limited constraint on the discretion of government decision-makers to appoint a preferred candidate.

The trigger for institutional change in Ireland was a political crisis. The instrument of institutional change was legislation to introduce a new independent judicial screening commission. The institutional change did not, in a practical way, reduce the political discretion of key decision-makers in judicial selection. This is a result of the hybrid model of judicial selection created and its institutional design that enabled institutional drift and change to the institutional functioning of the JAAB over time – with important implications for the role of government in judicial selection.

Some questions remain before we have fully explained the Irish government's hybrid reforms. The system of judicial appointment combined the delegation of powers to recommend suitable judicial candidates with continued executive discretion in selecting nominees for judicial appointment. Questions about the government's ability and willingness to give effect to consistent and systematic reform might be explored in the light of two countervailing experiences.

On the one hand, we might consider a different situation – reform of a different aspect of the legal system – in which the Irish government did indeed create a new institution with fully delegated powers in an important area of the justice system. The specific instance in question here concerns the creation of the Office of the Director of Public Prosecutions.

On the other hand, we might consider the same situation – the delegation of powers to nominate judicial appointees – in a different political jurisdiction, specifically in Scotland, a legal system very like that of Ireland, where the reforms involved the creation of a fully independent judicial nominations process that functioned in a way that really did constrain the political discretion available to the political authorities. Chapter 4 presents this counter-factual consideration.

CHAPTER 4

Reforming politically sensitive elements of the administration of justice: independent prosecutions office in Ireland and judicial selection in Scotland

Earlier chapters have shown that, while common law systems feature different institutional arrangements for appointing senior members of the judiciary, the issue of reducing the discretion of the political authorities has arisen as an important point of political interest in quite a few jurisdictions. We have analysed the circumstances in which governments have, in fact, introduced institutional change in a manner that reduces their political discretion in judicial selection and have discovered that Ireland was an outlier – both in terms of the circumstances of the introduction of the institutional change in 1995 and in terms of the lack of reduction of political discretion in judicial appointments. The next phase of the analysis involves looking at the conditions under which reform initiatives involving areas of political sensitivity to governments are undertaken from a different perspective. Here we seek to understand how and why far-reaching reforms have, in fact, taken place. This chapter examines a reform initiative in Ireland that reduced the role of the political system in criminal prosecutions. Next, it examines reform of the judicial selection system in Scotland to determine how it was implemented there focusing, in particular, on the impact this has had on the role of political discretion in judicial selection.

INSTITUTIONAL REFORM IN THE ADMINISTRATION OF JUSTICE IN IRELAND

In 1974, responsibility for the prosecution of criminal offences in Ireland was removed from the Office of the Attorney General and vested in an independent office for criminal prosecutions.[1] This removed the power of the Attorney General to make decisions in relation to the conduct of criminal cases. The Attorney General is appointed by the government of the day, sits at Cabinet meetings and, as legal adviser to the government, has a close professional relationship with members of Cabinet.

1 Article 30.3 of the Irish Constitution provides: 'All crimes and offences prosecuted in any court constituted under Article 34 of this Constitution other than a court of summary jurisdiction shall be prosecuted in the name of the People and at the suit of the Attorney General or some other person authorized in accordance with law to act for that purpose.'

In 1970, these competing roles of the Attorney General – as legal adviser to the government and prosecutor of criminal offences – came into sharp political focus in the course of criminal allegations made against members of the then Fianna Fáil government.[2] The question of whether the Attorney General would pursue these prosecutions came to the fore in public debate. Following a general election in 1973, the incoming government – formed by Fine Gael and the Labour Party – initiated the establishment of an independent prosecution office.

The institutional change introduced to remove criminal prosecution from the functions of the Attorney General was initiated by the Attorney General of the day, Declan Costello, in a letter to the Taoiseach, Liam Cosgrave, dated 20 November 1973.[3] In this letter Costello sets out his reasons for recommending the establishment of an independent prosecution office which were:

1 the risk of a public perception of the lack of independence of the criminal prosecution system,
2 the increased workload of the Office of the Attorney General arising from Ireland's forthcoming membership of the European Economic Community,
3 the recent successful establishment of a similar office in Northern Ireland.

This letter was the first step that resulted in a policy process involving the Office of the Attorney General, the Department of the Taoiseach and the Department of Justice that culminated in the publication of legislation to create an independent prosecution office. The Office of Director of Public Prosecutions was thus created by the Prosecution of Offences Act 1974. In creating this Office, the Act followed other common law countries. Indeed, in England and Wales, an independent prosecution office had existed since 1879. The legislation establishing the Office of Director of Public Prosecutions completely removed any political control from the prosecution of offences and the Director was conferred with complete independence.

The introduction of this reform is distinguished from the case of judicial appointments in two ways. First, unlike the change to the judicial selection system which occurred immediately after a significant political crisis, it was developed over time between the Office of the Attorney General, the Department of the Taoiseach and the Department of Justice. The consultations

2 The issue involved the aftermath of the highly controversial 'Arms Crisis' in Ireland, during which key government ministers were suspected of having diverted public funds for the relief of the minority Catholic population in Northern Ireland (exposed to systematic sectarian violence as the 'Troubles' began), in order to purchase arms which would be made available for citizens' defence initiatives. The accused persons in connection with these allegations were acquitted at the trial. For further reading: O'Donnell, C. (2007) *Fianna Fáil, Irish Republicanism and the Northern Ireland Troubles, 1968–2005*. Dublin: Irish Academic Press; McKittrick, D. and McVea, D. (2001) *Making sense of the Troubles*. London: Penguin.
3 Department of An Taoiseach (1973) National Archive File 2005/7/430.

took place over a period of about nine months.[4] The correspondence between the relevant departments and members of government is clearly detailed in both the files of the Department of the Taoiseach and the Office of the Attorney General. This correspondence details the incremental development of this institutional change over this period, culminating in an agreed draft Bill to implement these changes.[5]

Second, this reform was initiated because of policy-based concerns of the Attorney General that reflected his concerns at that time for the proper administration of justice, best-practice international comparison and the practical demands on his office.

The decision to remove responsibility for prosecution of criminal offences from the Attorney General was significant because it removed the scope for discretionary decision-making on the part of the Attorney General in two areas. Previously, the Attorney General was exposed to the possibility of pressure by members of Cabinet or members of parliament not to prosecute criminal offences. The Attorney General also had the discretion to distribute a certain amount of political patronage to politically connected lawyers who could be briefed by the Attorney General in criminal trials.

The independence of the criminal justice system was in focus following the serious political crisis in 1970 involving allegations that two members of Cabinet, unbeknownst to the Taoiseach or government, had been involved in the illegal importing of arms and ammunition into Ireland for use in the conflict in Northern Ireland.

> It is alleged that two senior Ministers of Government who were pledged to uphold the State, and whose job it was to see that the State was properly run, made arrangements to have imported into this country large quantities of arms for the use of an illegal organization. One of the objects of that illegal organization is the overthrow of this State. (Deputy James Tully, Dáil Debates, 7 May 1970, line 733)

The crisis was described as

> A situation of such gravity for the nation that it is without parallel in this country since the foundation of the state. (Deputy Liam Cosgrave, Dáil Debates, 7 May 1970, line 463).

The two ministers in question were removed from their ministerial positions and ultimately, criminal proceedings were brought against them by the Attorney General.[6] However, the immediate issue of debate was whether the

4 Ibid. 5 Ibid. 6 James Hamilton, the Director of Public Prosecutions from 1999 to 2011, observed in a speech at a seminar on Accountability in the Public Sector in 2008: 'A curious feature of the debate (on the Bill) is the absence of any reference whatsoever in it to

Attorney General was likely to bring such prosecutions at all against a backdrop of accusations that criminal prosecutions had been dropped in other cases for accused persons who were politically well connected.[7]

It had been a practice for members of the Oireachtas to make representations to the Attorney General in respect of their constituents who might be charged with offences – particularly minor criminal offences and road traffic offences. While it may well have been the case that such representations had little or no effect, the fact that they continued to be made indicated that the general public and their political representatives seemed to have a belief in their possible usefulness.[8] The events of 1970 brought into sharp focus the conflict that may be created in the Office of the Attorney General by it both acting as legal adviser to the government and having responsibility for the prosecution of criminal offences – including those alleged to have been committed by members of his government.

In the two days of debate that followed the announcement by the Taoiseach of the dismissal of the two ministers from his government several members of parliament asked whether the Attorney General was going to prosecute the two former ministers.[9] They also raised previous instances where criminal prosecutions had not progressed or had been dropped without, in their view, sufficient explanation. The assertion of members of parliament was that these

the Arms Trial which had taken place only four years previously, when the then Taoiseach, Jack Lynch, TD, had dismissed three members of his government from office, two of whom subsequently had prosecutions initiated against them for alleged conspiracy to import firearms. One of these ministers, Charles Haughey, TD, was returned for trial, and was subsequently acquitted by a jury. In the case of Deputy Neil Blaney the District Court found there was insufficient evidence to return him for trial. While the Attorney General of the day behaved with unquestioned propriety and impartiality it must have been a difficult and even an invidious task for him to have had to bring a prosecution against two colleagues who had sat with him very recently at the Cabinet table. At the very least it is difficult to believe that this experience would not have highlighted for many people the possible difficulties inherent in asking a political appointee of the Taoiseach to act as chief prosecutor. It is curious, however, that if such thoughts were present to any deputy's mind, and it is hard to believe that they were not, nobody at all thought it fit to mention them' (Hamilton, 2008). 7 Dáil Debates, 8 May 1970: Deputy Ryan (at line 665) 'There have been a number of cases brought to the notice of the Taoiseach and this House in which the Attorney General deliberately withdrew charges which were already before the courts. There had been complaints by district justices that, where criminal charges against a person were withdrawn, no explanation was given to the courts. Yet we now have a situation in which that Attorney general is presumably supposed to investigate the possible criminality of members of Government'; Deputy Fitzpatrick (at line 711) 'Does the Taoiseach intend to prosecute these men? Does he intend to ask his Attorney General to apply to them the same law as applies to everyone else, or does he intend to have one law for his Cabinet Ministers and their wealthy friends and another law for the ordinary people of this country?' 8 Hamilton (2008). 9 Dáil Debates, 7 May 1970: Deputy Cosgrave (leader of Fine Gael) (at line 646) 'What action is proposed to be taken against the persons concerned?'; Deputy Corish (leader of the Labour Party) (at line 651) 'Will these Minister be accused by the Attorney General?'

cases often involved people who were politically well-connected.[10] There was significant pressure in parliament on the Taoiseach and the Attorney General to ensure that appropriate prosecutions were initiated in the case of the alleged offences arising from the Arms Crisis. What is important for this study is that it shows how public perception of the criminal prosecutions system had been affected by this crisis and how it brought the competing functions of the Attorney General into sharp relief in the public debate. The crisis formed the background to the institutional change initiated by the new government. In contrast to the judicial selection reform that occurred in Ireland in 1994, the crisis of 1970 did not result in immediate institutional reform. The government of the day was not sufficiently motivated to introduce institutional change despite it being clearly demonstrated to the public that the system was sub-optimal.

Rather, the issue was taken up as a reform initiative by the subsequent government who had recognized and raised the problems inherent in the old system. The new government had committed itself to introducing institutional change that addressed these issues by effectively separating government from criminal prosecutions.

Neither the government files concerning the development of the legislation to establish an independent prosecution office nor the debate on that Bill in parliament explicitly references the Arms Trial.[11] In the parliamentary debate

10 Dáil Debates, 8 May 1970: Deputy Flanagan (at line 1156) 'I have known cases in which the rulings of the Attorney General were rather questionable and I honestly feel that the law is not administered as fairly as it might be'; Deputy L'Estrange (line 1259–60) 'I have said here before, and I repeat it now, that the Gardaí are frustrated in their efforts to administer the laws of this land. The vast majority of them do their duty conscientiously. They are being frustrated because, having spent time and money hunting criminals, drunken drivers and so on, they very often find that when the papers are sent to the Attorney General they are very often forgotten. If a case is so bad that political influence cannot help, there is unfortunately connivance in the courts and very often malefactors get off on a technicality. Singer got away on a technicality. We know he paid well for it.

'I will give an example of a case not far from my own county. A young man, drunk in charge of a car, killed an unfortunate man. I knew someone connected with the family and I was asked to approach the Minister for Justice. I said it was a thing I did not do, that I never brought pressure to bear on anyone but, if the person insisted, I would mention it, telling the Minister that I had been asked to do this but I was not asking him to do anything for the particular individual since I believed the law should take its course. The Minister, when I approached him, told me that there had been plenty of representation. I knew there would because the father was one of the head men in the cumann. Actually nothing could be done. The case went to trial. The witnesses were brought in. The evidence was given but nobody was called to give evidence of identification of the dead man and the moment the case for the State closed counsel for the defence got up and said: "On a point of law, your honour, the body has not been identified" and the justice said: "That is right" and the man walked out scot-free. That man could tell for months before that his case was being fixed and he would be allowed out scot-free. I know plenty of others.' 11 Department of An Taoiseach (1973) National Archive File 2005/7/430–3.

on the legislation the government parliamentary secretary, John Kelly TD, explained that the purpose of the legislation should be to ensure that the prosecution system:

> Should not only be impartial but should be seen to be so and that it should not only be free from outside influence but should be manifestly so. (Dáil Debates, 11 June 1974, line 803)

This reflects concerns expressed by government in a statement of 28 January 1974.[12]

> The government are very conscious of the necessity for the establishment of a system for the prosecution of crime that is not only free from political influence, but is manifestly so, and they believe that the establishment of an office for the direction of prosecutions would help enhance public confidence in the administration of the law.
>
> The government propose to ensure that the making of representations to the Attorney General, State Solicitors, members of the Garda Siochana and others officially concerned in relation to criminal proceedings shall cease. The making of similar representations to the Director of Public Prosecutions will likewise not be acceptable. The proposed legislation will include provisions for this proposal.[13]

This is a striking indication of the problems inherent in a government having control over operational elements of the administration of justice. This instance of institutional reform shows that an Irish government is not fundamentally opposed, in general, to reforms that limit their influence on the judicial system. This was a reform that limited the government's discretion in an important function. Nevertheless, the government enacted this reform despite government backbenchers losing a form of potential political influence that they could exert, or purport to be exerting, on behalf of their constituents. It also removed from the gift of the government the opportunity to give favour to political considerations in the briefing of barristers to act for the State in criminal work.[14]

12 Department of An Taoiseach (1973) National Archive File 2005/7/430. 13 Department of An Taoiseach (1973) National Archive File 2005/7/430. 14 Backbench lobbying on fines and sentences continued until the process was challenged by a District Court Judge in 1995 – *Brennan v. Minister for Justice* (1995) 1 IR 612 – in which the Minister for Justice's exercise of the power to remit penalties that had been imposed by the District Court judge on defendants appearing in his Court was challenged. Geoghegan J. found the power exercised by the Minister to be constitutional and executive in nature but improperly exercised.

> Happily, one of the effects of the establishment of the Independent Office of the Director of Public Prosecutions is that considerations of what side of the political fence a barrister may be on have since then played no part whatsoever in the allocation of criminal work to act on behalf of the People in prosecuting crime before the court. (Hamilton, 2008)

RECRUITMENT OF OTHER CONSTITUTIONAL OFFICE-HOLDERS IN IRELAND

It could be argued that it is the issue of recruitment of constitutional office-holders that is generally problematic for the government in Ireland. In the next section we will consider recruitment of the judiciary in Scotland as a counter-factual analysis of institutional change of judicial selection. Before that, it is worth reflecting on the recruitment practices for another constitutional office-holder in Ireland. That office is the Comptroller and Auditor General.

Article 33 of the Irish Constitution provides for a 'Comptroller and Auditor General to control on behalf of the State all disbursements and to audit all accounts of moneys administered by or under the authority of the Oireachtas'. Article 33.2 provides that 'The Comptroller and Auditor General shall be appointed by the President on the nomination of Dáil Éireann.' Other than a requirement that the Comptroller and Auditor General is not a member of either House of the Oireachtas, there is no other constitutional guidance as to how the person should be recruited or selected. The individual is appointed by the President but, in contrast to the selection of judges, the nomination comes from Dáil Éireann as opposed to the government.

The current Comptroller and Auditor General was selected following an interview process and consultation with opposition party leaders. There were fifteen candidates interviewed for the position. The interview board was composed of leading figures in financial services and public service including the Central Bank Governor, the Comptroller and Auditor General from Northern Ireland and the former Irish Comptroller and Auditor General.[15]

The process is a comparable recruitment process to that for judicial selection in Ireland in that it is the recruitment of a constitutional office-holder and the practices of this recruitment are organized by government. Both the judiciary and the Comptroller and Auditor General hold important roles in Irish governance by having the powers to hold government and state bodies to account in different ways. The government is responsible for the rules and practices that govern the selection of both positions. The recruitment process

15 Press statement, Department of Finance, 12 May 2012; Dáil Éireann Debate, 24 May 2012, vol. 766, no. 3.

for the Comptroller and Auditor General is organized, transparent and rigorous. Candidates undergo a rigorous assessment process, involving an interview with senior figures in comparable regulatory bodies. The important point is that the Irish government has the capacity to organize rigorous selection processes for constitutional office-holders.

Summary

The Office of the Director of Public Prosecutions has operated without interruption since its establishment in 1974. There has never been any question raised over its independence or separation from the political system. Nor have there been calls at a political level to return the function of the prosecution of criminal offences to the Office of the Attorney General.

How does this fit with our analysis of successful institutional reform? In Chapter 1 we saw that the motivations of politicians in introducing institutional change was an important determinant of whether institutional change would be likely to reduce the discretion of government in important elements of the administration of justice. We want to know how politicians designed the new institutional model and with what objectives. How did these objectives compare to the actual design of the new institutional model and how was it given effect in legislation?

The above instance of institutional reform demonstrates that there was clear political commitment on the part of government and, in particular, senior members of government to bring about far-reaching change in the processes for the prosecution of criminal offences. The establishment of an independent office for criminal prosecutions in Ireland shows that the Irish government can implement effective institutional change. This came about because there was a political commitment to the reform initiative and a willingness to remove political control from the process of criminal prosecution. An impartial, independent and enduring institutional model for managing criminal prosecutions was the product of deliberate and careful policy development by government.

The next instance of institutional reform to consider is the reform of judicial selection processes in another jurisdiction.

INSTITUTIONAL REFORM IN THE ADMINISTRATION OF JUSTICE IN SCOTLAND

Both Ireland and Scotland introduced changes to their respective systems of appointing judges. They did so in similar ways through the establishment of a judicial screening body. Chapters 2 and 3 showed that the effects of the Irish reforms were limited for three reasons.

First, the reform was introduced in Ireland as a result of a political crisis relating to a judicial appointment. The legislation was prepared quickly and with little in the way of a consultative process. Second, the legislation contained considerable scope for governments to find a preferred candidate among the names to be recommended by the new Judicial Appointments Advisory Board. Third, the JAAB itself made decisions that further extended the discretionary scope of government decisions over judicial nominations.

It is important to examine a comparable case to determine whether there is something particular about reform of judicial selection systems to reduce the role of government that is problematic or difficult, or whether a different approach in the design and implementation of such reform can have a different impact on the role of government in judicial selection. How was a comparable reform initiative undertaken in a comparable country and how effective was that reform in practice?

Therefore, the second instance of institutional reform to be considered in this chapter is the changes that were introduced to the institutions governing judicial selection in Scotland. It was effected in a manner that was similar to Ireland but with different outcomes for the political discretion of government in judicial selection.

Scotland was the first jurisdiction in the United Kingdom to change its judicial selection process in order to reduce the role of government in judicial selection. The Scottish experience informed the subsequent reforms in England and Wales and Northern Ireland, where practices that are similar to the Scottish system were adopted. Each system established a Judicial Screening Commission (JSC) to provide a formal structure within which judicial aspirants could apply for consideration for judicial office. The JSC was charged with performing an analysis of the suitability of applicants for judicial office and making specified recommendations to government about which candidate or candidates should be appointed.

To understand the significance of the Scottish reforms, we need first to understand something about the judicial appointments processes in Scotland historically (prior to the reform process that began in 1998). We will then consider the political genesis of the institutional change introduced, the legislation governing the new institutional arrangements for judicial selection in Scotland and the implementation of the new processes by the new 'Judicial Appointments Board for Scotland' (JABS).

JUDICIAL APPOINTMENTS IN SCOTLAND HISTORICALLY

Prior to the introduction of institutional change in 2001, judicial appointments in Scotland – just like Ireland – followed the executive nomination and appointment system that is described in Chapter 1. Although the senior government representative – the Secretary for State for Scotland – was formally vested with power of appointment, in practice, judicial appointments were made by the chief law officer of Scotland, the Lord Advocate.[16]

> The main criticism of the old appointments system was the lack of transparency in the appointment process. (The Judicial Appointments Board for Scotland Annual Report 2002–3, p. 7)

The Scotland Act 1998 made the first change to the judicial selection process in Scotland. This Act provided that appointments would be made by the First Minister, without any requirement to consult the Lord Advocate. Until then, the Lord Advocate had effective control over the process. This change was part of a larger set of reforms of the institutions of Scotland that followed devolution from the Westminster parliament. It was not a change that emerged from or was related to significant prior concerns about political influence in judicial appointments.

Other reforms of a different nature were beginning to take shape at the same time. When a new government was elected in England in 1997, Scottish politicians began to talk publicly about reform of the judicial appointments process – including the possibility of introducing a judicial appointments commission. The drive for change was given real momentum when the coalition partners in the new Scottish parliament made a formal commitment in their 1999 programme for government to consult on the judicial appointments system. It was the stated policy preference of the politicians in government, and it was rooted in the context of wider concerns of politicians about the need for reform of legal and constitutional structures.

In the summer of 2000, a public consultation exercise was carried out under the auspices of the Scottish Executive which produced the consultation paper, 'Judicial appointments: an inclusive approach'.[17]

Here we had institutional change driven by political leadership, as opposed to a response to a crisis or a response to the demands of the electorate. The Scottish government led the case for institutional change from the front and embarked on a consultative process to engage public interest and shore up support for the policy preferences of the government. Chapter 1 described how consultative processes can be used by governments to enhance support and understanding for a reform to which they are already publicly committed. This is one such example of institutional change that was delivered in the absence of a crisis or public demand for change. It was driven exclusively through political commitment to policy changes, even though those policy changes would result in a reduction of the discretion of government in an important function.

16 This is the equivalent of the Attorney General in Ireland. 17 Scotland. Scottish Government. (2000) *Judicial appointments: an inclusive approach*. Available at http://www.scotland.gov.uk/Publications/2000/04/5626/File-1 (accessed 16 Nov. 2015).

The submissions received during the consultative process demonstrated substantial support for the creation of an independent Judicial Appointments Board. In March 2001, the Justice Minister (who was also the Deputy First Minister), Jim Wallace, announced the setting up of such a Board to create more open and accessible arrangements for judicial appointments in Scotland. In the autumn of 2001, the Judicial Appointments Board for Scotland (JABS) was set up as an ad hoc organization to deal with judicial appointments that were due to be made.[18] The Scottish Executive published notices inviting applications from both legal and lay people to serve on the Board. It was the first initiative of this kind in the United Kingdom.

> The creation of this independent body is a landmark in the Scottish judicial appointments system and the Board is the first of its kind in the United Kingdom. (Judicial Appointments Board for Scotland Annual Report 2002–3, p. 6)

In June 2002, the JABS was formally established as an administrative body but without statutory backing. However, there was a strong political commitment that the JABS would be placed on a statutory footing after operating successfully for an undefined period. In 2003, the Scottish Executive asked the JABS to consider what might be included in the legislation that would put it on a statutory footing.[19] This was important, because it allowed the JABS to influence the structure of what would become established on a statutory basis. Inviting the JABS to contribute to the development of legislation was an important statement about the political commitment to the JABS in its continuing form. By inviting the JABS to contribute, the executive made an implicit statement of commitment to its continued operation. It would have been politically invidious thereafter to draft legislation that was materially inconsistent with the recommendations of the JABS or legislation that gave government a greater role in the judicial selection process than they had under the JABS structure since its establishment.

In February 2006, after 172 judicial appointments had been made on the basis of recommendations from JABS, the Scottish government published a paper, 'Independence in a Modern Scotland', that included a proposal to establish the Judicial Appointments Board for Scotland on a statutory basis, with its equal mix of lay and legal membership (Scottish Government, 2006). In February 2007, the Scottish Executive published a White Paper, 'Proposals for a Judiciary (Scotland) Bill' (Scottish Government, 2007). In its 2006–7

18 Judicial Appointments Board for Scotland (2009) *Framework document*. Available at http://www.judicialappointmentsscotland.org.uk/Publications/Corporate_and_Business_Plans2/Framework_Document.pdf (accessed 16 Nov. 2015). 19 Judicial Appointments Board for Scotland Annual Report 2003–4, p. 20.

Annual Report, the Board commented that they hoped that the new administration, that was to be formed in the wake of the 2007 election, would take the incoming Bill early in their legislative programme.[20]

The Judiciary and Courts (Scotland) Bill 2008 was introduced to the Scottish parliament in January 2008 (just seven months into the term of office of the new government) and it included provisions to establish, in statute, the Judicial Appointments Board for Scotland. The Judiciary and Courts (Scotland) Act 2008 (the 2008 Act) became law on 29 October 2008. The Judicial Appointments Board of Scotland is now established as an advisory non-departmental public body.

JUDICIARY AND COURTS (SCOTLAND) ACT 2008

The Judicial Appointments Board for Scotland (JABS) was established by Chapter 3 of the 2008 Act. Section 9(2) established the functions of the JABS as being 'to recommend to members of the Scottish Executive individuals for appointment to judicial offices within the Board's remit' and to 'provide advice to members of the Scottish Executive in connection with such appointments.' Section 9 makes clear that the JABS is to be independent of the Scottish Executive and all other persons.

Section 11 of the 2008 Act establishes the process by which the JABS makes recommendations and the role of the Scottish Executive on receipt of such recommendations. Section 11 provides that the relevant Minister may appoint an individual to a judicial office within the JABS's remit '*only* if the Board has recommended the individual for appointment to the office' (emphasis added).

This is different from the Irish system, which allows the government to nominate an individual who had not applied for consideration by the JAAB or, indeed, to choose not to refer the vacancy to the JAAB for consideration in the first place. Furthermore, in contrast to Ireland where the government receive a large number of names, the Scottish system provides that, if the relevant Minister does not accept the recommendation of the JABS for appointment, he or she *must* give notice of that decision and the reasons for that decision. Following receipt of such notice the JABS must 'reconsider its recommendation, and make a further recommendation (whether of the same or a different individual).'

Section 12 of the 2008 Act provides that the selection of an individual to be recommended for appointment must be 'solely on merit'. The JABS may only select an individual if it is 'satisfied that the individual is of good character'. Section 13 of the 2008 Act provides that only the judicial and legal members of the JABS can take part in any assessment by the JABS of an individual's

20 Judicial Appointments Board for Scotland Annual Report 2006–7, p. 7.

knowledge of the law or their skill and competence in the interpretation or application of the law.

The 2008 Act establishes that the JABS, in exercising its functions, must have 'regard to the need to encourage diversity in the range of individuals available for selection to be recommended for appointment to a judicial office' (section 14). It also provides for the procedures and disclosures of the JABS to be confidential (section 17) and that it should present annual reports to the Scottish Executive who will lay a copy of that report before the Scottish parliament.

Schedule 1 of the 2008 Act provides further detail on the role and operation of the JABS. It provides for the composition of the JABS, their terms of office and the manner in which they may be removed, ethical requirements and the management of conflicts of interest involving members of the JABS. It provides that there are to be three judicial members, two legal members and an equal number of lay members to the legal and judicial members. In contrast to Ireland, the judicial members on the JABS are not specified office-holders (for example, a Court President). They are members of different courts appointed by the Lord President (of the Court of Session). The legal members represent the advocate and solicitor branches of the legal profession and the lay members are required to be residents of Scotland who are neither lawyers nor judicial office-holders. The legal and lay members alike are appointed by the Scottish Executive. The Chairperson of the JABS must be a lay member – chosen by the Scottish Executive. The JABS is given the freedom to establish its own processes on all matters but may receive guidance from the Scottish Executive from time to time.

PROCEDURES OF THE JUDICIAL APPOINTMENTS BOARD FOR SCOTLAND

The JABS was established with a broad remit:[21]

1 to provide the First Minister with a list of candidates recommended for appointment to the offices of Senator of the College of Justice, Sheriff Principal, Sheriff and Part-time Sheriff,
2 to make such recommendations on merit, but in addition to consider ways of recruiting a judiciary which is as representative as possible of the communities which they serve,
3 to undertake the recruitment and assessment process in an efficient and effective way.

21 Judicial Appointments Board for Scotland (2009) *Framework document*.

In its institutional design, politicians ensured that there would be an equal number of lay and legal representatives on the JABS. It was made clear by the executive that merit selection was to be the paramount concern but the JABS was also expected to fashion a judiciary that was as representative as possible of the communities that they would serve. Although the Scottish ministers gave it general guidance, it was for the JABS to develop its own processes and procedures. In so doing, the JABS exercised particular care to ensure that the network-effects of being known to members on the JABS were minimized to avoid the threat of self-selection. There was an important contrast between the role of the lay members of the Judicial Appointments Advisory Board in Ireland and the Judicial Appointments Board for Scotland. The Scottish system accorded lay members a good deal more status than did the Irish system, both formally in terms of the relative numbers involved, and procedurally, by the relative weight of their input to discussions about candidates.

The JABS held its first meeting on 12 June 2002. At the outset it was agreed to meet on a monthly basis to discuss general business. The Scottish ministers gave the JABS general guidance, but it had a free hand in developing its own policies and procedures. Having followed the Scottish executive process for the first year of its operation, the JABS then reviewed their processes and revised both the application and referee assessment forms. These were changed to include competency-based assessments for judicial applicants. The forms were framed in such a way that applicants and referees were asked to provide examples to demonstrate how the applicant met the published criteria. The JABS also decided to consider applications without first calling for referees' reports so that they could do an initial screening of candidates before being required to provide such reports.

These initial recruitment exercises are open competitions with the onus on the applicant to present a convincing application to persuade the JABS that they should be shortlisted for interview. Applicants must therefore provide sufficient relevant information and evidence to convince the JABS of their suitability for judicial appointment before referees are asked for their assessment of a candidate.

While the underlying principle of the system is that appointment should be on merit, a key further aspect of the Board's remit was to consider ways of recruiting a judiciary that would be as reflective as possible of society. The Board was given a remit to proactively consider ways of encouraging applications from minority groups. From the outset, the Board made it explicit in its Annual Reports that it welcomed applications from individuals who met the statutory qualification for judicial office from all branches of the legal profession, whatever their age, gender, ethnic background, sexual orientation, political affiliation or religious beliefs. The Board also made explicit that disability would not rule out a candidate for judicial office, except where the disability prevented the fulfilment of the physical requirements of the office and where reasonable adjustments could not be made.[22]

The JABS took a series of steps to fulfil its function of monitoring diversity in the judicial appointments system. All of the applicants were asked to complete an equal opportunities questionnaire focusing on gender, nationality, ethnicity and disability. Since its establishment, the JABS maintained statistical data on applications received with particular reference to these criteria to assist in the monitoring of diversity in the judicial appointments system.[23] In their Annual Reports, the JABS published data in relation to the age and gender distribution of applicants and in relation to the number of those applicants declaring whether they suffered from a disability.

On observing the low numbers of applications from minority groups, the JABS committed to a programme of independent research to identify whether and what structural barriers existed to achieving a balance of applications from both genders and more diverse ethnic backgrounds.

> The Board is anxious to ensure it plays its part in securing a judiciary that is reflective of the communities it serves. Given the dearth of applications from members of ethnic minorities and the number of applications received from female candidates, a particular priority for the Board will be to inquire whether there are any institutional or procedural barriers to the recruitment of a judiciary which reflects the make-up of our communities. We envisage this being the subject of appropriate research coupled with consultation with relevant bodies. (Judicial Appointments Board for Scotland Annual Report 2002–3, p. 11)

The JABS was conscious of the close networks present in a small legal community and of the ways in which personal acquaintance of the JABS members with potential candidates might appear to favour one candidate over another. This contrasts with Ireland. As shown in Chapter 3, being known to a member of the Judicial Appointments Advisory Board was an important element of the assessment of judicial candidates (in the absence of interviews). In Ireland, being known to a member of the JAAB was a key determinant in whether an applicant was likely to be recommended to government.

As a further safeguard against network effects, it was established that the lay members of the JABS would give their views first during the assessment stages involved in the shortlisting, interviewing and Board review of candidates. As noted in Chapter 3, the JAAB operated with the views of judicial members generally heard first in the assessment of applicants.

22 Judicial Appointments Board for Scotland Annual Report 2002–3, p. 11. 23 Ibid.

The most marked contrast to the operation of the JAAB in Ireland is that the JABS conducts interviews of applicants. Following the interview those on the panel review the candidate and discuss their comparative merits. At the conclusion of each day of interviews a further discussion takes place to arrive at a consensus view of the panel. Upon the completion of the full interview process the JABS reaches its final conclusions as to the ranking of all candidates. The JABS also offers feedback to all unsuccessful applicants. Those who have been interviewed but not recommended for appointment are offered the opportunity to discuss their performance at interview with a member of the interview panel.[24]

The JABS produces Annual Reports of its activities, as well as the agenda and minutes of monthly meetings. It commissions and publishes working papers on matters connected to judicial appointments, as well as formal academic reviews of its work and studies on public perceptions of judicial appointments. It is an active and well-resourced body with a permanent secretariat.

Summary

The Judicial Appointments Board for Scotland is a body that was created as a response to the political preferences of the Scottish Executive between 1998 and 2002. In 2008 it was given statutory underpinning. That provided evidence of ongoing political support of the Scottish Executive to maintaining a stable, non-political body for the delegated governance of judicial selection processes.

The JABS has had a marked impact on the political discretion of the Scottish government in judicial selection. This is a result of its institutional design, which tightly binds the Scottish Executive to the recommendations of the JABS. The processes of the JABS are designed to ensure that there is a rigorous assessment of judicial applicants. Conscious of the threat of self-selection, the JABS has deliberately structured its processes to ensure that the views of lay members are clearly heard. It is important to understand how these structures, which seem on the face of it to look similar to the institutional structure in Ireland, differ in ways that impact on political decision-making.

COMPARABLE REFORM; CONTRASTING RESULTS

The contrast of the structure, purpose and operation of the Judicial Appointments Advisory Board in Ireland and the Judicial Appointments Board for Scotland is summarized in Table 4.1 below.

24 Judicial Appointments Board for Scotland Annual Report 2004–5, p. 26.

Table 4.1: Contrasting Irish and Scottish reform of judicial selection

	Ireland	Scotland
Genesis	Political crisis related to specific individual judicial appointment.	Programme for government political commitment.
External consultation	No.	Yes.
Timeline for establishment	One year.	Two Years.
Purpose	Reduce executive discretion in judicial appointments.	Reduce executive discretion in judicial appointments and enhance diversity of judiciary.
Other contemporaneous constitutional or legal reforms?	None.	Significant legal and institutional changes following devolution from Westminster.
Independence from executive	Established on statutory basis; AG and 3 Ministerial Appointees on Board.	Established on administrative basis initially, then on statutory basis; guidance on lay members to ensure not 'political men'.
Composition	Seven legal, three lay.	Five legal, five lay.
Number recommended	Legislation says that JAAB should recommend at least seven names in respect of each vacancy but this has been implemented differently over time.[25]	JABS makes one recommendation which the Minister is obliged to accept or write back stating reasons why not. JABS can make a second recommendation (which may be the same person) which the Minister must then accept.
Effect on political discretion of government	Little.	Significant.
Post-implementation review	Minister for Justice invited submissions on possible changes to the judicial selection system in 2014 in the context of broader reforms to the court system.	Functions and processes formally reviewed with input of JABS and Board was upgraded to statutory body in 2009.

Scotland is similar to Ireland in that they are both common law systems and are both parliamentary democracies with dominant executives. They both had an identical judicial selection process prior to their respective reforms in 1995 and 2002. Both had judicial selection systems that provided maximum discretion for the executive to appoint their preferred candidate. They have legal systems of broadly comparable size and structure.

25 See Chapter 3.

Ireland and Scotland had similar historical judicial selection processes that had heavily favoured executive preferences. In both countries, the reasons for reform are identical (removing judicial appointment form political control). The nature of the reform (the establishment of an independent screening and recommendation process) is similar in both countries.

However, the initial conditions that triggered the perceived need for reform differed. In Scotland, there was a sustained period of policy and political development prior to the introduction of reform, whereas the Irish reform occurred quickly and as a response to a specific intra-coalition political crisis.

The two reform outcomes display marked contrast in the extent to which the government was ultimately bound by the recommendations of the delegated body and the impact that had on the constraints placed on the discretion of the executives in both jurisdictions. Although the institutional design of the two systems is generally similar, there is a marked difference in the impact of the two systems on political discretion in judicial selection. This is the result of the institutional design as it relates to the number of names to be recommended by the delegated body to government.

This study argued that the explanation for the contrast in institutional design lay in the different political commitment behind each system. Chapter 1 showed that Ireland had a low political commitment score (the lowest in the analysis), whereas Scotland had a high political commitment score (one of the highest in the analysis). In Chapter 1 (Table 1.13) we saw that there was a link between the level of political commitment to institutional change and the impact of the judicial selection commission on the discretion of government in judicial selection.

The Scottish judicial selection reform process was more effective than its Irish predecessor in changing the role of the executive in the selection of judges from one that was heavily influenced by the preferences of the executive to one in which judges were selected based on the recommendations of an independent body. What is particularly interesting in the Scottish case is that the politicians had only recently acquired all of the power in relation to judicial appointments for themselves, yet they chose immediately and voluntarily to divest themselves of such power in a new institutional arrangement.

The principal reason why the Scottish reform functioned in a manner that so greatly reduced political discretion in judicial selection was because the system was intentionally and deliberately designed to have this effect from the outset. Providing in statute that the government *must* choose the person recommended by the JABS and that the government had no capacity to make appointments outside of this process, bound the government into a practice in which it would thereafter be unable to exercise discretionary influence.

Why did institutional change of the judicial selection process in Scotland have this effect, whereas comparable institutional change in Ireland resulted in much less reduction in the political discretion of governments in judicial selection? The institutional design of the new process was critical to the impact that reform could and would have on political discretion in judicial selection. The choice of institutional design was a product of the level of political commitment behind the institutional change. The Scottish reform had political support at the time of its initiation. The reform was the product of the political preferences of the executive, clearly set out in the programme for government of the day.

CONCLUSIONS

In both the case of the establishment of the Office of the Director of Public Prosecutions in Ireland and the establishment of the Judicial Appointments Board for Scotland, strong political commitment underpinned the introduction of institutional change. Where reform occurred, it was driven by the centre of political power and was introduced by a new government who had observed that there had been deficiencies in the previous institutional arrangements.

Political commitment is essential to bringing about effective institutional change that is intended to reduce the power of governing politicians. This may seem obvious, but it is something that must be recognized in trying to understand the process of institutional reform in areas that are deemed sensitive and that affect the core competences of government. The importance of political commitment to institutional change in these areas is central to understanding the contrast between the design of the Judicial Appointments Board for Scotland and the design of the Judicial Appointments Advisory Board in Ireland. Moreover, in the Irish case, neither of the governments involved in institutional change proposals in 1994 and 1995 had expressed any prior principled commitment to delegated governance of judicial selection in Ireland.

This analysis is important because it sheds light on the introduction and implementation of institutional change to judicial selection processes in Ireland. Chapter 2 argued that the form taken by the new institutional design in Ireland was such that it could have little impact on the discretion of government in future judicial appointments. Chapter 3 deepened this analysis by showing that the introduction of institutional change in 1995 had little impact on members of government engaged in judicial selection; and that furthermore, whatever scope the JAAB had had to constrain government choice was, in fact, voluntarily relinquished over time.

Was there something about Ireland or something about judicial selection systems that was problematic? This chapter has shown that the answer to each of these questions is no. Ireland introduced effective institutional change to reduce the discretion of politicians in the criminal justice system. Scotland introduced effective institutional change to reduce the discretion of politicians in judicial selection. Matters could also have been different in Ireland in the case of judicial appointment systems.

So what were the factors at play in Ireland that were different? Effective institutional change was introduced in Ireland and Scotland when it was led by politicians. In Ireland, sensitivities in the criminal justice system had been the subject of public discourse in 1970 but it was not until a new government, unconnected to the previous scandal and with the political commitment to make institutional changes as a response to the controversy, came into office – some three years later – that there was any serious move to change these processes. In Scotland, although there had initially been little public debate about the merits of alternative judicial selection systems – it appears to have been championed by an incoming government who had specific policy preferences. The new government in Scotland then conducted a public consultation and engagement, which increased support for their preferred position and which enabled them to introduce institutional change without significant resistance.

In both of these examples, political commitment by government was core to introducing these institutional changes. Such political commitment was not present in relation to the institutional change of the judicial selection system in Ireland. As a result, the institutional change that was introduced and eventually implemented was ultimately ineffective in its objective of reducing government discretion in judicial selection. It is important to re-emphasize that this book does not say whether one judicial selection system or other is a good or bad system. Rather it affirms the core democratic principle that law-making majorities in stable democracies are entitled to make and change the rules regarding their own political institutions. The purpose of this analysis is to assess the impact of a given institutional change relative to the stated objective of its introduction.

CHAPTER 5

Prospects for further reform in Ireland

Between 1995 and 2013 there was little further political debate about the judicial selection process in Ireland. Judicial selection processes had been periodically raised by academics, civil society groups and, occasionally, by judges,[1] but generally in the context of a broader discussion about the administration of justice and governance of the judiciary or within the context of general constitutional review. In 1996 the Constitution Review Group considered whether the power to appoint judges should be taken out of the hands of government and given to the President or some other body. It considered the provisions of the Courts and Court Officers Act 1995 and concluded:

> The Courts and Court Officers Act 1995 provides for the establishment of the Judicial Appointments Advisory Board to advise the Government on the selection of judges. The Review Group is of the opinion that time should be allowed for a build-up of experience of the operation of the Board on this statutory basis before the issue of whether it should be placed on a constitutional basis is considered. The Review Group considers it desirable that judges continue to be appointed by the Government, the authority directly responsible to the Oireachtas and the people. (Constitution Review Group, 1996, p. 158)

In 1999 the All-Party Oireachtas Committee on the Constitution in its Fourth Progress Report examined the Irish model of judicial selection. It noted that the 'shortlisting procedure in Ireland compares favourably with those in other common law countries because the opportunity has been taken to combine the best features of those systems' (All-Party Oireachtas Committee on the Constitution, 1999, p. 7). The Committee concluded that the judicial selection system should be retained in its existing form with its role for the elected government.

> The independence of the judiciary might suggest that the executive should have no discretion in the appointment of judges. But, since the judiciary is an organ of state, it must ultimately be held accountable to the people ... The Committee takes the view that our present system of appointing judges should be retained. It feels that the government has

1 Meenan, D. (2007); Carroll (2005b); Irish Council for Civil Liberties (2007); Clarke, J. (2013) 'A difficult balance', lecture delivered at Griffith College, Dublin, 10 April 2013.

> sufficient non-partisan advice from the Judicial Appointments Advisory Board and that it, as the executive of the elected representatives of the people, should retain the final decision. It is significant because the judicial candidates are already shortlisted by the board strictly on merit, the government cannot be open to criticism that it appoints only its own supporters rather than suitably qualified persons when it chooses from a list. (All-Party Oireachtas Committee on the Constitution, 1999, pp. 7–8)

The Committee further commented that 'this procedure supersedes the rather informal process pursued by successive governments who were seen to appoint, almost invariably, their own supporters to judicial office. There is no evidence, it should be noted, that such appointees displayed favouritism to the party that appointed them. The new procedures were introduced because there was pressure on governments to ensure transparency in appointments' (All-Party Oireachtas Committee on the Constitution, 1999, p. 7). The Committee also observed that the independence of the judiciary was protected elsewhere in the Constitution (Article 35.2) irrespective of the method of appointing judges.

> The independence of the judiciary might suggest that the executive should have no discretion in the appointment of judges. But, since the judiciary is an organ of state, it must ultimately be held accountable to the people. As Chief Justice Finlay put it [in 1998] 'At the end of the day somebody must be accountable for the standard and type of judiciary that is appointed. There is a significant amount to be said for making politicians accountable for the standard and type of judiciary that is appointed. They are the ones to whom people in general can turn if bad appointments are being made by some body of people who are relatively anonymous then there is no-one to turn to and blame.'[2] (All-Party Oireachtas Committee on the Constitution, 1999, pp 7–8)

In 2007, the Irish Council of Civil Liberties (ICCL) conducted a wide ranging study of the Irish judiciary and judicial independence in Ireland.[3] It examined the judicial selection system in the context of assessing the personal independence of the Irish judiciary. It found that

> Similar to other well-established liberal democracies, the personal independence of Irish judges is very well protected, particularly in relation to conditions of service and tenure and remuneration. However, this section also indicates that recent reforms in judicial appointments

2 Finlay CJ interview, Sturgess and Chubb (1998) *Judging the world* (Oxford: Butterworths), pp 413–14. 3 Ward (2007) *Justice matters* (Dublin: Irish Council for Civil Liberties).

> still allow for political affiliation to play a part in appointments and that criteria for judicial selection is imprecise and ill-defined. (Ward, 2007, p. 46)

In relation to judicial selection, the ICCL recommends that:

- criteria for judicial selection should be replaced with criteria and competencies that are transparently meritocratic and precise.
- minority or under-represented status should be treated as a component of competence for the purpose of increasing diversity on the Bench.
- the criteria of 'awareness of diversity, racial and gender issues' should be added as a competency for judicial appointments.
- when advising the Government on judicial appointments, the number of persons shortlisted by the JAAB should be reduced to three. The JAAB should also be involved in advising the Government on promotions.
- criteria for recommending a judge for appointment or elevation by Government must be transparent and defined. The Government should consider publishing reports indicating why it has recommended a person for appointment or elevation. (Ward, 2007, p. 98)

In 1999, the Department of Justice and Equality examined the operation of the new judicial selection model in the course of a broader review of eligibility requirements for appointment as a judge of the High Court or Supreme Court but did not review the judicial selection system itself.[4] The question of the structure of the process for judicial selection did not return to the political agenda until 2013 when the Minister for Justice and Equality indicated it was something which he was going to review.[5] It did not feature in the manifestos of the political parties in the preceding election in 2011 and did not form part of the subsequent agreed programme for government between the governing coalition parties. The statements by the then Minister provided a starting

4 Report of the Working Group on qualifications for appointment as judges of the High and Supreme Courts (1999). 5 The Minister also made reference to judicial appointments at the Law Society of Ireland Annual Conference 2013. 'The development of a new system of judicial appointments is something I have been considering carefully. My own view, having had the experience over the past two years of observing the JAAB system in action, is that it is very much of its time and we could do better. I should be clear that this is not a criticism of the Judicial Appointments Board itself, they merely operate within the legislative framework they are given and the candidates for judicial office are without doubt of a very high calibre. But there is certainly scope for a much more transparent and accountable system which could promote more diversity in our judiciary and serve to uphold the very high opinion in which the Irish people hold the judiciary.' Minister Alan Shatter TD: 'A Time of Change' delivered at the Law Society of Ireland Annual Conference, Killarney, Co. Kerry, 11 May 2013 (http://www.justice.ie/en/JELR/Pages/SP13000187) accessed 22 June 2015.

point for renewed political debate, culminating in the Department of Justice and Equality establishing a formal consultation process on the system of judicial selection in December 2013. This contrasted with the previous instance of political debate in Ireland on judicial selection, which was the product of political crisis between coalition partners in government. The political debate of 2013–14 took place during the formal consultation process initiated by the Department of Justice and Equality in 2013 and also during the parliamentary discussions on the proposed legislation changes to the judicial selection process in 2013 and 2014.

This chapter examines this renewed political debate on judicial selection systems in Ireland and the legislative and procedural improvements that may now be desirable twenty years after the establishment of the Judicial Appointments Advisory Board.

REVIEW OF PROCEDURES FOR APPOINTMENT AS A JUDGE

As we have mentioned, in December 2013, the Department of Justice and Equality established a consultation process and invited submissions on the system of judicial appointments, including eligibility for appointment, the need to ensure and protect the principle of judicial independence, and also the need to promote equality and diversity. The role of the Judicial Appointments Advisory Board, including its membership and its procedures were also issues to be considered. This review requested that submissions should be made having regard to the existing constitutional parameters.[6] In the course of the research for this book, the author interviewed the former Minister for Justice and Equality, Alan Shatter TD, on his reasons for initiating the review.[7]

The Minister's reasons for establishing the review can be summarized as follows:

1 The statutory mechanisms for the JAAB had been in place for 20 years and it was time to review its operation.
2 The operation of the JAAB process was different to his expectations prior to becoming Minister.

6 'I would like to encourage public debate on elements of reform that should be considered in the public interest with regard to how we go about appointing judges … while the JAAB process was a model of best practice in its day, it seems to me that it would be worthwhile now to review the operation of the judicial appointments system to ensure it reflects current best practice, that it is open, transparent and accountable and that it promotes diversity.' Minister for Justice and Equality Alan Shatter TD, press statement issued 6 December 2013 at http://www.justice.ie/en/JELR/Pages/PR13000413 (accessed 13 Nov. 2015). 7 See Appendix 2.

3 The position of the lay people on the JAAB was unclear and their capacity to contribute to debate about judicial candidates was unknown.
4 The JAAB had never interviewed anybody despite its statutory power to do so. An interview process might enable the lay members of the JAAB to gain a stronger perspective of the candidates.
5 The JAAB recommended a large number of names which provided larger than expected political discretion to government in making selection decisions.
6 Gaps of expertise on the judiciary had to be considered when making judicial appointments and this may be something the JAAB should be asked to consider.
7 The statutory mechanism for judicial selection system did not include promotions between courts or appointments to European courts.

The Department of Justice received 27 responses in the consultation process including from the judiciary, the Bar Council of Ireland, the Law Society of Ireland, the Irish Council for Civil Liberties, individual constitutional office-holders, political parties and other individuals and groups and public representatives.[8] Some of these submissions were published by their authors.[9] It is suggested the Review provided a natural opportunity for the Judicial Appointments Advisory Board to publish an account of its institutional experience since 1995 to help inform the public debate about judicial selection processes.

A committee of senior judges made a submission on behalf of the Irish judiciary – the Judicial Appointments Review Committee (JARC). Its members included the Chief Justice and Presidents of the High Court, Circuit Court and District Court – all of whom were members of the JAAB. As such, the submission carried an additional level of authority derived from the personal experience of those members of the intricacies of the judicial selection system as members of JAAB. The JARC submission was also significant because it is unusual for the judiciary in Ireland to comment in such a structured way about a matter of political importance and the administration of justice.

> The report of the JARC was characterized by a serious concern that the institutional arrangements for judicial selection in Ireland risked compromising the high standards of judicial independence enjoyed by the

8 Dáil Debate, 6 June 2014 (http://oireachtasdebates.oireachtas.ie/debates%20authoring/debateswebpack.nsf/takes/dail2014060600015?opendocument – accessed 22 June 2015).
9 Judicial Appointments Review Committee, Preliminary Submission to the Department of Justice and Equality's Public Consultation on the Judicial Appointments Process, January 2014; Law Society of Ireland, Submission of the Law Society of Ireland, January 2014; Bar Council of Ireland, Submissions on the Procedures for Appointment as a Judge, January 2014; Irish Council for Civil Liberties, Submission on Review of Procedures for Appointment as a Judge, February 2014; Free Legal Advice Centre, Preliminary Submission on Review of Procedures for Appointment as a Judge, January 2014.

> Irish judiciary for many years. Any reformed system of judicial appointment must at a minimum seek to maintain and ideally enhance those qualities of the Irish judicial system while addressing deficiencies in the appointment and selection process. It is increasingly clear that the relative success of the administration of justice in Ireland has been achieved in spite of, rather than because of the appointment system. The system of judicial appointment in Ireland is by now demonstrably deficient, fails to meet international standards of best practice, and must be reformed if in more challenging times it is to achieve the objective of securing the selection of the very best candidates for appointment to the Irish judiciary and thus contributing to the administration of justice in a manner which will sustain and enhance public confidence. (Judicial Appointments Review Committee, 2014, pp 8–9)

The concern identified was that judicial appointments were based on party political considerations and that this was corrosive of public confidence in the judiciary.

> It appears that the area of the judicial appointments process which has attracted most public comment, and criticism, and which, it may perhaps be inferred, is the matter of greatest public concern, is the fact, that the appointment decision is still largely a political decision made by the Cabinet, and the fact that it is perceived that to a greater or lesser extent, political connection with, or allegiance to, the parties then in Government, can favourably affect the appointment decision … Furthermore, the perception of political appointment is corrosive of public confidence in the administration of justice which is itself a vital component in ensuring acceptance of decisions, and at a more fundamental level, the stability of the State. The problem it is submitted is twofold. First, a perception that political allegiance influences the appointment decision, and second the lack of any identifiable criteria designed to ensure that the appointment made is of the highest quality. Political affiliation is a matter which is logically irrelevant for appointment to a judicial post. No one now suggests that the political affiliation or support for a political party is in any way indicative of judicial merit. But if appointment is made by the Cabinet which is necessarily highly attuned to political considerations, then if political affiliation is relevant, it becomes a significant and potentially dominating factor.
>
> This has not been true for all appointments but it is sufficiently true to attract public comment. By reason of a series of factors however, the appointment process in Ireland has not led to a polarized or a politicized judiciary. Ireland has in general been very well served by its judiciary, which has a high reputation for independence. Some public commentary

> has been simplistic and on occasions unfair. But all of this, while true is not relevant to the present discussion. Public confidence in the system of appointment is essential. It is simply wrong in principle that consideration of political considerations should form any part of the decision process. (Judicial Appointments Review Committee, 2014, pp 16–17)

The JARC argued that judicial independence would be best protected by a reduction of the role of politics in judicial appointments. It suggested that the legislation should be changed so that the JAAB would recommend three names per judicial vacancy to government, as opposed to the statutory provision of at least seven names per vacancy. It also recommended that the merit principle be enshrined in legislation, that the JAAB needed to be significantly better resourced to perform its functions, that the JAAB should be specifically empowered to rank certain candidates as outstanding or to say when there were no suitable candidates, and that promotions between courts should be subject to the advisory process of the JAAB. The JARC also recommended that the eligibility for all courts should be extended to fifteen years' experience, that retirement ages should be harmonized across all courts and that a formal judicial council be established.

These suggested reforms, along with those of other submissions, are discussed later in this chapter. In the interim, I would make the following observations. The judiciary, along with the legislature and government, is charged with the defence of the Constitution and the responsibility to protect the administration of justice. It is clear that the members of the JARC were gravely concerned about judicial appointments at the time of writing the submission in December 2013–January 2014. It is right that the judiciary should have the opportunity to set out its concerns and it was valuable that there was a public consultation process in being that provided a formal platform within which such concerns could be publicly expressed.

However, the content of the submission presents challenges. Factually, the submission makes a number of charges about the over-politicization of judicial appointments in Ireland without acknowledging the full picture of the judicial selection system.

As the JAAB did not make a contribution to the political debate of 2013–14, the JARC (which had four members of the JAAB among its authors) submission was an opportunity to make some comment on the current process of judicial selection at JAAB level and to describe any legislative difficulties that may be faced by the JAAB in the application of the Courts and Court Officer Act 1995. The JARC makes a recommendation that the number of recommended candidates be reduced to three in order to reduce the role of political influence in judicial selection, but omits to comment on the practice of the JAAB recommending many multiples of the current statutory provision of seven names to government from which to make a nomination. In the absence of that information, the JARC recommendation is missing important and relevant context.

As we know, judges are consistently chosen by government from the recommendations of the JAAB. And as we also know, the JAAB has broad powers to set its own selection criteria and recruitment practices and standards. Additionally, the JAAB has the power to recommend a smaller number of candidates than it has chosen to recommend over the past fifteen years or so. Governments can be faulted for *breaking* the rules, but cannot be faulted for *following* the rules of a system which gives so much power to the JAAB which it has not, for various reasons, chosen to use.

Further, the JARC submission overreaches in its assertions about international practices and standards. As will be discussed later in this chapter, international principles of judicial independence respect the role of the political majority in judicial selection. As we have seen in earlier chapters, international practice on the role of government in judicial selection varies considerably and the Irish statutory model (if it were more rigidly applied by the JAAB) offers a good middle ground position within that spectrum of practice. As will be shown in this chapter, in stable democracies such as the jurisdictions examined in this book, judicial independence and the role of the political majority in judicial selection is not really linked - because of the tenure of the judge until a set retirement age and because of the behaviour of the judges appointed has had no connection to any political circumstances of their appointments. The jurisdiction that has come first in recent international assessments of relative judicial independence, New Zealand, operates a system of judicial selection that gives greatly more power to politicians than the Irish system. Ireland, as the JARC observed, was ranked third in Europe and fourth globally in the same assessment (World Economic Forum Global Competitiveness Report 2013–14, 2014–15).

The observations made by the JARC on the role of the political majority in judicial selection sit somewhat contrary to earlier observations made by the Constitution Review Group, the All-Party Oireachtas Committee on the Constitution and Chief Justice Finlay. Finally, it is simply inconsistent to argue that Ireland has been 'universally well served by its judiciary' in spite of an 'unsatisfactory' and 'demonstrably deficient' appointments process by which all of its members were selected.

Notwithstanding these challenges to the arguments made by the JARC, its concerns were clearly serious and sincerely held. However, it is important to reflect that these concerns were also informed by a separate concern for judicial independence held by the JARC (p. 6) arising from the consequences of a series of changes to judicial pay and pensions introduced between 2011 and 2013. In this period judicial pay had been substantially reduced[10] and changes to pension arrangements for would-be judges were introduced. As the JARC described (p. 19), judges would now have to make a significant and upfront contribution of a large sum of money to fund their public sector pension and would have to serve a longer period as a judge (20 years instead of 15 years before a mandatory retirement age of 70) before obtaining full pension provision from the State.[11] The argument is that the impact of these financial changes resulted in some of the then leaders of the legal profession reasoning that the new financial cost, added to the usual opportunity cost, of accepting a judicial appointment was now too great. These changes occurred at a time of severe economic recession in Ireland during which property values and the value of pensions and shares plummeted and many professional people were in a different financial position than they may have expected. Put simply, within a very short space of time, becoming a judge may have became too expensive for certain senior people at the Bar who might otherwise have been expected to seek judicial office at that stage of their career, especially in the High Court. This resulted, in some cases, in a very slightly more junior cohort of lawyers than usual applying for judicial office and being appointed. Consequently, certain lawyers appearing before some of those newer judges will have had more experience or, in some cases, greater perceived 'standing'. That is not to say that such a scenario had never happened before or that justice cannot function in that way but in this case it was felt that the very best of the legal profession were, within a short period, seemingly collectively deciding to withdraw from consideration for the judiciary. The concern was that the impact on the administration of justice of this new behaviour by the 'best' candidates for judicial office was a threat to judicial independence.

As the JARC observed, public confidence in the administration of justice requires securing the very best quality and the most efficient management of the courts. Getting the appointments right is not just about appointing from the people who make themselves available at a given time, but ensuring the best candidates become applicants in the system. This is an understandable concern and one that either needs to be revisited by policy makers or simply accepted as part of a once in a generation change to public sector pensions.

10 Following a referendum in November 2011 which passed the Twenty-Ninth Amendment of the Constitution (*Judges' Pay*) Act 2011. 11 'A newly appointed judge of the High Court will receive take home pay of less than 50 per cent of that paid in 2008, and will face an accrual period 1/3 longer to accrue a full pension, and while at the same time incurring substantial additional liability to tax in respect of the judicial pension, and any savings for private pension provision made in practice. In such a context it is particularly important to enhance the significance of judicial appointments as recognition of quality. The converse is also true. If it is perceived that persons of quality are not being appointed then such candidates will be further dissuaded. Furthermore, the entire concept of a learned judiciary requires that by and large the persons deciding cases be more experienced and more knowledgeable than the persons arguing them' (Judicial Appointments Review Committee, p. 19).

But, crucially, the JARC leaned too far in linking this perceived threat to judicial independence to problems in the machinations of the current system of judicial appointment that have been in place for considerably longer than this recent question about attracting judicial candidates. In summary, the JARC submission omits to acknowledge the reality of the operation of the JAAB and wrongly conflates two unrelated elements of judicial selection and judicial independence.

The submission of the Law Society of Ireland, which represents the vast majority of practising lawyers in Ireland, suggested the JAAB system be retained but with some modifications. The Law Society called for a change in composition that would increase the number of lay members from three to six and the number of solicitor representatives on the Board from one to two in order to reflect their greater numbers in the Irish legal profession and to 'assist in addressing the continuing emphasis on appointing barristers to the Circuit and Superior Courts' (Law Society of Ireland, 2014, p. 5). The Law Society also recommended that the eligibility for membership of all courts should be harmonized at ten years' experience in practice.

The Law Society of Ireland called for more formalized processes to be adopted within the JAAB in its consideration of candidates.[12] It also recommended that the JAAB should carry out its process with 'the ultimate aim of providing the Government with a shortlist of three candidates for each vacancy or proposed appointment; ranked on the basis of qualifications and suitability' (Law Society of Ireland, 2014, p. 4). The Law Society echoed the view of the JARC in calling for the merit principle to be specifically enshrined in legislation.

> The Society considers that the alteration of the role of the JAAB such that it would conduct an assessment of 'merit criteria' and therefore select the most able candidates on this basis would serve to greatly strengthen the protection of judicial independence in the State as it would greatly minimize the discretionary role of the Minister for Justice and Government in the area of judicial appointment whilst still ensuring that candidates of the highest quality are chosen. (Law Society of Ireland, 2014, p. 4)

12 'A formal evaluation process should be carried out by the JAAB in respect of each eligible applicant; such evaluation should consist of each candidate being assessed on the basis of published categories of "merit criteria" and involve review of a detailed curriculum vitae, online preliminary testing, an interview process, questionnaire based professional references, and peer review, in order to ensure that the most able and suitable candidates are selected on a meritorious basis' (Law Society of Ireland, Submission of the Law Society of Ireland, January 2014, p. 4).

The Bar Council of Ireland also made a submission to the review process which recommended that any review of the judicial selection process be carried out by an independent group – as opposed to the Minister – in order to ensure the independence of the judiciary and to ensure that the review is not 'overly influenced by the concerns and interests of the Government' (Bar Council of Ireland, 2014, p. 4). This echoed concerns stated by the JARC that such a review should be conducted by a body outside of government because 'the process itself is being initiated by a member of the Executive, and will apparently be decided upon by the Executive without further discussion' (Judicial Appointments Review Committee, 2014, p. 14). The Bar Council of Ireland recommended that the JAAB conduct interviews for the purpose of establishing suitable candidates and produce more objective criteria by which an applicant's personal experience of litigation in courts could be assessed as part of the basis of the assessment of their suitability for judicial office. In particular the Bar Council made recommendation to ensure that applicants for the High Court and Supreme Court provide information in their application and supporting references that explicitly addresses their knowledge and experience of superior court practice and procedure.

In addition, the Bar Council recommended that the JAAB be the 'sole body for selecting candidates for judicial appointment, and the JAAB process should be followed for all judicial appointments, including elevation from lower to higher courts' (Bar Council of Ireland, 2014, p. 1). More specifically, the Bar Council recommended that there be statutory change to provide that the JAAB would recommend three candidates to government in respect of each appointment, ranked in order of merit, and that the JAAB should be free to recommend no candidate where it felt there was no suitable candidate. It recommended that the government should retain a discretion in relation to which candidates recommended by the Board are ultimately appointed to office, but that only candidates recommended by the JAAB should be eligible for appointment. The Bar Council of Ireland also expressed concern about the perception of a link between judicial appointments and cronyism.[13]

The submission of the Irish Council for Civil Liberties (ICCL) called for the abolition of the JAAB and its replacement with a non-political body dominated by lay people with powers to cover all judicial appointments,

13 'The Bar Council is of the opinion that in order to dispel the apprehension that party politics plays a role in the appointment of judges, it would be wise to include an explicit statutory prohibition on consideration of a person's political affiliation in determining their suitability for appointment. It is important that judicial appointments are, and are seen to be, politically neutral. The Bar Council does not consider it necessary that persons who were previously involved in party politics or who have held positions in local or national government should be excluded from appointment to judicial office. However, appointments must be based solely on the merit of the candidate' (Bar Council of Ireland, Submission on Procedures for Appointment as a Judge, 2014, p. 13).

including Court Presidents and 'promotions' of a judge from one court to another.[14] It called for a more transparent set of merit-based assessment criteria and the use of interviews in such assessments. It also called for an express prohibition against lobbying of political representatives in relation to judicial selection as well as an explicit bar on membership of a political organization forming part of a determination of the suitability of an applicant for a judicial position. A key concern of the ICCL was the need for better representation of minorities in the judicial selection process and the enhancement of diversity, particularly gender diversity. According to the ICCL, without this concern for diversity, the independence and legitimacy of the judiciary in the eyes of the public was potentially threatened.

The submission of the Free Legal Advice Centre[15] called for the retention of the current system in which the JAAB would make recommendations to government. It suggested that the JAAB send forward three recommendations to the government in respect of each vacancy.

> The Government should select one of the three nominees except for specific reasons which should be communicated to the Board. In the event that the Government decides not to appoint any of the persons nominated, the Judicial Appointments Advisory Board should be asked to make further nominations. (Free Legal Advice Centre, 2014, p. 1)

The Free Legal Advice Centre also recommended extending the size of the JAAB to include five members to be nominated by the government to represent civil society, including organizations with a particular interest in the justice system. Concerned with promoting enhanced diversity on the judiciary, the Free Legal Advice Centre recommended that the membership of the Board should be gender balanced and to the extent possible reflect the diversity of Irish society. Finally, the Free Legal Advice Centre recommended that the JAAB adopt objective assessment criteria 'similar to those developed by the Scottish Judicial Appointments Board, including knowledge of the law; skill and competence in the interpretation and application of the law; intellectual capacity and powers of reasoning; personal characteristics; case management skills and communication skills.'[16] The Free Legal Advice Centre was of the view that lack of diversity in the judiciary was as serious an issue as perceptions of political influence in judicial appointments.

14 www.iccl.ie. 15 http://www.flac.ie/download/pdf/20140131_flac_submission_on_judicial_appointments.pdf (accessed 1 July 2015). 16 Free Legal Advice Centre, 2014, p. 1.

> The current system of appointments has been criticized as ineffective and there have been criticisms that the appointment of some judges has been influenced by their political affiliations. Despite these concerns, it must be acknowledged that the Irish judiciary has served the people and the State well, with very few exceptions, but our justice system must have the confidence of the people. That confidence may be undermined if people feel that some have been appointed for political reasons. Similarly sections of society may lose confidence in the justice system if they feel people of their gender, ethnicity or other characteristics are seriously underrepresented in the judiciary. We believe the system of appointing the judiciary should be and should be seen to be free from political patronage and should aim to ensure that the judiciary is broadly representative of all sections of society and is appointed on a basis of merit and experience alone. (Free Legal Advice Centre, 2014, p. 2)

The following table (5.2) summarizes the principal recommendations made in the submissions during the consultation process and provides some contextual analysis of the recommendations having regard to the statutory provisions and operation of the JAAB to date.

Table 5.2: Proposed reforms to judicial selection in Ireland in the consultation process

Proposed reform	Source	Comment
The number of candidates for a single judicial post submitted by the Judicial Appointments Advisory Board for governmental decision should be reduced to three, or three per vacancy.	Judicial Appointments Review Committee Bar Council of Ireland Law Society of Ireland Free Legal Advice Centre	It is believed that it is already in the statutory powers of the JAAB to recommend fewer than seven names where it believes it to be appropriate (as was the practice of the JAAB in its early years). The evidence is that the JAAB was recommending greatly in excess of seven candidates per vacancy – up to 100 names per District Court vacancy. However, there seems to be an institutional difficulty within the JAAB in reverting to its original practice (recommending about seven names or less), which reflected a literal reading of the Courts and Court Officers Act 1995. Legislation may be needed to clarify the intended operational practice by the JAAB.

Table 5.2: Proposed reforms to judicial selection in Ireland in the consultation process *(contd)*

Proposed reform	Source	Comment
Where it is proposed to fill a judicial position by promotion, including to the positions of Chief Justice and Presidents of the other courts, applications from serving judges should be processed through the JAAB.	Judicial Appointments Review Committee Bar Council of Ireland Irish Council for Civil Liberties	The government is already required by statute to consider sitting members of the judiciary when making an appointment to Court President and has done so in each instance since 1995. A formal mechanism for considering judges who wish to be promoted to another court is necessary. Such a system has been established in the Office of the Attorney General. However, the JAAB, as it currently operates, may not be the appropriate body to perform this function as it is comprised of Court Presidents and members of the legal profession who would then be required to make an assessment of a sitting judge. This may pose a risk to the independence of that judge and cause embarrassment for the judge either in applying or in making an unsuccessful application. While there have been excellent Court Presidents in office historically, for a judge of a given court to apply for a position on another court, and for the President to be aware of that, could cause practical difficulties for that judge if there is not a good working relationship in situ. Yet some system is needed involving members of the judiciary. If, instead, the judge were to make an application to a body comprising the Chief Justice, Attorney General and a number of lay people (i.e., not members of the legal profession or the President of the Court of which they are a member) this could provide a useful means of communicating such a request officially and leave sufficient separation for the candidate judge and his or her Court President.
The JAAB should be empowered to rank candidates and to designate any particular candidate as 'outstanding'.	Judicial Appointments Review Committee Bar Council of Ireland	The JAAB should be able to provide more complex information to government in making its recommendations than is currently provided (names and CVs). The JAAB could have greater influence by providing more detailed assessments of candidates and arguments for their appointment. The JAAB would need to employ more rigorous selection tools to achieve this. There may be a concern that ranking candidates could be unconstitutional if it binds the government in its selection of judges for appointment but the circumstances and implications of making such a declaration about a candidate could be clarified in legislation. The government would benefit from more detailed information about judicial candidates in its decision-making process.

Table 5.2: Proposed reforms to judicial selection in Ireland in the consultation process *(contd)*

Proposed reform	Source	Comment
The JAAB should be specifically empowered to inform the government when it considers that there are no candidates of sufficient quality.	Judicial Appointments Review Committee	It could be argued that the JAAB has this power already but there is no evidence of it ever having taken this approach in its recommendations. It could be made further explicit in legislation. However, in practice it would leave government in a difficult position, with a court vacancy which they should, in the interests of the efficient administration of justice, fill with reasonable expediency. In this scenario the government may have no option but to fill the vacancy either with someone who has either not applied to or not been recommended by the JAAB, or by the promotion of a judge of a different court.
The Judicial Appointments Advisory Board requires adequate financial resources to enable it to carry out its functions. A reformed appointments system will require adequate resources.	Judicial Appointments Review Committee	Since its establishment the JAAB has been limited in the procedures it can implement to assess candidates. A properly resourced body, with a full time secretariat or multiple periodically seconded staff, is necessary to employ standard professionalized recruitment practices consistent with best practice internationally. By way of comparison, the Judicial Appointments Board for Scotland has four civil servants periodically assigned to it to assist its operation and had expenditure of over £360,000 in the year to 31 March 2015.[17]
Criteria for being eligible to be a judge should be set out in greater detail.	Judicial Appointments Review Committee Bar Council of Ireland Law Society of Ireland Irish Council for Civil Liberties	Some guidance is provided in statute as regard temperament, experience and character but it is left to the JAAB to interpret and apply these guiding standards. It is within the power of the JAAB to formally set out the detail of the eligibility criteria it uses in assessing candidates. The JAAB is given unlimited discretion to set its own standards for recommending candidates and is free to publish these standards at any time. Any statutory expression of such standards may risk being a restriction on the untrammelled discretion the JAAB currently enjoys in this regard. Nevertheless, the merit principle, which is recommended by most submissions, could

17 Judicial Appointments Board for Scotland Annual Report 2014–15, http://www. judicialappointmentsscotland.org.uk/files/AnnualReport2014–15.pdf (accessed 13 Nov. 2015).

Table 5.2: Proposed reforms to judicial selection in Ireland in the consultation process *(contd)*

Proposed reform	Source	Comment
Criteria for being eligible to be a judge should be set out in greater detail *(continued)*.	Free Legal Advice Centre	be established in legislation. It is argued that the research shows that merit is already a key consideration in judicial selection in Ireland. Further statutory expression of the merit principle is possible, but how should this be done? Is merit the dominant requirement for the JAAB or the government or both? How does merit interact with temperament or character and what weight should these be afforded vis-à-vis merit? Does merit refer to technical expertise or personal skills or courtroom management? Should different definitions of merit be applied to different courts? What about other political considerations in appointments such as the filling of particular gaps of expertise or achieving diversity goals? This would require very careful consideration and statutory drafting.[18]
A more formalized evaluation process should be carried out by the JAAB in respect of each eligible applicant; including being assessed on the basis of published categories of 'merit criteria' and involve a review of a detailed curriculum vitae, online preliminary testing, an interview process, questionnaire based professional references, and peer review.	Law Society of Ireland Bar Council of Ireland Irish Council for Civil Liberties	This should be the cornerstone of reform of judicial selection processes in Ireland and is discussed in detail later in this chapter. Such formalized processes should include professional screening of candidates, shortlisting and interviewing and the use of other standard professional recruitment tools (such as assessment centres or psychometric training). If, when these processes are designed, legislative change is determined to be required to underpin this, such change should be made.
Personal experience of litigation should be necessary for appointments to higher courts.	Bar Council of Ireland	Section 8 of the Courts and Court Officers Act 2002 states that 'appropriate knowledge and experience of superior court practice and procedures' is necessary for an individual to be appointed to higher courts. Further clarity on how this should be determined would be helpful both to judicial applicants and for the purposes of transparency in judicial selection

18 See Judicial Appointments Review Committee, Preliminary Submission to the Department of Justice and Equality's Public Consultation on the Judicial Appointments Process, January 2014, pp 56–8, for a detailed review of merit criteria.

Table 5.2: Proposed reforms to judicial selection in Ireland in the consultation process *(contd)*

Proposed reform	Source	Comment
Personal experience of litigation should be necessary for appointments to higher courts *(continued)*.		generally. Ideally, maximum flexibility should be left with the JAAB to determine a set of standards that would constitute 'appropriate knowledge and experience', and these criteria would be published by the JAAB. If necessary, the Oireachtas could provide further definition in legislation. However, the risk with providing too much detail in legislation is that it may constrain an otherwise institutionally powerful JAAB to set its own standards and change them as necessary or appropriate without recourse to the Oireachtas.
Experience requirements should be harmonized.	Judicial Appointments Review Committee Law Society of Ireland	The basic experience requirements, in terms of the number of years' practice experience, should be consistent across courts. This is especially important given the practice of judges being promoted between courts. Certain anomalies should also be addressed such as the ineligibility of District Court judges for appointment to the High Court and the ineligibility of lawyers not in 'practice' immediately before their appointment. It may be timely to review the case of lawyers working in house or in the service of the state and their ineligibility for judicial office.[19]
The composition of the membership of the JAAB should become more open and focused on representing the public interest by (i) increasing the lay membership, and (ii) introducing a requirement that all lay members be selected by a public and open competition rather than by the Minister for Justice, and (iii) including a broader range of representatives of civil society groups with an interest in the administration of justice.	Law Society of Ireland Free Legal Advice Centre	Increasing the involvement of the lay members on the JAAB is a crucial element for the development of the judicial selection process in Ireland. Lay members should play a more substantive role in the selection process by having access to better quality information about candidates and better opportunity to assess candidates through enhanced recruitment processes such as assessment centres, interviewing or observation at role play. Consideration could be given to the use of providing a lay report to government regarding judicial candidates to complement that of the JAAB. Members of the public may now apply to be members of the JAAB following a broader change in the process for appointment to state boards in 2014.

19 The Report of the Working Group on qualifications for appointment to the High Court and Supreme Court 1999 stated (p. 67) that for barristers no period of working in the service of the state should constitute reckonable experience for the purposes of eligibility for judicial office at the Bar, whereas solicitors may gain up to five years' experience in the service of the state as reckonable for eligibility for judicial office. In *Gender injustice* (2003), Bacik et al.

Table 5.2: Proposed reforms to judicial selection in Ireland in the consultation process *(contd)*

Proposed reform	Source	Comment
Two nominees of the Law Society of Ireland should be appointed to the JAAB.	Law Society of Ireland	This should be considered in the context of calls for new assessment processes to be adopted by the JAAB, especially in the context of the very large proportion of applications from solicitors (see Table 5.5).
The JAAB should have specific processes to enhance judicial diversity or have as part of its remit the need to promote diversity in the judiciary.	Irish Council for Civil Liberties Free Legal Advice Centre	There is divergence in the submissions regarding the promotion of diversity in the judiciary. The ICCL and FLAC strongly recommend that the promotion of diversity be included as part of the remit of the JAAB whereas the JARC argued that Ireland may not face the same racial diversity challenges as other jurisdictions.[20] In Northern Ireland, Scotland and England and Wales, a focus on enhancing diversity is a key objective of the judicial selection commissions.[21] The tension between selecting judges exclusively on merit and enhancing diversity is discussed in greater detail later in this chapter.
Express prohibition on lobbying political actors and on membership of a political organization being a determinative factor in judicial appointment.	Irish Council for Civil Liberties	There is an express prohibition in the 1995 Act on canvassing members of the JAAB. This could be extended to a prohibition on canvassing members of government and the Oireachtas. It is unclear how a statutory provision providing that being a member of a political organization cannot be a determinative factor in judicial appointment would operate in circumstances where the decision-maker is choosing between two candidates of equal professional standing. It is hard to see why a decision-maker would concede that decisions were determined in this way.

Source: Judicial Appointments Review Committee, Preliminary Submission to the Department of Justice and Equality's Public Consultation on the Judicial Appointments Process, January 2014; Law Society of Ireland, Submission of the Law Society of Ireland, January 2014; Bar Council of Ireland, Submissions on the Procedures for Appointment as a Judge, January 2014; Irish Council for Civil Liberties, Submission on Review of Procedures for Appointment as a Judge, February 2014; Free Legal Advice Centre, Preliminary Submission on Review of Procedures for Appointment as a Judge, January 2014.

describe the difficulties inherent in legal professional practice, particularly during family bearing years for professional women. Another view may therefore be that if there is a higher proportion of women taking legal positions in the service of the state, as a consequence of the impact of repeated maternity leave on a sole professional practice either at the Bar or as a solicitor, then this decreases the pool of female candidates for judicial office, making the goal of gender diversity, or even parity, on the superior courts ever more difficult. **20** For a discussion on the concerns regarding diversity in other jurisdictions see the Judicial Appointments Review Committee, Preliminary Submission to the Department of Justice and Equality's Public Consultation on the Judicial Appointments Process, January 2014, pp 62–5. **21** See Judicial Appointments Board for Scotland, Diversity Strategy Group, 2014 *Diversity Conference Report*, http://www.judicialappointmentsscotland.org.uk/files/diversity conferencereport.pdf (accessed 14 Nov. 2015); MVA Consultancy (2013) Profile of the

PROPOSED LEGISLATION AND OIREACHTAS DEBATE ON JUDICIAL SELECTION, 2013–14

Between January 2013 and February 2014 three Private Member's Bills were published to reform the judicial selection system. These were published by members of the three opposition groups in parliament – Fianna Fáil, Sinn Féin and the Technical Group.[22]

Chapter 1 presented an analytical framework for assessing political power in judicial selection systems in which we determined that judicial selection systems could be assessed based on the power to nominate a person for judicial appointment and the power to ensure that the nominated candidate is the one who fills the vacancy. The three Bills published in 2013–14 took slightly different approaches within this framework. Both the Sinn Féin and Fianna Fáil Private Member's Bills sought to retain the existing structure whereby the Judicial Appointments Advisory Board would make nominations to government with government retaining power to choose a candidate to recommend to the President who would make the appointment. Both bills sought to make certain amendments to the structure, powers and functions of the Judicial Appointments Advisory Board but the fundamental structure was to be maintained.

The Thirty-Fourth Amendment to the Constitution (Judicial Appointments) Bill 2013 proposed by the Technical Group member, Deputy Shane Ross TD, proposed a different system in which the Constitution would be changed to provide that the President would appoint a judge following a nomination from a joint committee of both Houses of the Oireachtas (as opposed to the government). The joint committee would receive nominations of 'suitably qualified candidates on merit' from a newly created Judicial Appointments Council, composed of 'persons drawn from a broad spectrum in society' but would not contain any members of a 'judicial or legal representative body'.[23] The Bill proposed that the joint committee shall have a majority of members who 'are not affiliated to the political parties who form the Government'.[24]

This Bill was debated in Dáil Éireann in February 2014. In the course of that debate, Deputy Ross stated that his purpose in bringing the Bill was to 'address this in a radical but extremely effective way and, unfortunately, it is necessary to address it in a constitutional way because some of us on the

Profession 2013: Demographics and Work Patterns of Scottish Solicitors (Law Society and Scotland); MVA Consultancy (2009) Continuous Improvement – An Analysis of Scotland's Judicial Appointments Process, Judicial Appointments Board for Scotland; see the Judicial Appointments Commission's 'Equal Merit Provision' https://jac.judiciary.gov.uk/equal-merit-provision (accessed 14 Nov. 2015). **22** This is a group of independent members of Dáil Éireann who have formed a technical group under the Standing Orders of Dáil Éireann for the purposes of obtaining regular speaking time on legislation and other matters of business of Dáil Éireann. **23** Thirty-Fourth Amendment to the Constitution (Judicial Appointments) Bill 2013. **24** Ibid.

Independent benches do not trust the political parties to implement a Bill which guarantees the independence of the Judiciary' (Deputy Shane Ross, Dáil Debate, 21 February 2014).

> I propose in my Bill that judges should be introduced on merit and should guarantee their independence. I will outline the two layers of selection that are suggested and constitutionally imposed in this Bill. JAAB should be abolished and replaced by a judicial appointments council or board, whichever the Minister wants to call it, which is drawn from a broad spectrum of society. There would be no room in that judicial appointments council for any judges because the Bar Council and the entire legal profession is a home for insiders. There would be no room for any judges or any *ex officio* legal representatives from the Law Society of Ireland or the Bar Council but rather candidates would be drawn from a broad spectrum of society. That could include legal academics who would have a knowledge of the law and of the people. It could include ordinary citizens and community groups, but it would not allow insiders to push their nominees onto the bench.
>
> The second layer would be an Oireachtas committee which would receive the names of those who had applied to be judges, debate those names and then send them to the President. The Government would be bypassed completely. The Oireachtas would have a role in this but the security in this particular committee is that there would be an Opposition majority on that Oireachtas committee. There would be no way the Government could impose its way as it did in the past, and the Opposition would have a veto on that. That is the most important part of this Bill. The rest of the detail could be provided by law but if there was an Opposition majority, we would no longer have a system where political patronage would rule. People would be nominated by citizens and a judicial council. They would then go before an Oireachtas committee which would hold interviews, unlike JAAB, and would then nominate individuals and send the names to the President. Those interviews could be held in public. (Deputy Shane Ross, Dáil Debate, 21 February 2014)

The Bill amends the Constitution but, in practice, supporting legislation would be necessary to give detail on how such a radically different structure would operate. For example, who would select the members of the Judicial Appointments Committee? What is its processes and tenure? How would it guard against its own patronage? As the underlying legislation is not provided, further comment is not possible. But the central and fundamental difficulty with this Bill is that it provides for a system of judicial selection in which the law-making majority is not accountable. This approach is not one adopted in judicial selection models internationally where the principle of direct or indirect democratic participation is recognized as being a legitimate element of the selection of judges.[25] The second issue is the question of the Oireachtas committee debating the names that would be put forward by the Judicial Appointments Committee and whether that debate is to happen in public or private, whether the recommended names will be invited to appear before the Committee. If it is to be a system of parliamentary confirmation hearings then it is one that reflects the United States Supreme Court Senate Justice Committee hearings – a system that has led to a highly publicly politicized judicial appointments process[26] requiring candidates to face questions on issues that they may face as judges of the Court and which, it is suggested, is very far from a model of international best practice.

The Reform of Judicial Appointments Procedures Bill 2013 (the 2013 Bill) published by Sinn Féin in 2013 retained the existing structure of the Judicial Appointments Advisory Board but increased its membership by two to include an additional representative of the Minster for Justice (an additional lay person) and a new Chairperson who would be the Chair of the Irish Human Rights Commission (now the Irish Human Rights and Equality Commission).[27]

The core amendment made by the 2013 Bill is the reduction in the number of names to be recommended to the Minister to three persons in respect of each vacancy (reduced from at least seven names in respect of each vacancy in the 1995 Act) and the Board will make public the reasons for recommending these candidates.[28] It is not clear from the Bill if it is proposed to also make the names of the candidates recommended public. The government, in making an appointment, is not bound to make the appointment from the recommended candidates, nor say whether or not the person to be appointed has been recommended by the JAAB, but must instead, '14 days in advance of their appointment, publish a report indicating why it has recommended a person for

25 The Mount Scopus International Standards of Judicial Independence 2008 address judicial appointments as follows: '2.14. The principle of democratic accountability should be respected and therefore it is legitimate for the legislature to play a role in judicial appointments and central administration of justice provided that due consideration is given to the principle of judicial independence. 4.1. The method of judicial selection shall safeguard against judicial appointments for improper motives and shall not threaten judicial independence. 4.2. a) The principle of democratic accountability should be respected and therefore it is legitimate for the Executive and the Legislature to play a role in judicial appointments provided that due consideration is given to the principle of judicial independence. b) The recent trend of establishing judicial selection boards or commissions in which members or representatives of the Legislature, the Executive, the Judiciary and the legal profession take part, should be viewed favourably, provided that a proper balance is maintained in the composition of such boards or commissions of each of the branches of government'. **26** See Chapter 1. **27** Section 7, Reform of Judicial Appointments Procedures Bill 2013. **28** Section 8, Reform of Judicial Appointments

appointment or promotion'.[29] The Board is also required to advise the government on promotions of members of the judiciary; however no further detail is given on how this would be done in practice.[30] In the course of Oireachtas hearings on judicial selection, Deputy Pádraig MacLochlainn, the sponsor of the 2013 Bill, commented on his Bill as follows:

> The issue of appointments is one of perception. Whether justified or not, there has been a perception that some judges have been politically appointed, and that has undermined the work they have been involved in. I put forward a Private Member's Bill which essentially recommended a shortlist of three and looked at the issue of diversity. I do not have a massive objection to the fact it was not voted for because there is a review process under way at the moment ... To be frank, there has been a criticism of the Supreme Court historically that it was too conservative in its compositions and, therefore, its interpretation of the Constitution would be a conservative interpretation. How do we get to the point at which it is reflective of society in the very fundamentally important role it performs? (Deputy Pádraig MacLochlainn, Joint Oireachtas Committee on Justice Defence and Equality, Discussion on Judicial Appointments, 26 November 2014)

The 2013 Bill also makes certain declaratory references to international standards on judicial independence and to principles of equality.[31] These are not matters generally contained in legislation but the purpose of a Private Member's Bill is not always simply to make direct statutory changes, but rather to provide a vehicle and a platform through which members of parliament can raise different issues for political discussion. In this vein, the 2013 Bill requires the Board to ensure the judiciary is reflective of society[32] and that 'methods of judicial selection shall safeguard against judicial appointments for improper motives',[33] but further detail on how this would operate is not expressed.

The 2013 Bill is a positive contribution to the debate on proposed reforms of judicial selection. It provides that control of judicial appointments remain in the hands of the law-making majority, but with a broader societal representation on the JAAB. However, a significant risk is inherent in requiring government to publish reasons for promoting one judge or another.

Procedures Bill 2013. **29** Section 10, Reform of Judicial Appointments Procedures Bill 2013. **30** Section 9, Reform of Judicial Appointments Procedures Bill 2013. **31** Equality Act 2004, the United Nations Basic Principles on the Independence of the Judiciary (1985) and the Bangalore Draft Code of Judicial Conduct (2001). Section 2, Reform of Judicial Appointments Procedures Bill 2013. **32** Section 5, Reform of Judicial Appointments Procedures Bill 2013. **33** Section 6, Reform of Judicial Appointments Procedures Bill 2013.

The Judicial Appointments Bill 2014 (the 2014 Bill) published by Fianna Fáil was a consolidating Bill that restates many of the provisions of the 1995 Act but replaces others.[34] It establishes a Judicial Appointments Advisory Board with the same composition as the current Board (but it reduced the number of ministerial appointments from three to one and provided for one appointment by the Chairperson of the National Consumer Agency). It extends the judicial offices covered by the selection process to include Irish nominations to the Court of Justice of the European Union, the General Court of the European Union and the European Court of Human Rights. Like the 1995 Act, it provides that candidates shall be recommended solely on merit but then sets out more detailed considerations that the Board shall use in making such an assessment about a candidate compared to those provided in the 1995 Act. These considerations include high intellectual quality, a proper work ethic, analytical capacity, personal skills of a high quality including independence, persuasiveness, integrity, social ability and unflappability.[35] The Courts and Court Officers Act 1995 currently gives JAAB a broad discretion in this regard by including a general criterion that the candidate 'is otherwise suitable'. This arguably covers the more detailed criteria set out in the Fianna Fáil 2014 Bill and, in fact, gives JAAB greater flexibility to determine its own

34 Speaking in the Dáil on the occasion of the second stage debate of the Thirty-Fourth Amendment to the Constitution (Judicial Appointments) Bill 2013, the sponsor of the Bill, Deputy Niall Collins TD, described the approach of the Bill in the following terms: 'Fianna Fáil believes we can take a constructive approach to changing the system without the need for a referendum. Fianna Fáil has introduced legislation to tackle the long-standing problems in the judicial appointments process. Our Bill is based on the declaration of the European Network of Councils for the Judiciary on the recruitment and appointment of members of the Judiciary. At present, the law simply requires the Judicial Appointments Advisory Board to recommend to the Minister for Justice and Equality at least seven persons for appointment to that judicial office. The Minister may or may not accept the recommendation. Under our Bill, a new judicial appointments board would be established and the existing Judicial Appointments Advisory Board would be abolished. Instead of recommending seven persons for appointment to judicial office, the judicial appointments board would recommend for appointment by the Government candidates who it would certify as the best candidates for appointment to that judicial office. This would ensure high calibre candidates are drawn upon to fill judicial vacancies. This process would be fully open and transparent, in contrast to the behind the door approach taken to date with the Judicial Appointments Advisory Board.' (Deputy Niall Collins, Dáil Debate, 21 February 2014 – http://oireachtasdebates.oireachtas.ie/debates%20authoring/debateswebpack.nsf/takes/dail2014022100005?opendocument (accessed 30 June 2015)). 35 Section 8(2)(a–d), Judicial Appointments Bill 2014 – these criteria are presumed to have been drawn from the Report of the Working Group on 'Development of Minimum Judicial Standards' 2010–2011 and recommendation 2.5 of the European Network of Councils for the Judiciary, Development of Minimal Judicial Standards II Report 2011–2012 (the Dublin Declaration of 2012), which states 'There should be personal skills of a high quality, such as the ability to assume responsibility in the performance of his/her duties as well as qualities of equanimity, independence, persuasiveness, sensibility, sociability, integrity, unflappability and the ability to co-operate.'

assessment processes and standards. Legislation containing such specifics may limit the capacity of JAAB to set these standards and change them as it deems appropriate over time.

As with the 1995 Act, the Fianna Fáil 2014 Bill provides that a candidate should provide a tax clearance certificate in order to be nominated and must, if appointed, agree to undertake such course of training as may be deemed appropriate by the Chief Justice or the President of the Court to which they are appointed. As with the 1995 Act, the 2014 Bill prohibits canvassing of members of JAAB and demands confidentiality and independence of the Board in the performance of its functions.

The 2014 Bill differs from the 1995 Act in certain important respects. The Bill enables the Board to recommend sitting judges for judicial vacancies[36] and reduces to three the number of candidates to be recommended to government from which they may choose for appointment by the President. If the candidate chosen by government is not one who has been recommended by the Board, the government must issue a written reason as to why the recommendation was not followed and must also publish the Board's reasons for recommending the candidates.[37]

The 2014 Bill also establishes a separate procedure for the appointment of the Chief Justice; it provides that the Board recommend three names for the vacancy and its deliberations should not include the President of the High Court whose name may be submitted. The government then must consider the recommendations of the Board and must, on the appointment of the Chief Justice, publish whether or not the appointment was one of the three names recommended.[38]

Finally, the 2014 Bill places stronger statutory obligations on the Board to maintain records of its process, and to engage with candidates and, if requested, give written reasons as to why their application was not successful and not recommended to government.[39]

The 2014 Bill is a detailed and positive contribution to the development of judicial selection reform proposals. It contains practical suggestions to increase the robustness of the analysis of applicants for judicial vacancies and provides for more formalized processes for assessing judges for European courts. However, there should be no necessity to legislate for more detailed selection

36 Section 7, Judicial Appointments Bill 2014, but prohibits the recommendation of its own members for judicial vacancies. The 1995 Act provides that the Attorney General may be recommended but must not participate in the deliberations about their candidacy. The 1995 Act is silent on its application to other members of the JAAB, but in practice could only affect the candidacy of the representative of the Law Society or Ireland, the Bar Council of Ireland or the representative of the Minister for Justice as the 1995 Act does not apply to judicial appointments of sitting judges, whereas these appointments would fall under the rubric of the 2014 Bill (section 7). 37 Section 6 (5) and (8), Judicial Appointments Bill 2014. 38 Section 16, Judicial Appointments Bill 2014. 39 Section 15, Judicial Appointments Bill 2014.

criteria to be used by the JAAB – and the JAAB should retain the freedom to establish and publish these criteria as it sees fit over time. The Bill requires JAAB to provide written analysis of candidates to government along with the particulars of their CVs.

Table 5.3 below summarizes the different statutory approaches taken by the 1995 Act and the 2013 and 2014 Private Member's Bills.

Table 5.3: Differences between Courts and Court Officers Act 1995 and Sinn Féin and Fianna Fáil Private Member's Bills published in 2013–14

	Courts and Court Officers Act 1995	Sinn Féin Reform of Judicial Appointments Procedures Bill 2013	Fianna Fáil Judicial Appointments Bill 2014
Number of names to be recommended to government	On the request of the Minister, the JAAB to recommend at least seven names in respect of each vacancy for nomination by government for appointment to judicial office.	Reduces number of recommendations to three for nomination by government for appointment to judicial office.	Reduces number of recommendations to three for nomination by government for appointment to judicial office.
Is recommendation binding on government?	No requirement for government to seek recommendations.[40] Government may make an appointment of a person who has not been recommended by the JAAB but must publish a notice to this effect. Filling of a vacancy by the appointment of a judge of another court is not governed by the Act and government may make such appointments without reference to the JAAB.	No requirement for government to seek recommendations. Government may make an appointment of a person who has not been recommended by the JAAB without reference to that fact but must publish a report on why it has appointed the candidate chosen. The JAAB is to advise the government on the filling of a vacancy by the appointment of a judge of another court, but it is not specified how this is to be done.	Government is obliged to refer a judicial vacancy to JAAB and to seek three nominations for that vacancy. Government is obliged to consider the names recommended by the JAAB when advising the President on a judicial appointment. Government may make an appointment of a person who has not been recommended by the JAAB but must publish a notice to this effect.

40 In practice this is deemed politically necessary. As was shown in Chapter 3, the government has used the JAAB process for judicial vacancies, referring 92 per cent of vacancies to the JAAB for nominations.

Table 5.3: Differences between Courts and Court Officers Act 1995 *(contd)*

	Courts and Court Officers Act 1995	Sinn Féin Reform of Judicial Appointments Procedures Bill 2013	Fianna Fáil Judicial Appointments Bill 2014
Composition of the JAAB	Chief Justice (Chairperson), President of the High Court, President of the Circuit Court, President of the District Court, President of the Law Society of Ireland, President of the Bar Council of Ireland, Attorney General, three individuals nominated by the Minister for Justice. All members to be involved in all deliberations (except the Attorney General if discussing his or her candidacy for judicial office).	Chairperson of the Irish Human Rights and Equality Commission (Chairperson), Chief Justice, President of the High Court, President of the Circuit Court, President of the District Court, President of the Law Society of Ireland, President of the Bar Council of Ireland, Attorney General, three individuals nominated by the Minister for Justice. All members to be involved in all deliberations (except the Attorney General if discussing his or her candidacy for judicial office).	Chief Justice (Chairperson), President of the High Court, President of the Circuit Court, President of the District Court, President of the Law Society of Ireland, President of the Bar Council of Ireland, Attorney General, one individual nominated by the Minister for Justice, one individual nominated by the National Consumer Agency. All members to be involved in all deliberations, except the President of the High Court in relation to the appointment of a Chief Justice. Members of the Board may not be recommended by the Board, except the President of the High Court in relation to the appointment of a Chief Justice.
Role of the Attorney General on the JAAB and judicial selection process	Member of the JAAB who participates in the JAAB discussions and in government discussions on judicial selection.	No change to 1995 Act.	No change to 1995 Act.
Application of Act/Bill to judicial vacancies	Ordinary judge of the Supreme Court, ordinary judge of the High Court, ordinary judge of the Circuit Court, ordinary judge of the District Court. In making appointments to the Office of Chief Justice or President of another court, the government must first have regard to sitting members of the judiciary.	No change to 1995 Act.	Ordinary judge of the Supreme Court, President or ordinary judge of the High Court, President or ordinary judge of the Circuit Court, President or ordinary judge of the District Court, judge of the Court of Justice of the European Union, judge of the General Court of the European Union, judge of the European Court of Human Rights.

Table 5.3: Differences between Courts and Court Officers Act 1995 *(contd)*

	Courts and Court Officers Act 1995	Sinn Féin Reform of Judicial Appointments Procedures Bill 2013	Fianna Fáil Judicial Appointments Bill 2014
Criteria for recommendation of judicial candidates	In the opinion of the Board, the candidate has displayed in his or her practice as a barrister or solicitor a degree of competence and probity appropriate to and consistent with the appointment concerned. Is suitable on the grounds of character and temperament and is otherwise suitable.	No change to 1995 Act.	Solely on merit and capability.
Powers and processes of the JAAB	The Board may adopt such procedures as it thinks fit to carry out its functions under this Act (and may establish sub-committees of the Board to assist it) including advertise for applications for judicial appointment, require applicants to complete application forms, consult persons concerning the suitability of applicants, invite persons, identified by the Board, to submit their names for consideration by the Board, arrange for the interviewing of applicants who wish to be considered by the Board for appointment to judicial office, and do such other things as the Board considers necessary to enable it to discharge its functions.	No change to 1995 Act.	Shall publish a set of selection competencies for assessment of applicants for judicial office. Shall advertise for applications to judicial office. Shall require applicants to complete application form. Shall provide the government with reasons why recommended candidates are suitable for nomination and identify the best candidates that have applied. May conduct soundings on suitability of applicants. May invite persons to submit applications. May arrange for interviewing of applicants. May do such other things as the Board considers necessary to perform its functions.

Source: Courts and Court Officers Act 1995; Reform of Judicial Appointments Procedures Bill 2013; Judicial Appointments Bill 2014.

Oireachtas debate

The question of possible reform to the judicial selection system in Ireland was also considered by the Joint Oireachtas Committee on Justice, Defence and Equality in November 2014.[41] The Committee considered the judicial selection processes in operation since the institutional change of 1995 and possible areas for reform.[42] The issues that dominated the discussion were judicial diversity,[43] the operation of the JAAB[44] and the appropriate role of politicians in judicial selection.[45] This was the first occasion since the enactment of the Courts and

41 The discussion included the two opposition spokespersons on Justice who produced Private Member's Bills on judicial selection processes, Deputy Niall Collins of Fianna Fáil and Deputy Pádraig MacLochlainn of Sinn Féin. 42 The Committee decided to engage in this discussion at the suggestion of Senator Ivana Bacik: 'It was after hearing the three of them give presentations at the Law and Government conference in DCU that I felt we should invite them to come before the committee to explore this issue. It is in the context of the review of judicial appointments, which I hope this committee will feed into, because the witnesses have offered worthwhile insights.' (Senator Ivana Bacik, Joint Oireachtas Committee on Justice Defence and Equality, Discussion on Judicial Appointments, 26 Nov. 2014). 43 Senator Denis O'Donovan: 'On the ratio of women in the judiciary, I am a solicitor by profession and I am aware there are now more women than men who are qualified solicitors. As far as I know only one solicitor has ever been appointed to the High Court. In terms of the Circuit Court, the High Court and particularly the Supreme Court, unless one comes from the Bar Council one's chances of being appointed are slim to nil. There are some excellent solicitors with a great deal of experience who are being ignored for appointment and that is not necessarily for political reasons.' (Senator Denis O'Donovan, Joint Oireachtas Committee on Justice, Defence and Equality, Discussion on Judicial Appointments, 26 Nov. 2014).

Dr David Kenny: 'In terms of perspectives, diversity is very important because I believe judging is a dialogue between a group of people, and the assumptions and suppositions the judges have together end up influencing sentencing and everything else, including the way the people judge. While there are definitely questions for the Legislature in terms of whether a sentencing council is a good idea, the diversity of the people on the bench will inevitably alter the way people engage in issues like sentencing, because different perspectives will force the judicial dialogue to be broader and include different perspectives that previously would have been heard as irrelevant, beside the point or whatever else. When someone is a colleague and is telling you something you might not have taken very seriously, that will gradually change perceptions. Therefore, from sentencing all the way up to constitutional adjudication at the Supreme Court, diversity matters. I believe there are definitely questions in that regard.' (Dr David Kenny, Joint Oireachtas Committee on Justice, Defence and Equality, Discussion on Judicial Appointments, 26 Nov. 2014). 44 Senator Ivana Bacik: 'I read the Judicial Appointments Review Committee's report and was struck by what Dr Cahillane has referred to as self-perpetuation by the judiciary. That seems to be the danger of many of the recommendations the review committee has made. Dr Kenny also picked up on the report's suggestion of increasing the requirement for professional practice. It seems this is just picking more of the same rather than increasing diversity. In Dr Carroll MacNeill's presentation, she pointed out that the Judicial Appointments Advisory Board, JAAB, is not using the powers that are provided to it in the legislation. If one looks at the JAAB reports, one sees this straight away. For example, where there is a pool of perhaps 100 applicants for the District Court, rather than recommending seven names, which significantly narrows government's choice, the JAAB is recommending many more than seven.' (Senator Ivana Bacik, Joint Oireachtas Committee on Justice, Defence and Equality, Discussion on Judicial Appointments, 26 Nov. 2014). 45 Deputy Niall Collins: 'My view is that the

Court Officers Act 1995 in which the Joint Oireachtas Committee on Justice reviewed the processes of judicial selection and the operation of the 1995 Act. The Committee was surprised to learn that the JAAB had adopted substantially different institutional practices to those established in the 1995 Act.

This shows that more parliamentary oversight of the operation of statutory bodies is appropriate in monitoring institutional functioning. Legislators should review the operation of the legislation under their remit. Later in this chapter, there are a number of suggestions for procedural and statutory reforms of the judicial selection system in Ireland. These reforms retain, at their core, a reasonably strong role for the elected politicians of the law-making majority, which, it is suggested, is a democratic imperative. However, these suggestions also highlight the need for some political accountability of such politicians. If it is determined that political involvement in judicial selection is desirable, then it is important that the role of politicians is not limited to the ultimate selection of judges, but includes parliamentary monitoring of those processes over time. The Joint Oireachtas Committee on Justice is a forum where both the Minister for Justice, on behalf of the government, and the JAAB, as the independent statutory assessment body, may provide some account of the operation of the judicial selection model of the day.

2014 PROCESS CHANGES BY THE JAAB AND GOVERNMENT

On the same day that the submission of the Judicial Appointments Review Committee was submitted to the then Minister for Justice, the Chief Justice (and Chairperson of the JAAB) wrote to the Minister for Justice to inform him that the JAAB would henceforth begin to use its statutory powers to conduct interviews. This was reported in the Dáil Debate on the 34th Amendment to the Constitution Bill by the then Minister for State Paschal Donohoe:

> It should be remembered that the board is given complete freedom to establish its own processes. Indeed, it is given express statutory power to engage in certain functions to assist it in the performance of its critical task, including a remit to interview applicants for judicial office.

system needs to be reformed. It is not entirely broken; it has worked with a degree of merit, but certainly what we and the delegates have been saying points to some of its deficiencies, particularly on diversity. Ultimately, judges should be appointed by the government because there is then a layer of accountability and responsibility, to which governments have to live up. How to go about selecting the best candidates is where we come into the debate. Whenever political appointments are made, there will always be criticism, for example, in the case of the chair of the independent policing board who was appointed recently. I do not think one could have found a more independent or suitably qualified person, yet there was criticism of her appointment. Taking her as a candidate, one would go far and wide to find somebody more suitably qualified for the job and independent, yet there was criticism. There will always be criticism, which we have to accept as a starting point'. (Joint Oireachtas Committee on Justice,

> Unfortunately, this has not happened to date, but in a recent letter to the Minister, the Chief Justice said the board was now considering doing so, and the Minister welcomes this proposed initiative. The manner in which the board fulfils its statutory functions is, of course, the responsibility of the Chief Justice.[46] (Minister of State Paschal Donohoe, Dáil Debate, 21 February 2014)

This is an important development in the implementation by the JAAB of their statutory powers and, it is suggested, an unforeseen one because in the 2013 Annual Report of the JAAB, the Board gave no indication that its position on interviewing was likely to shift.

> The Board has also not availed of its power to arrange for the interviewing of applicants. There are serious practical obstacles to the Board conducting such a process routinely and generally the Board has sufficient information in particular which is provided by the applicants themselves to carry out its function in each instance. (Judicial Appointments Advisory Board Annual Report 2013, p. 15)

The communication by the Chief Justice to the Minister for Justice was the second indication by the JAAB that it would begin to use the power to interview provided by the 1995 Act (the first was in the Annual Report for 2003). There was some speculation as to whether the JAAB would immediately begin to use this new process in the assessment of judicial candidates, particularly given the very large number of judicial vacancies created by the establishment of the Court of Appeal in 2014.[47] However, in its Annual Report 2014, the JAAB noted that it has not to date availed of its power to arrange for the interviewing of applicants. Consistent with its earlier concerns regarding interviewing (expressed in Chapter 3), the Board observed that there were serious practical difficulties associated with conducting such a process[48] and that 'additional financial and human resources would be required to fully implement the relevant provision of the 1995 Act pertaining to the interviewing of applicants'.[49] This underlines the absolute necessity of the provision of more extensive professional recruitment supports to the JAAB to enable it to use its powers to greatest effect.[50]

Defence and Equality, Discussion on Judicial Appointments, 26 Nov. 2014). **46** This speech is reported slightly differently on the website of the Department of Justice in one material respect as follows: 'The manner in which the Board fulfils its statutory functions is, of course, the responsibility of the Chief Justice, who chairs the Board, and the other members of the Board.' http://www.justice.ie/en/JELR/Pages/SP14000045 (accessed 15 June 2015). **47** http://oireachtasdebates. oireachtas.ie/Debates%20 Authoring/DebatesWeb Pack.nsf/ committeetakes/JUJ2014112600011?opendocument (accessed 6 July 2015). **48** Judicial Appointments Advisory Board Annual Report 2014, p. 17. **49** Judicial Appointments Advisory Board Annual Report 2014, p. 6. **50** A second change was an attempt to effect a

Within government, a change to the judicial appointment process was introduced in 2013. This change involved the establishment of a process in the Office of the Attorney General by which a sitting judge could signal to the Attorney General that they were interested in being appointed to another position on the judiciary. This arose because of an ongoing concern that in the absence of some formalized system to provide such a facility for judges, representations were being made informally to a range of members of government, who were not necessarily pleased to have received them and who had concerns about the appropriateness of such representations having regard to the separation of government and the judiciary. But in the absence of such a process, how does a judge properly communicate such a sentiment to government?

> I was concerned about promotions because the judiciary are rightly independent of the executive. There was no official or unofficial mechanism around promotions. You would have had a small, a very very small number of members of the judiciary who one might meet on social occasions who would very expressly make it known to you as Minister that they would like to get promoted to a higher court and I thought it was an inappropriate procedure. I was concerned about the implications of it for judicial independence, as well as the position that it put the Minister in. If anyone so approached me I always treated them courteously but I was never influenced in any recommendation I brought to Cabinet by that type of approach. One could have taken a perspective on it that that type of approach was inappropriate, on the other hand I was very conscious that no real mechanism existed and that was unfair to members of the judiciary. I wanted to create a different structure that couldn't be suggested to compromise either the judiciary or Minister in any shape or form. I didn't like the idea that it could at some point be interpreted as a judge trying to curry favour with a Minister, I thought that was very dangerous and taking the number of judges who are appointed to conduct inquiries, there were inherent dangers in that system.
>
> I think the judges are in a very difficult position on this. If you are appointed to a particular court and you've been in it for five or ten years and you work extremely hard and you are a good judge, you're good at what you do, if there is a possibility of promotion, it shouldn't simply be

slight reduction in the number of names provided to government in respect of judicial vacancies. Multiple unofficial reports suggest that the JAAB in the summer 2014 sought to return to recommending a smaller number of names to government. The institutional view that there is a difficulty with the legislation in this regard persists and that in adhering more closely to the number prescribed in the Courts and Court Officers Act 1995 the JAAB may be open to judicial review by judicial applicants.

> a matter of luck or because the Minister for Justice of the day happens to have been in your court at some stage and believes you to be competent or because other people have been telling you what a good person you are – there has to be some formal mechanism. I had some concerns around the JAAB doing it because as members of the judiciary are on the JAAB and as the Presidents of the different courts are on the JAAB I didn't want a member of judiciary within any particular court level to feel embarrassed by making that application to a body which included the President of their court. And if their name wasn't put forward could that be seen as a vote of no confidence in them? Giving the Attorney a role in this removed the possibility of somebody being embarrassed in front of their peers in the JAAB and removed the difficulty for a judge in feeling there was something irregular in the manner in which they otherwise had to approach people. It would have come back to me that there were judges who were obviously aware that this happened and they themselves regarded it as completely inappropriate and something they would never engage in. So this was something that the Attorney and I discussed and we put in place an informal mechanism. (Interview with Alan Shatter, Dublin, 25 June 2015)

The new process provided that if a serving judge wished to express interest in another judicial position, such as one on another court or in the Office of President of a court, then the judge should write in confidence to the Attorney General, enclosing an up-to-date curriculum vitae.[51] This was a significant institutional development that formalized a process by which sitting judges could communicate with government. Prior to this, judges who wished to be so considered either chose to remain silent, and risked being overlooked for such positions, or found some way to informally communicate their wishes to the Attorney General or a member of the government, which risked being an inappropriate communication between the judiciary and executive. While government was statutorily obliged to consider sitting judges of a given court for the position of President of a court, there was no manner in which interest could be expressed to government by members of a court.

51 In October 2013, the Chief Justice wrote to all members of the judiciary regarding elevation to higher courts and senior judicial appointments. The Chief Justice issued guidance, stating that if a serving judge wished to express an interest in another judicial position such as elevation to a higher court, or appointment as President of a court when a vacancy arises, then expressions of interest should be made in writing by way of letter, and not otherwise, and sent, in confidence, to the Attorney General. An up-to-date curriculum vitae should be attached to the letter. (Judicial Appointments Review Committee, Preliminary Submission to the Department of Justice and Equality's Public Consultation on the Judicial Appointments Process, January 2014, pp 50–1).

A second institutional change was introduced by government at this time which was the establishment of a new system for choosing judges for appointments to various European courts. This new process was used in the assessment of candidates and the making of recommendations for the European Court of Human Rights and the European Court of Justice in 2015.[52] The new process was primarily established because of a concern that such European court appointments were outside of any formal judicial selection mechanism and that Irish nominees may not succeed at the next stage of assessment unless there was a more rigorous and transparent domestic selection process to choose the name or names to be recommended by government for appointment to the European Court of Justice or the European Court of Human Rights.[53] This is a real concern, the process is one that carries risks for member governments – the Article 255 panel exercises a thorough jurisdiction: 22 per cent of candidatures assessed by the panel since its establishment in 2010 have been found to be unfavorable,[54] with other senior European judicial nominees finding it better to withdraw their candidacy before the Committee.

The new process provided that vacancies would be advertised and applications sought for consideration. Applicants are required to submit a CV. A small panel is established on an ad hoc basis in the Office of the Attorney General, comprised of a retired judge, the Director General of the Office of the Attorney General and one other person. A shortlist of names is considered by the panel. Applicants may be interviewed. The panel will then make its recommendation to government. In the case of the European Court of Human Rights, three names are submitted by government to the Council of Europe which makes the decision on who to appoint. In the case of proposed appointments to the European Court of Justice, candidates are recommended to government who may then put forward a single candidate for consideration by a suitability committee established under the Treaty on the Functioning of the European Union for the purpose of assessing the candidature of proposed nominees.[55]

52 http://www.justice.ie/en/JELR/Pages/PB15000069 (accessed 17 Nov. 2015). 53 'There was no mechanism available – you might have well have pulled a name out of a hat and this was something I wanted to change and include in the legislation. It was who knew who and so on. We're fortunate in that very good people have been appointed to the European courts, but it's quite bizarre that this was a free floating thing that didn't feature in any formal structure at all and the idea was to get away from that.' (Interview with Alan Shatter, Dublin, 25 June 2015.) 54 Third Activity Report (December 2013) published by the Panel provided for by Article 255 of the Treaty on the Functioning of the European Union, p. 9. 55 Article 255 of the Treaty on the Functioning of the European Union establishes a panel to 'give an opinion on candidates' suitability to perform the duties of Judge and Advocate-General of the Court of Justice and the General Court before the

AN APPROACH TO FURTHER INSTITUTIONAL DEVELOPMENT TO JUDICIAL SELECTION IN IRELAND

Following the Review in 2014, the Minister and government made statements to the effect that they would consider what changes may now be appropriate.[56]

> A report on the consultation process that is being finalized by my Department will inform the provisions of the forthcoming judicial appointments Bill, which will reform and update judicial appointments procedures. I intend to submit this Bill to the Government and publish it later this year. (Minister Frances Fitzgerald, Dáil Éireann, 2 April 2015)

It is clear that the political system in Ireland may be open to further reform of the judicial selection system. Refinements of the existing system were proposed in the 2016 election manifestos of the Labour Party and Sinn Féin, but neither of the large political parties made reference to it. It is suggested that there are a number of procedural reforms and supports that can be provided to the JAAB to enhance its institutional operation prior to considering substantive structural change to the judicial selection process in Ireland. What is currently in law in Ireland is a good hybrid judicial selection system involving both political accountability through democratically elected governments and an important element of independent screening that governments have, since its establishment, consistently used. There is a danger that in rushing to substantially overhaul the structural arrangements for judicial selection, an opportunity to incrementally, but substantially, enhance the institutional functioning of this hybrid system may be missed. It is clear from the debate of 2013–14 that there is strong interest and multifaceted concern about the quality of the judicial selection process in Ireland. Before

governments of the Member States make the appointments referred to in Articles 253 and 254' of that Treaty. See Activity Reports published by the Panel provided for by Article 255 of the Treaty on the Functioning of the European Union. **56** Minister Frances Fitzgerald: 'While the Judicial Appointments Advisory Board that we currently have was a model of best practice, it would be timely to review the operation of the judicial appointments system to ensure it reflects current best practice, is open, transparent and accountable and promotes diversity. We got a significant response to our call for submissions. We have those submissions now. They cover many different areas, including criteria for eligibility and the appointment process. A report on the consultation process that is being finalized by my Department will inform the provisions of the forthcoming judicial appointments Bill, which will reform and update judicial appointments procedures. I intend to submit this Bill to the Government and publish it later this year. The review and reform of this area which is critical to the functioning of our system of justice provides an opportunity to determine what type of system can best respond to the expectations and needs of a modern state.' (Minister Frances Fitzgerald, Dáil Debate, 2 April 2015, http://oireachtasdebates.oireachtas.ie/debates%20authoring/debateswebpack.nsf/takes/dail2015040200009#G003 00 (accessed 24 June 2015)).

proposing an approach to development of the judicial selection process in Ireland, this section summarizes what matters should be of concern to policy makers engaged in further development of the process and what matters are, it is gently suggested, perhaps not as problematic as suggested in the debate of 2013–14.

Problems with judicial selection system in Ireland

1. The problem is a perception of political party influence on judicial appointments

It is clear that there are ongoing concerns about politics in judicial selection in Ireland. This is evident from the analysis of the submissions to the Department of Justice and the Private Members Bills of 2013 and 2014 described in this chapter, and other academic and civil society analysis that followed the implementation of the 1995 Act.[57] The consensus that has emerged is that judicial selection is overly politicized. Yet, academic research evidence actually shows that over the period 1969 to 2004 a decreasing number of judges self-identify as having links to the political parties in government at the time of their appointment.[58] Notwithstanding this, the reality is that there is a perception that judicial appointments are 'political' but precisely what is meant by this has not been explained.

- Does it mean that judicial appointment is not possible without being a member or supporter of a political party that is in government?
- Does it mean that most people who receive judicial appointments are members or supporters of a political party that is in government?
- Does this charge apply equally to all judges of all courts?
- Does it mean that people who are judged to be of insufficient calibre are appointed to the judiciary because of their links to a political party that is in government?
- Does it mean that the selection of Court Presidents or judges who are promoted are judges who have in the past been members or supporters of a political party in government or who have made decisions that are perceived to have been in some way favourable to a political party that is in government?[59]

57 Carroll (2005b: 188), Irish Council for Civil Liberties, *Justice matters: independence, accountability and the Irish judiciary* (Dublin: Irish Council for Civil Liberties, 2007: 98). 58 Bartholomew (1971); Carroll (2005 a and b). 59 'It has been alleged that there is political interference in how our Judiciary operates. I want Deputy Ross to give me an example of this. He referred to the fact that an accident has never happened. I want an example of an accident that might have happened. I suggest that an accident has not happened because we have an independent Judiciary which has exercised its powers throughout the history of our State independently of political influence from this or any other Government. In the remainder of my contribution I will address the substance of the

Or does it mean something else entirely? Is the charge that governments make political appointments extended to the political decision-making of governments in appointing people of a particular religion, gender or race or people of a particular ideological or social persuasion? Another form of political decision-making may be choosing candidates with specific legal experience. This may be motivated by perceived public concerns about, for example, inefficiencies in family law or an insensitivity in relation to victims of sexual abuse in criminal trials. Yet political decision-making of this type is broadly accepted as legitimate and an appropriate response by the law-making majority to these public concerns. These types of political decision-making tend not to feature in the debate about politics in judicial selection. The challenge for policy makers is how to retain sufficient political involvement in judicial appointments to enable this legitimate political activity in judicial selection, but remove decisions perceived to be based on political party allegiance.

What specifically are the underlying concerns about politics in judicial selection in Ireland, why is this problematic and what institutional changes can be effected to reduce its influence? It is suggested that when we talk about politics in judicial appointments what is specifically meant is that where a person is appointed to the judiciary, or promoted within the judiciary, and that, person has a close association with the political party in government at the time a charge of political appointment may be levelled. This is generally done subtly and without too close a reference to the individual in question, but the cumulative impact of such appointments or perceived appointments is what leads to the charge that judicial appointments in Ireland are political.

The reality is that some appointments in Ireland are political. There are clear examples of people who, having met the eligibility criteria and been recommended by the JAAB, have been appointed and who have had a clear and open association with the political party that appointed them. The question in this instance is whether they would have been appointed in the absence of that political connection. Could they have been appointed by an

Bill introduced by Deputy Ross but I still want him to provide an example that would underpin his claims. Since 1922 we have had a robust and independent judiciary but apparently Deputy Ross and his Independent colleagues believe they are the only people who can be trusted to appoint our judges. Members of the Irish judiciary point out that they are ranked among the most independent in the world. I assume Deputy Ross is not saying otherwise in respect of our judges.' (Minister of State Paschal Donohoe, Dáil Debate, 21 February 2014). Deputy Shane Ross TD: 'We are lucky that we have not as yet had a very obvious accident in which a judge has made what is quite obviously a political judgment. That is true. I cannot point to one. It would be very difficult to prove that a judge had made a decision because he or she was a member of a political party and that affected the verdict. It cannot be proved because it is in the mind. It is obviously a possibility and a system which is vulnerable to that criticism.' (Deputy Shane Ross, Dáil Debate, 21 February 2014, http://oireachtasdebates.oireachtas.ie/debates%20authoring/debateswebpack.nsf/takes/dail2014022100005?opendocument (accessed 30 June 2015)).

entirely independent selection process? The submissions of the JARC and the ICCL make clear that membership of a political party is not in itself a problem, because it if was it would be an unjustifiable restriction of an individual's political participation as citizens. So how do we deal with the simple reality that there will be lawyers in Ireland who are also supporters of political parties? How do we ensure that lawyers who are not supporters of political parties have an equal opportunity for judicial appointment?

The way to manage this is to establish an independent body to screen judicial applications and make recommendations to government as to who would be the most suitable for appointment to a given position and for the government to consistently use this system as the basis for the judicial selection decisions. This is the system that was established in 1995. Although the government is not obliged in statute to refer vacancies to this system, the evidence shows that it was the overwhelming practice. Once a person is recommended by the JAAB the government should have complete political cover in nominating that person for appointment. The crucial thing about such a system is that, even at its present construction of seven names per vacancy, it greatly reduces the discretion of the government in choosing judges. However, as we have seen, the reality of the operation of that system is that the JAAB, at its own initiative, has recommended greatly more names than was envisaged by the legislation, providing (at least in theory) compete political cover to the governments since 1995 in making their appointments. Yet the charge of political appointments persists and this, as is noted in the debate of 2013–14, is said to undermine confidence in the judicial system generally.

The tension is that where any person is in a decision-making position and has to choose between two or more candidates who have been determined to be of objectively equal standing, that person must make a decision based on certain subjective grounds. The evidence in this book shows that the decision-makers in judicial selection, both on the JAAB and in government, are interested in ensuring that good quality candidates are appointed to the bench. At each stage, they have to make certain subjective assessments. For example, presented with two senior lawyers, both having broadly similar qualifications and comparable professional experience, how does one choose the 'better' judicial candidate? Even applying a detailed competency based assessment will result in cases showing that two candidates, who may have different technical or personal strengths, are equally meritorious and both entirely suitable for judicial appointment. Even with a 'merit' principle enshrined in legislation, most decisions will still require a measure of subjective assessment. For example, 'Nuala' is just obviously better intellectually at dealing with technical matters of commercial law but she can be personally very acerbic or difficult. 'Nora' has good general legal experience and her temperament is solid and reliable with a broad range of witnesses and litigants. Somebody has to make a decision between Nuala and Nora.

The research evidence in this book is that both in Cabinet and on the JAAB, those decisions tend to be made based on the personal knowledge of the candidates held by the decision-makers. It is suggested that the real determinant in judicial selection in Ireland is not necessarily a connection to party politics, but a personal or professional connection to the relevant decision-maker. Party politics is a relevant factor in judicial selection in Ireland, but it is only one of several factors in government decision-making. What is actually more important is perceived competence and 'being known' to the decision-makers.

2. The problem for judicial aspirants is an opaque process

From the perspective of the judicial aspirant, the judicial selection system in Ireland is truly opaque. The applicant prepares and submits the application form which is acknowledged by the JAAB. They receive no subsequent formal communication from the JAAB. If they are ultimately recommended by the JAAB and chosen for judicial appointment, they will be contacted by the Minister for Justice following the Cabinet meeting that confirms their nomination. Otherwise, they receive no formal (but occasionally informal) communication in relation to the success or otherwise of their application. In addition, the candidate has no opportunity, in practice, to participate in or contribute to the deliberations relating to their application.

Judicial applicants should have better information about the standards of assessment used by the JAAB at each court level. They should also have the opportunity to directly contribute to their own assessment either through interviews held with shortlisted candidates or other assessment tools involving the judicial candidate.

As we have seen, the JAAB has broad statutory powers to conduct interviews or take soundings about individual applicants. It has actually never conducted any such interviews. The reasons given have been practical difficulties relating to confidentiality and concerns about what could or should be asked in those interviews. The JAAB has used its powers to take soundings to obtain more information on candidates. From the perspective of the candidate, this means that persons unknown may be asked their professional or personal opinion of the candidate and the candidate has no right of reply.

In its submission to the Review of the Appointment Process for Judicial Selection the JARC noted that

> applications for appointments follow what might at least in the abstract appear a surprising pattern. The largest number of applications is for positions at the lower level of the judiciary, and the smallest number for appointment to the higher courts. For example, in 2012 there were 8 vacancies in the District Court which attracted 193 applicants. There were 7 vacancies in the Circuit Court which attracted 155 applicants,

while there were two vacancies in the High Court which attracted 20 applicants. (JARC, p. 10)

There is some evidence of a pattern of self-selection by judicial candidates. There are more applicants per vacancy for District Court positions than High Court positions. This may simply be an interesting example of self-selection by members of the legal profession who understand their likely prospects for judicial advancement. There is a smaller cohort of lawyers who are likely to be of a quality suitable for appointment to the High Court. This pattern, which is repeated throughout the Annual Reports of the JAAB from 1995 to 2013, may be evidence that lawyers decide whether to put themselves forward based on their own assessment of their likely chances of appointment.[60] An alternative explanation is that fewer lawyers actually want to be High Court rather than District Court judges. We can see in Table 5.4 that the numbers of applicants for vacancies support the point raised by the JARC.

Table 5.4: Number of vacancies and applications considered by the JAAB, 1996–2014[61]

	Vacancies	Applications	Applications per vacancy
Supreme Court	13	26	2
Court of Appeal[62]	1	24	24
High Court	62	765	12
Circuit Court	59	2834	48
District Court	59	5320	90

Source: Judicial Appointments Advisory Board Annual Reports, 2002–14.

As is shown in Table 5.4 above there is a very large body of applications to be considered by the JAAB. It is clear that the JAAB needs professional institutional supports if it is to engage in robust and appropriate analysis of each candidate, even acknowledging that some candidates are duplicated in these figures.

There is also evidence that solicitors took a similarly self-selecting approach to judicial vacancies on the High Court and Supreme Court in the period after

60 Appendix (ii) of the Judicial Appointments Advisory Board Annual Report 2014 lists the number of applications per vacancy considered at each board meeting since 1995. Based on our understanding of the procedure adopted by the JAAB where applications remain valid for one year, it is expected there will be some duplication of applicants per vacancy. They are not necessarily different applicants considered at each meeting. The variation in numbers of applications for the different courts is a useful demonstration of the point made by the JARC in regard to self-selection. **61** Appendix (ii) of the Judicial Appointments Advisory Board Annual Report 2014, pp 22–4. **62** A new Court of Appeal was established in 2014.

2002 when they first became eligible for direct appointment to these courts.[63] The Courts and Court Officers Act 2002 provides for the direct appointment of solicitors to the superior courts. This statute considerably widens the pool of individuals entitled to apply to the JAAB for consideration for appointment to the superior courts. Despite this theoretical extension to solicitors, in practice it is limited by section 8 of the 2002 Act. This section requires that the candidates that are recommended to the Minister by the JAAB are individuals who have 'an appropriate knowledge of the decisions, and an appropriate knowledge and appropriate experience of the practice and procedure, of the Supreme Court and the High Court'. Section 8(7) (b) (ii) spells out this requirement by instructing the JAAB, in determining whether such an appropriate knowledge exists, to have regard to the nature and extent of the practice of the person concerned, insofar as it relates to his or her personal conduct of proceedings in the Supreme Court and the High Court, whether as an advocate or as a solicitor instructing counsel in such proceedings. In its 2006 Annual Report, the JAAB noted that the purpose of this provision seems to be to ensure that solicitors appointed to the Supreme and High Courts are sufficiently conversant with practice and procedure in the superior courts.[64]

Analysis of the number of applications made by practising solicitors showed that the introduction of this change in 2002 resulted in an initial surge in the number of applications being made by solicitors to the JAAB, but that this declined in the years that followed (Carroll, 2007). Despite solicitors constituting approximately 80 per cent of practising lawyers in Ireland eligible for appointment, this trend continued up to 2014 when there was a second surge in applications from solicitors. This may be as a result of a concerted effort on the part of the Law Society of Ireland to encourage solicitors to apply for the large number of High Court vacancies that were anticipated as a result of the establishment of the Court of Appeal.[65]

63 Carroll (2007) http://www.lawsociety.ie/Documents/Gazette/Gazette%202007/August September2007.pdf (accessed 30 June 2015). 64 Judicial Appointments Advisory Board Annual Report 2006, p. 10. 65 'Now is the time to act if you, or any solicitor colleague that you know, have ever considered applying to become a judge of the High Court or of the Court of Appeal. Never in the history of the State have anything even remotely close to the number of such positions been in the process of appointment, at one time, as is the case today. Indeed it is difficult to envisage such an opportunity ever occurring again. No less than seven appointments to the High Court, together with three appointments to the Court of Appeal, are open for suitably qualified applicants at present. Thursday, 11 September 2014 at 4.00pm has been set by the Judicial Appointments Advisory Board as the deadline for receipt of applications ... In my President's message in the April 2014 issue of the Society's Gazette, I pointed out that of the 49 High and Supreme Court appointments made since solicitors became eligible in 2002, just four of the Judges appointed were solicitors. Throughout this period solicitors have constituted in excess of 80 per cent of the practising lawyers in this jurisdiction. When the Society has raised this shocking imbalance as an issue over the years with successive Ministers for Justice and others we have been told that solicitor candidates for appointment to the High Court and the Supreme Court have

Tables 5.5 below shows the percentage of applications coming from solicitors at each of the court levels.[66]

Table 5.5: Applications by solicitors for High Court, Circuit Court and District Court vacancies

Year	2002	2003	2004	2005	2006	2007	2008	2009	2010	2011	2012	2013	2014
High Court applications by solicitors (%)	37	No vacancy	26	31	25	27	20	No vacancy	15	21	25	21	46
Circuit Court applications by solicitors (%)	57	60	57	61	No vacancy	50	70	36	No vacancy	64	48	49	49
District Court applications by solicitors (%)	96	94	87	92	84	80	81	88	88	88	82	87	82

Source: Judicial Appointments Advisory Board Annual Reports, 2002–14.

The JAAB performs an important decision-making function that has a direct bearing on the career prospects of an individual applying for constitutional and statutory positions. Its processes should be more transparent and engaged with candidates.

3. The problem for government is quality of information and ensuring sufficient choice

In making decisions relating to judicial appointments the evidence is that the government has, over many years, made its decisions from the recommendations of the JAAB, except in the cases where it has promoted a judge from another court. In order to make this decision the government is provided with

been insufficient in number. There is no doubt, in the view of the Society, that a great many practising solicitors would have all the professional and personal qualities required to make excellent Judges of the Superior Courts. If you believe you are such a solicitor, there may never be an opportunity like this again to put your name forward. If you are interested, now is the time to act.' John P. Shaw, President of the Law Society of Ireland, E-Bulletin, 3 September 2014; https://www. lawsociety.ie/Documents/Gazette/Gazette%202014/April2014.pdf (accessed 6 July 2015). **66** Supreme Court vacancies are not included because of the overwhelming trend for the government to promote judges of the High Court to fill such vacancies, with only two exceptions since 2000.

a list of suitable candidates and their CVs by the JAAB. What additional information or value could the JAAB provide to assist government in making decisions beyond the simple provision of CVs?

Properly supported and resourced, the JAAB could offer the government a much deeper analysis of the recommended candidates and their attributes. The JAAB could assess and provide comment on an applicant's technical skills and experience or evidence of their temperament and character. It would also be interesting to get a direct report from the lay members of the JAAB who have, through interviews or other interactions, had an opportunity to form a personal view of the candidates.

4. The problem for the JAAB is the absence of professional institutional supports to enable more rigorous assessment processes

Judicial selection commissions in other jurisdictions employ a range of tools to assess the suitability of judicial candidates. In Chapter 4 we saw evidence of the types of professional recruitment supports that are provided to these judicial screening commissions. We also saw the level of institutional support that is provided to resource the activities of these commissions.

Since its establishment the JAAB has operated on an extremely limited institutional basis with little secretariat or other administrative or financial support to assist it in exercising its very broad statutory powers and administrative demands. We have seen evidence in Chapter 3 of the difficulty faced by members of the JAAB who wanted to introduce more rigorous assessment of candidates including an interview process. The JAAB has now said it will begin such a process but notes that there remain the same practical difficulties.[67] Other appropriate evaluation tools used elsewhere include interviews or the use of role-playing in assessment centres. The use of these tools can only occur with specific professional recruitment input and expertise.

5. The problem for policy makers is institutional drift

It is problematic for policy makers when bodies established by law do not operate the way legislators thought they would. When the process change in the JAAB occurred in the early 2000s, there is no evidence that the government questioned this change or made objections to it. The suspicion may be that the government was very pleased by this process change that widened its discretion in judicial selection almost to pre-1995 levels. Such an example of institutional drift should have triggered some response either by government or by the Oireachtas. Had members of the Oireachtas been aware of the change it is likely that it would have prompted some response, perhaps in the form of a Private Member's Bill to correct the anomaly that permitted this process change. This raises reasonable questions about post-legislative scrutiny by the political system of the operation of statutory bodies and their processes.

67 Judicial Appointments Advisory Board Annual Report 2014, p. 17.

The operation of the JAAB is an important example of institutional drift for policy makers interested in further reform of the judicial selection process and for policy makers involved in institutional design generally. The institutional design of the JAAB had certain weaknesses that may not have been anticipated. This capacity for institutional drift was facilitated by the drafting of the legislation which provides that the JAAB is to recommend at least seven names in respect of each vacancy. This allows a broad range of interpretations. One interesting interpretation of the Courts and Court Officers Act 1995 with regard to institutional drift was made in the submission of the Bar Council of Ireland:

> As pointed out in the invitation for public submission, specifying a minimum number of recommendations rather than a maximum number of recommendations may result in long lists of candidates being sent to the Minister for consideration. (Bar Council of Ireland, 2014, p. 9)

This institutional drift is also problematic due to the lack of transparency. It also raises important questions for policy makers engaged in any proposed changes to the judicial selection regime. For example, in the future, how much interpretive flexibility should be given in statute to an independent board designed to operate at arm's length from the legislature without incurring the sort of institutional drift that has been evident in the JAAB? What post-legislative review structures should be in place to enable ongoing parliamentary oversight of the operation of bodies created by statute? How should the judicial selection system be best improved based on how it has actually operated rather than how it is perceived it has operated?

6. The problem is *not* a threat to judicial independence

Judicial independence is a crucial element of constitutional democracy and should be protected with vigilance.[68] Judicial selection is the point that marks the end of the direct interaction between an individual judge and the political system, unless the judge is seeking re-appointment, promotion or reconfirmation.[69] The World Economic Forum Global Competitiveness Reports of

68 See, in particular, the Preface and Chapter 32 of Shetreet, S. (ed.) (2014) *The culture of judicial independence; rule of law and world peace* (Boston: Martinus Nijhoff-Brill).
69 Examples of links between judicial selection and judicial behaviour are considered in the extensive literature on US judicial elections including Hall, M. (1992), 'Electoral politics and strategic voting in State Supreme Courts'; Huber, Gregory A. and Sanford, Gordon C. (2004), 'Accountability and coercion: is justice blind when it runs for office?' all in Epstein, L. (2013) *The economics of judicial behaviour* (Edward Elgar: Cheltenham); Unah, R., 'Race and death sentencing' in McGuire, K. (ed.) *New direction in judicial politics* (Routledge: New York); Hall, M. (1995) 'Justices as representatives: elections and judicial politics in the American States'. *American Politics Quarterly* 23 (October): 485–503; Huber, G. and Sanford, G. (2004) 'Accountability and coercion: is justice blind when it runs for office?' in

2013–14 and 2014–15[70] credit New Zealand as having the most independent judiciary globally. As we saw in Chapter 1, New Zealand and Australia have a system of judicial selection in which government has greatest power and discretion to choose its preferred candidates, with no role for independent judicial selection commissions. England and Wales, which has the least such discretion for government in judicial selection of the jurisdictions assessed in Chapter 1, was placed behind Ireland (fourth) at sixth in the world in terms of judicial independence.

What is important for judicial independence is that judges can make individual decisions free from external influence. This might include political influence, the influence of legal practitioners or other judges, the threat of financial hardship that could be exploited, or the impact of public comment by other public officials or representatives.[71]

The role of the political majority in the selection of judges is an important international principle and should not be diminished or overly criticized, especially by the judiciary which is itself an agent of interest in the debate about institutional rules governing judicial selection. Judicial selection is the moment at which the courts and the political system most visibly intersect (Volcansek, 2007). It is the link between the judiciary and the people (All-Party Oireachtas Committee on the Constitution, 1999). The Mount Scopus International Standards of Judicial Independence, which consolidate and develop international principles of judicial independence dating back to 1982,[72] make clear that the role of elected governments in judicial selection is legitimate.

Epstein, L. (2013) *The economics of judicial behaviour*; Sanford, G. and Huber, A. (2007) 'The effect of electoral competitiveness on incumbent behavior', *Quarterly Journal of Political Science*, 2 (May): 107–38. **70** World Economic Forum Global Competitiveness Report 2013–14, 2014–15. **71** Murray (2014) summarizes the four tenets of judicial independence as being security of tenure, financial security, the institutional independence of the courts with respect to matters of administration bearing directly on the exercise of the judicial function, and adjudicative independence, or the freedom of judges to perform their adjudicative role without interference from the other branches of government (Murray, B. (2014) 'Judges: institutional independence and financial security' in Ruane, B., O'Callaghan, J. and Barniville, D. (eds), *Law and government: a tribute to Rory Brady* (Dublin: Round Hall), p. 73). **72** Including the New Delhi Minimum Standards on Judicial Independence 1982, the Montréal Universal Declaration on the Independence of Justice 1983, the UN Basic Principles of Judicial Independence 1985 and the long series of sets of other international rules and standards relating to judicial independence and the right to a fair trial; and the Burgh House Principles of Judicial Independence in International Law (for the international judiciary). 'Inspiration has also been drawn from the Tokyo Law Asia Principles; Council of Europe statements on judicial independence, particularly the Recommendation of the Committee of Ministers to Member States on the independence, efficiency and role of judges by the Council of Europe 1998, the Bangalore Principles of Judicial Conduct November 2002, and the American Bar Association's revision of its ethical standards for judges.' International Project of Judicial Independence of the International Association of Judicial Independence and World Peace – http://www.jiwp.org/#!mt-scopus-standards/c14de (accessed 17 Nov. 2015).

Mount Scopus International Standards of Judicial Independence

Key principles on judicial appointment

2.4. Judicial appointments and promotions by the Executive are not inconsistent with judicial independence as long as they are in accordance with Principles 4.
2.14. The principle of democratic accountability should be respected and therefore it is legitimate for the legislature to play a role in judicial appointments and central administration of justice provided that due consideration is given to the principle of judicial independence.

4. TERMS AND NATURE OF JUDICIAL APPOINTMENTS
4.1. The method of judicial selection shall safeguard against judicial appointments for improper motives and shall not threaten judicial independence.
4.2. a) The principle of democratic accountability should be respected and therefore it is legitimate for the Executive and the Legislature to play a role in judicial appointments provided that due consideration is given to the principle of Judicial Independence.
b) The recent trend of establishing judicial selection boards or commissions in which members or representatives of the Legislature, the Executive, the Judiciary and the legal profession take part, should be viewed favourably, provided that a proper balance is maintained in the composition of such boards or commissions of each of the branches of government.
4.3. Judicial appointments should generally be for life, subject to removal for cause and compulsory retirement at an age fixed by law at the date of appointment.
4.3.1. Retirement age shall not be reduced for existing judges.
4.4. Promotion of judges shall be based on objective factors, in particular merit, integrity and experience.
4.5. Judicial appointments and promotions shall be based on transparency of the procedures and standards and shall be based on professional qualifications, integrity, ability and efficiency.
4.6. Judges should not be appointed for probationary periods except in legal systems in which appointments of judges do not depend on having practical experience in the profession as a condition of appointment, and provided that permanent appointment will be granted on merit.
4.7. The institution of temporary judges should be avoided as far as possible except where there exists a long historic democratic tradition.
4.8. Part-time judges should be appointed only with proper safeguards secured by law.
4.9. The number of the members of the highest court should be fixed, with the exception of courts modeled after the courts of cassion, and in the case of all courts, should not be altered for improper motives.
4.10. Legislatures should formulate special procedures for the appointment of Chief Justices and Presidents of courts.

Ireland is a stable constitutional democracy that respects and protects the rule of law and international evidence shows it to be a global leader in the independence of its courts and judicial processes. The judicial selection system has been unchanged in statute since 1995. During this period both domestic and international observers have noted the independence of the Irish judiciary.[73]

73 Constitution Review Group (1996); All-Party Oireachtas Committee on the Constitution

So why then was a concern for judicial independence such a strong feature of the political debate in 2013–14, in particular in the submission of the JARC? It is suggested that the context in which the JARC submission was prepared sheds light on the weight placed by the JARC on the potential threat to judicial independence in Ireland posed by the judicial selection system. The period 2011–13 was characterized as one of unprecedented tension between the government and the judiciary. This tension was largely caused by a series of institutional changes to the judiciary effected in response to the severe economic difficulties of the day, and included a referendum to reduce the pay of serving members of the judiciary, changes to pension arrangements for judges and a pay differential between judges on the same court.[74] The net effect of these changes was that taking a judicial appointment became a severely different economic prospect.

> The Committee is concerned that recent changes to pension provisions may have little fiscal benefit and may disproportionately deter excellent candidates from applying for judicial office. Since 2008 there have been seven distinct changes to the pay and pension provision of judges, all of them adverse. The cumulative effect is severe. The take home pay of a new High Court Judge for example is 50 per cent of an equivalent in 2008, and is now for example very considerably less in gross and even more so in net terms than comparators in other common law countries. (Judicial Appointments Review Committee, 2014, p. 66)

The effect of this, according to the Judicial Appointments Review Committee, was that the traditional leaders of the legal profession, those who were regarded by the judges as the leading technical lawyers of the day, were less likely to seek judicial office. The impact of this was that instead of having first tier appointments being made in the bulk of judicial appointments, especially

(1999); Ward (2007). World Economic Forum Global Competitiveness Report 2013–14, 2014–15 and the European Union Justice Scoreboard for 2013 records the findings of the World Economic Forum that Ireland has the third-highest perception of independence of the judiciary in the then 27 member states of the European Union, and is ranked fourth among 144 countries surveyed; Minister Frances Fitzgerald: 'With regard to the independence of the judiciary, I was pleased to note the conclusions in the recent report of the Council of Europe's anti-corruption group, which is known as GRECO. Its fourth round evaluation report on Ireland found that our judiciary is among the most trusted public institutions in the country. It was gratifying that the principle of judicial independence in this country was recognized by the international evaluation team – GRECO – that did this work and that the independence and professionalism of our judges was not disputed. (Minister Frances Fitzgerald, Dáil Debate, 2 April 2015 – http://oireachtasdebates.oireachtas.ie/debates%20authoring/debatesweb pack.nsf/takes/dail2015040200009#G00300 (accessed 24 June 2015)). **74** 'A newly appointed judge of the High Court will receive take home pay of less than 50 per cent of that paid in 2008, and will face an accrual period ⅓ longer to accrue a full pension, and while at the same time incurring substantial additional

to the High Court, there was a perception that those appointments were going to second tier candidates who were less experienced and less technically proficient than the traditional candidate for judicial office. This was compounded by unofficial reports of senior lawyers withdrawing their application from the JAAB following the introduction of further pay and pension changes by the government.

> A closely related issue is the widespread perception within the legal profession, that it is increasingly difficult to attract candidates of the highest calibre ... In such a context it is particularly important to enhance the significance of judicial appointments as recognition of quality. The converse is also true. If it is perceived that persons of quality are not being appointed then such candidates will be further dissuaded. Furthermore, the entire concept of a learned judiciary requires that by and large the persons deciding cases be more experienced and more knowledgeable than the persons arguing them ... The quality and reputation of any judicial system depends on the willingness of outstanding individuals to accept appointment. For solicitors and barristers, by the time that they have built up their practice and developed expertise, they are generally aged in their 50s. (Judicial Appointments Review Committee, 2014, pp 19, 66)

The reduction of judicial pay is regarded as acceptable in certain limited cases.

Mount Scopus International Standards on Judicial Independence

Key principles on judicial pay

2.20. Judicial salaries and pensions shall be adequate at all times, fixed by law, and should be periodically reviewed independently of Executive control.
2.21. The position of the judges, their independence, their security of tenure, and their adequate remuneration shall be entrenched constitutionally or secured by law.
2.22. Judicial salaries, pensions, and benefits cannot be decreased during judges' service except as a coherent part of an overall public economic measure.

In Ireland, the reduction of judicial pay as part of a public service wide adjustment in response to the economic problem was legitimated and entrenched by a constitutional referendum and so may be said to be in keeping with key international principles on judicial pay. Nevertheless, the cumulative impact of the pay reduction, and, in particular, the cut to the pension, was a possibly unforeseen consequence, with leading lawyers behaving differently and not seeking judicial office in the way that might have been expected.[75] It

liability to tax in respect of the judicial pension, and any savings for private pension provision made in practice.' (Judicial Appointments Review Committee, 2014, p. 66). **75** 'This was this unforeseen consequence that led, it is suggested, to the heightened concern about judicial independence and the judicial selection system rather than the machinations of the process itself which were unchanged in statute since 1995.

Suggested developments to the judicial selection system in Ireland

The issues of concern in relation to the judicial selection system in Ireland are multifaceted. What we should want is an efficient, effective, transparent and accountable model of judicial selection. Chapter 1 shows us that there are different models of judicial selection used in common law jurisdictions that work very well, with varying roles for government and independent judicial selection commissions. There are numerous different comparative models and many work quite satisfactorily (Malleson, 2003; Bell, 2003).

What model then may work best for Ireland? There is a democratic imperative in retaining a measure of discretion for the political majority in judicial selection. In this regard, the Irish judicial selection model, as designed in statute, offers a good balance between the purely executive appointment judicial selection models (such as New Zealand and Australia) and models of judicial selection where the role of the political majority is minimal (such as England and Wales). This is because the limited element of political discretion provided in the Irish statutory system allows a limited but indirect popular participation in judicial selection and the capacity for governments to respond to a range of political concerns through judicial appointments.

In practice the operation of the Irish model has veered too far away from its statutory design. The quality of the analysis of judicial candidates provided to government by the JAAB falls short of the sort of information we might think governments should have in making these decisions. By providing more detailed information and evaluation about recommended candidates, the JAAB could enhance their influence over who may be chosen by government. We should be slow to react to concerns about judicial selection by reducing the role of the law-making majority.

The JAAB has been given a broad remit in statute to adopt processes it sees fit in recommending candidates according to standards that it itself deter-

submission does not question in any way the need to make severe adjustments to the public pay bill or any of the reductions in judicial pay and pension in the past years. There has however been no comprehensive review of the cumulative impact of all changes, and no opportunity for a consideration of the impact on recruitment. Some changes which affect only the judiciary, or have a disproportionate impact on the judiciary such as the imposition of penal taxation provisions on private pension provision made while in private practice, may have little fiscal benefit, but may be a significant deterrent to applicants. A provision which imposes an unquantifiable, unpredictable, but substantial tax charge upon an appointee with private pension savings, is likely to be a serious deterrent to such applicants.' (Judicial Appointments Review Committee, 2014, pp 66–7).

mines. We should be slow to make changes that restrict the breadth of the powers given to the JAAB before it has an opportunity, in a properly resourced manner, to fully utilize those powers. The Department of Justice has described the JAAB model as 'best practice in its day'[76] but the reality is that a inadequate provision of appropriate resources to the JAAB and a failure to adopt best practice recruitment processes has meant that this model cannot be said to have lived up to its 'best practice' billing.

It is suggested that steady incremental institutional development should be preferred over a statutory overhaul of judicial selection in Ireland. Further reform, or development, should be grouped under two headings. The first is process-based development and the second is statute-based development. It is suggested that process-based development should be adopted and tested for an interim period before the introduction of further statutory change to the general institutional design of the judicial selection model. This may be justified by the fact that the JAAB has been operating very far from its institutional design for close to fifteen years. A period in which it had the opportunity to exercise its powers more fully in performing its functions might be helpful in allowing policy makers and legislators to assess statutory developments that might then be appropriate. However, there are certain statutory changes that could be introduced immediately without compromising the JAAB's authority or narrowing the breadth of its powers.

Some contributors suggest that the JAAB has an ongoing institutional difficulty as regards the statutory interpretation of the Courts and Court Officers Act 1995 on the number of candidates to be recommended to government. If it is the view of the Board that there is a legal difficulty with the number of candidates that can be recommended to government – in that the Board could be opened to incurring a legal risk from those candidates who may apply and not be recommended – then it is clear that the JAAB will need some immediate statutory change to clarify the number of candidates that should be recommended to government. It is suggested that this be retained at about seven candidates for a single vacancy, to be reviewed following significant institutional development of the processes of the JAAB. This institutional development would be largely based on significant process-based development.

Process-based developments

1 The JAAB requires institutional resources and supports if it is to operate as a professional assessment body providing recommendations to government for senior constitutional and statutory office-holders. It is not sufficient to provide financial or personnel supports within the Courts Service. The JAAB should be served by the professional recruitment expertise available at other senior levels of the public service. This should involve the JAAB

76 http://www.justice.ie/en/JELR/Pages/PR13000413 (accessed 1 July 2015).

being supported by the operations of other public appointments services, such as the Top Level Appointments Commission.[77]

2 Empowered by such supports, the JAAB should immediately begin preparation of detailed recruitment standards for the different court levels. These should be published for the benefit of judicial candidates and to enhance transparency of the JAAB assessment process.

3 The JAAB should develop, in conjunction with the Top Level Appointments Commission, new processes for multi-stage assessment of candidates including detailed criteria for shortlisting of candidates, the development of an interview process and other assessment processes. The role of the laymembers of the JAAB should be at the forefront of these new assessment processes to enable them to develop a better analysis of the judicial candidates. Sitting Presidents of a given court should not be involved in interviewing candidates for vacancies on that court in order to protect the independence of both the judiciary and the legal profession. Procedures for conducting 'soundings' should be formalized and transparent.

4 New procedures should be developed by the JAAB for communicating with applicants for judicial vacancies at each stage of the assessment process. Making an application for a position as judicial office-holder is an act of enormous personal and professional importance and candidates should expect to receive appropriate communications on the status of their applications as they would for an application to other statutory positions through the Public Appointments Service or the Top Level Appointments Commission.

5 The Minister for Justice should engage with the JAAB at the earliest opportunity when it is known that a judicial vacancy will arise. The Minister should, when writing to the JAAB in respect of such a vacancy, highlight any areas of legal expertise that may at that time be desirable, for example, as a consequence of the retirement of a particular judge or the build-up of court cases in a particular area (arising from an economic crisis or other particular event). This approach would represent a more targeted engagement by the Minister with the JAAB in the judicial selection process. In the past, such information has been on occasion communicated informally by the Attorney General to the Board but such communication between government and the JAAB should be more formal. The JAAB may, when seeking applications, make particular reference to the desirability of candidates with such expertise and may tailor its recommendations according to the perceived gap on the court. Similarly, there must be a

77 http:// www.cpsa.ie/en/Publications/Audits-of-Recruitment-and-Selection-Activity/ Senior-Recruitment/TLAC.html.

suitable mechanism by which a Court President may highlight a particular gap of expertise on his or her court. This, again, is generally done informally through the Attorney General but should be formalized under new institutional processes.

6 The JAAB should operate in line with the provisions of the 1995 Act when making recommendations to government about candidates who are suitable for judicial office. Section 16(2) requires statutory clarification to assist the JAAB in this regard but the number recommended should remain in the realm of seven candidates per vacancy with a reasonable approach taken in the case of multiple concurrent vacancies.[78] The JAAB should retain its power to recommend fewer candidates if it thinks there are fewer than seven suitable candidates for judicial office.

7 Where there are multiple vacancies on a court, the Minister may use his or her authority under section 16(2) (5) of the 1995 Act to give guidance to the JAAB on the number of recommendations to make, in consultation with the Board.[79] The evidence in the research data is that such power has not been used to date. It is suggested that, for illustrative purposes only, receiving 28 recommended candidates for four vacancies on the same court is excessive unless the Minister has expressly asked the JAAB to consider judicial candidates with particular skills in diverse fields of legal expertise. For example, if it is known that the High Court is in need of two judges with extensive criminal law experience and a judge with significant commercial experience and a judge with general legal experience to cover multiple court lists, then to receive seven names may unduly restrict the government in its decisions. The government may be better served by receiving seven names of candidates with criminal experience, seven names with commercial experience. It is important to state that this example is for illustrative purposes only. The discretion should remain with the JAAB to implement the legislation as they see fit and having regard to the applications before them at any given time. What is suggested generally is a more targeted engagement between the Minister and the JAAB that serves the needs of the courts and the administration of justice and allows the executive of the law-making majority sufficient choice between recommended candidates.

78 This is unless there are fewer than seven applicants, or the JAAB thinks there are fewer than seven suitable applicants. 79 Section 16(2) (5) 'Where more than one judicial office in the same court stands vacant, or in advance of more than one vacancy arising in the same court, at the request of the Minister, the Board shall submit to the Minister the name of each person who has informed the Board of his or her wish to be considered for appointment to judicial office and shall recommend to the Minister the names of at least seven persons in respect of each vacancy or such lesser number of names as the Minister shall specify following consultation with the Board'.

8 The JAAB should in its Annual Reports provide an account of any request by the Minister to consider judges with particular legal expertise and experience.

9 Without making comments about individual judges or other named persons and within the appropriate bounds of separation of powers, Dáil Éireann should have an annual opportunity for general statements on judicial selection or the Minister should make an annual statement in the Joint Oireachtas Committee on Justice and Equality on judicial selection. This could include the number of judges appointed in the preceding year, any specific requests made by the Minister of the JAAB to recommend candidates with particular skills to fill gaps in the courts and any other matters of relevance within the appropriate bounds of separation of powers and the necessity to protect the judiciary and administration of justice from undue interference or attack by the legislature. If the argument for retaining political discretion in judicial selection is to be sustained seriously, there should greater political accountability, outside of elections, where the executive can account in routine and general terms to the law-making majority about the process of judicial selection and current trends and needs on the courts.

Statute-based developments

There are a number of statute-based developments that could be made to improve the functioning of the judicial selection system in Ireland. The intention with respect to this approach is to retain maximum institutional discretion for the JAAB in the performance of its functions and to allow it an opportunity to more fully fulfil its capacity with appropriate professional resources and supports. Some of the legislative reforms suggested in the 2013–14 political debate may have the effect of diluting these very broad powers given to the JAAB in the 1995 Act. Others focus on the outputs of the JAAB (the number of recommendations) without acknowledging the need for enhanced quality of information in relation to candidates that could be obtained through more rigorous assessment processes.

As such, the following suggested statutory reforms are divided into those that could be made immediately and those that might follow a period of enhanced institutional functioning by the JAAB, which may in itself throw up further desirable statutory reforms.

Immediate

1 Clarification of section 16(2) of the Courts and Court Officers Act 1995 to assist the JAAB in recommending seven names to government per vacancy.

2 Section 22 of the Public Service Pensions (Single Scheme and Other Provisions) Act 2012, and section 787TA of the Taxes Consolidation Act

1997 as amended, should be reviewed to consider the impact of the behaviour of leading would-be judges in applying for judicial office.

3 Section 20 of the 1995 Act[80] should be amended to make clear that the JAAB can communicate in general terms about its institutional functioning to approved bodies which may include the Top Level Appointments Commission and the Joint Oireachtas Committee on Justice. This should not include deliberations about individual persons or vacancies but should be restricted to generalized communications about standards and processes. This is necessary so that the JAAB, through its secretary or lay members, can communicate with the Oireachtas generally, and in particular, about its institutional needs and development prior to any further statutory change.

4 The eligibility criteria for applicants to judicial posts should be harmonized so that there is no distinction made between experience levels necessary for different courts.

5 Section 28(e) of the Courts and Court Officers Act 1995 should be amended to remove the provision whereby the District Court judges are ineligible for appointment to the High Court or the Supreme Court. As the JARC observes,[81] a person otherwise eligible for appointment should not lose it by appointment to another court.

Medium Term

It is envisaged that in this period the JAAB would be provided appropriate resources and professional support to enhance its processes and fully utilize its current statutory powers. Having established transparent selection criteria for each court, and developed a recruitment and assessment process that enables a new quality of analysis of judicial aspirants, the Board can then refine its recommendations to government to include this analysis. Following this, and following a review of these developments to include the Oireachtas, the JAAB and the Department of Justice, further statutory change may be desirable.

1 The 'merit principle' may be established in statute as the paramount consideration in judicial appointments. However, establishing such a statutory principle will not obviate the need for some person to make a necessarily subjective assessment between two candidates of equal merit. In making this decision such a person may have regard to the needs of the courts in terms of legal expertise or other political considerations such as the enhancement of diversity. The establishment of the merit principle is

80 Section 20. All proceedings of the Board and all communications to the Board shall be confidential and shall not be disclosed except for the purposes of this Act. **81** Judicial Appointments Review Committee, Preliminary Submission to the Department of Justice and Equality's Public Consultation on the Judicial Appointments Process, January 2014 p. 51.

one recommended by several groups in the consultation process. It is unarguably correct that it should be expressly stated in the legislation, but it is suggested that it is not a panacea for the eradication of the perception of political influence in judicial selection and its establishment will not delimit the need for ongoing subjective assessments about equally meritorious but different judicial candidates.

2 The legislation should be amended to include an express prohibition on lobbying by judicial candidates or persons on their behalf. It is already prohibited to lobby or canvass a member of the JAAB but this principle should apply to the lobbying of members of government and members of the Oireachtas. The new prohibition should include canvassing or lobbying by sitting members of the judiciary for positions on other courts, but exclude the new process established whereby sitting members of the judiciary may write to the Attorney General to express an interest in another judicial vacancy. The establishment of such a principle in legislation will, it is suspected, be of considerable relief to members of government who, since 1982, have expressed their unease at being lobbied for judicial office.

3 The new process that enables sitting judges to express an interest in other judicial vacancies could be refined to include the Chief Justice in addition to the Attorney General. This would then allow for the senior judiciary to be included in the process, yet avoid any risk, however remote, that a judge of a given court finds difficulty with the President of that Court having applied for another position. The use of the JAAB for this process should be approached with great caution – there is something invidious about members of the legal profession and judges of other courts making assessments about sitting judges. If the JAAB is to be involved in this process, its involvement should be restricted to the Chief Justice and the lay members of the Board. The new process should be tested for a period of three years at which point, the Minister for Justice, on behalf of the Attorney General and the government, should provide an account to the Joint Oireachtas Committee on Justice on the operation of this process. The Minister and the Joint Oireachtas Committee on Justice should give consideration to those elements of this process that should be put on a statutory footing.

4 Similarly, the new process for appointing judges to European courts should be tested for a similar period and then considered and debated by the Joint Oireachtas Committee on Justice with the Minister for Justice. As applicants for these positions may include sitting judges in Irish courts, similar issues of judicial independence arise when considering the involvement of the JAAB.

5 A number of bodies recommended changes to the composition of the JAAB in the course of the consultative and legislative debate in 2013–14. These suggestions included a greater representation of solicitors and an enhanced proportion of lay persons representing a range of civil society groups. The concern behind these recommendations was that the JAAB was over-represented by judicial and legal members and that some better balance should be struck to ensure greater diversity in judicial appointments. It is clear from the research evidence that judicial diversity has been a concern of certain government decision-makers over many years and that the political system is well placed to ensure that the judiciary is more reflective of society. It is suggested that before changes are made to the composition of the JAAB, that it be given the opportunity to improve its institutional functioning to ensure that lay members play a stronger role in the deliberations of the JAAB. Having made such changes, and assessed their impact in conjunction with the parliamentary oversight of the Joint Oireachtas Committee on Justice, further consideration could be given to the composition of the JAAB and the necessity, or otherwise, of increasing the proportion of lay members and solicitor members on the JAAB.

6 Having had a period of developed institutional functioning for the JAAB, there may be other statutory changes that are appropriate. They may include
   a statutory changes to eligibility criteria, including placing the criteria used by the JAAB in assessing candidates on a statutory footing,
   b changes to the number of recommended candidates to be made by the JAAB or the nature of those recommendations,
   c putting some of the new and developed process of the JAAB on a statutory footing,
   d an extension of the remit of the JAAB to judges of European courts or judicial promotions,
   e a stronger role for lay people on the Board through increased numbers or the creation of a lay chairperson of the Board.

7 Finally, eligibility for judicial office should be reviewed to reconsider the position of lawyers working in the service of the state and other in-house positions. It is suggested that this may assist in ensuring that senior female lawyers are fully represented in the pool of qualified applicants for judicial office.

The political debate about the judicial selection system in Ireland in 2013–14 was very welcome. It was the first such public debate involving consultation with stakeholders whose active participation has contributed to a rich debate and engagement on the development of a judicial selection system that operates at the highest standard internationally. It should be remembered that in all countries it is ultimately a matter for the law-making authority to determine the shape and structure of the judicial selection system. Consultation with the judiciary and other stakeholders demonstrates the type of political engagement that is desirable for such policy development. We can see from Chapter 1 that such engagement was present in all of the jurisdictions that considered institutional change,[82] whether or not the law-making authority ultimately made changes to the judicial selection system. Perhaps the political debate of 2013–14 may have benefitted from greater monitoring of the changed institutional functioning of the JAAB[83] from the early 2000s to 2014. The implication of this is that concerns about the capacity for political influence in judicial selection have to be read in the context of the JAAB providing greatly enhanced political discretion to government in making their recommendations – if the JAAB receives 150 applications for two vacancies on the District Court and makes 100 recommendations as opposed to seven or eight or nine, it entirely changes the impact of the JAAB on reducing political discretion in judicial selection.

There is an important distinction between political involvement in making a choice based on the subjective needs of the day as opposed to making a choice based on membership of or affiliation with a political party. The government needs more detailed information on judicial candidates and needs to retain the capacity to choose between candidates to achieve objective public policy goals such as those described in this chapter. We should not be afraid of political involvement in judicial selection – there is a democratic imperative in the political majority playing a role in the selection of judges. To balance this though, the system needs to be more transparent in its processes and held to more regular political account within the parliamentary structure.

82 Except Ireland where the unique political circumstances of 1994 promoted urgent institutional change. 83 Recommendations in excess of the statutory provision of 'at least seven'.

CONCLUSIONS

Implications for institutional change

Institutions shape political and human behaviour just as political and human behaviour shape institutions. The study of institutions can provide insights into the ways in which the strategic interactions of actors, within particular institutional frameworks, give rise to particular kinds of outcomes. As we have seen in this discussion, institutions themselves can be the subject of intentional change and they can evolve and change in ways that have important consequences. This book considers how judicial selection institutions change.

The independence of the judiciary is core to the credibility of a legal system and to constitutional governance. In countries where the independence of the judiciary is under threat, there can be serious risks to the protection of human rights and the rule of law. Governments should want to have an independent judiciary. The principle of separation of powers in a constitutional democracy means that governments can be held to account by an independent judiciary. The decisions of the judiciary can have far reaching consequences for government and the broader society. Judges have powers to find validly enacted legislation unconstitutional or to decide that the decision or acts of the government should be overturned because they are not in accordance with the principles of constitutional justice. Governments will therefore be interested in the membership of the judiciary and in its capacity to influence that membership.

Governments are also interested in judicial selection because, in systems where judges are appointed from the ranks of senior lawyers, it offers an opportunity to the members of government to disburse patronage among their supporters. Whether or not they choose to make appointments to reward political support, the *capacity* of government to make appointments in this way provides them with a useful means of rewarding political supporters and retaining their support over time. From the government's perspective, this can be a valuable political tool.

For both of these reasons, it could be expected that governments would want to retain the greatest level of discretion in the judicial selection process. Chapter 1 showed that there are different judicial selection processes operating in the common law countries examined. A typology was presented that categorized different types of judicial selection systems according to the level of government power in that process. It was clear that there was a spectrum of government discretion in the different systems – ranging from virtually full discretion over all elements of the judicial selection process to relatively little discretion in systems, where the power to choose a nominee had effectively been delegated to another decision-making body.

Notwithstanding the principle of separation of powers, there is an operational problem associated with judicial independence that must be acknowledged. The judicial system is dependent on government to facilitate the operation of the judiciary in different ways. The government controls the laws governing the selection and retention of judges. Somehow, judges have to be appointed to their positions and government has to be involved in the selection of judges in some manner. Such a function could not be outsourced to a private entity – given the role played by the judiciary in the constitutional order. Judges cannot appoint themselves. This puts the government in a conflicting position. There is recognition that judges cannot be functionaries of government and too much in its debt – either for appointment or possible promotion within the courts system. One solution to this dilemma is to have an arms-length body to perform elements of judicial selection.

Each country examined in this book had given consideration to changing the judicial selection system. Some countries did introduce change and, where they did, it happened in a way that was designed to reduce government discretion and create some separation between politics and judicial selection.

In these cases, governments delegated governance of elements of the judicial selection process to non-political bodies of delegated governance. Where they did so, the institutional design was important in ensuring that the motivations that drove institutional change were realized. Two principal findings emerged from the comparative analysis of the experience of reforming the judicial appointments system across common law countries.

1 Institutional reform requires explicit political commitment and a significant degree of consultation and preparation.
2 The original features of institutional design are critical for the way institutions function over time. Institutional drift may result in unanticipated change, such that political discretion in judicial appointments is actually increased rather than constrained.

COMPARATIVE ANALYSIS OF MOMENTS OF INSTITUTIONAL REFORM

Chapter 1 demonstrated two issues. First, that in most cases where a decision was made to introduce institutional change to the judicial selection process, the decision appears to have had the full support of the government. Indeed, in most cases, the impetus to introduce institutional change derived from the stated policy preferences of the government. The government was already committed to implementing change. Second, Chapter 1 also showed that in most of those cases where institutional change was introduced, it achieved the objective of reducing political influence over judicial selection by separating the process from the control of governments. Chapter 1 demonstrated a link between political commitment to institutional change and the degree to which the government was constrained by the design of the new model for judicial selection.

The challenge was to understand the reasons why governments would introduce institutional change in ways that reduced their power in a function that was important to them. We examined each of the jurisdictions and countries to understand how political debate about judicial selection processes had been generated and what pressures had existed to prompt governments to consider change. Such political debate occurred when there was:

1 government commitment to institutional change,
2 particular problems with the judiciary based on a series of controversial decisions, or
3 a context of wider legal and constitutional change.

It was shown that, where institutional change was introduced, there had been clear evidence of political commitment to such change from governments. Indeed, in each case (except one), the idea had been generated by the government in the first instance. In countries where no change was introduced, pressure for institutional change had generally come from sources external to government – such as commentary by interest groups or the media. In each case (except one), whether institutional change was introduced or not, the idea had received sustained public comment and debate – facilitated by government processes such as discussion papers and stakeholder consultation exercises.

The one exception in both cases was Ireland. As shown in Chapter 1, institutional change in Ireland was driven by government, but as a response to a political crisis rather than policy concerns about judicial selection. Ireland experienced a different institutional development process – there was no public debate, no stakeholder consultation or policy papers prepared. The impetus for institutional change in Ireland and the development of the new institutional model stood out as different from all of the jurisdictions with comparable judicial selection models and experiences of institutional change.

The initial motivation for institutional change in Ireland was to overcome a political crisis. The intention was to create a system that would not explicitly bind future governments. Between the moment of crisis in 1994 – when change was mooted – and the time it was established by the Courts and Court Officers Act 1995, the impact of this new system on government discretion in judicial selection had changed in ways that weakened the independent powers of the new Board. The institutional change introduced in Ireland had less impact on government discretion in judicial selection than was the case with analogous reforms in other jurisdictions.

It should not be concluded that Irish governments have always been unwilling to divest themselves of discretionary political influence over the functioning of the legal system. Political reform that committed government to distancing itself from key legal functions has in fact been undertaken. Chapter 4 presented an example of such effective reform in Ireland. This involved the reduction of the discretion of government in the prosecution of criminal offences by removing the general responsibility for such prosecutions from the Office of the Attorney General and establishing an independent prosecutions office – the Office of the Director of Public Prosecutions. Where government adopted a principled stance and prepared the case effectively, the reform was implemented successfully.

Nor is the issue of judicial selection necessarily more difficult to tackle than other issues of discretion-curbing reforms. Chapter 4 also considered the case of Scotland, where the discretion of government in judicial selection was effectively reduced through the establishment of a judicial selection commission. In this case, both in the institutional design and its implementation, the new model was such that there was a real separation between the political executive and the process of selecting judges. The new Scottish body functioned in ways that protected the public interest and actively guarded against some of the threats posed by judicial selection commissions, such as the threat of self-selection.

This book examined the centrally important role of political commitment in bringing about institutional reform. It examined the impact of government preferences in the introduction and implementation of institutional change that had the effect of reducing the power of governments in functions that are important to them. It provided important lessons about the institutional design of delegated institutions and comparative analysis showed that, when major reform is taken to delegate powers to a non-political body of delegated governance, two key issues emerge.

These key explanatory variables are explicit political commitment to major institutional change and a consultation process involving external stakeholders and public debate.

The Irish case is an outlier that can be fully accounted for in terms of the explanatory framework summarized here. The institutional model adopted in this instance had much less impact on government discretion than in comparable judicial selection commissions. It was shown that an absence of political commitment initially, combined with waning political necessity to introduce change over time, resulted in an institutional model that was a hybrid of judicial selection systems – a combination of an executive appointment model and a judicial selection commission model. Getting institutional design in major institutional reform right is important. Ireland did it in a particularly unusual way.

FUNCTIONING OF INSTITUTIONS OVER TIME

Institutions do not stay stable in the way they function over time but may shift and alter. The original institutional design may set up incentives for further change through institutional drift. The Irish experience also displays evidence of this sort of outcome.

The purpose of the establishment of the Judicial Appointments Advisory Board was to assist the government in identifying qualified people who were also, according to explicit statutory criteria, *suitable* for judicial appointment. Initially, when the new body, the JAAB, was established it adopted practices reasonably closely in line with the legislation. However, it was also shown that the Board took a decision in the early 2000s to change its processes in ways that changed its function. The Board adopted a new process that increased the discretion of the government, because it provided a longer list from which to choose a preferred name. This had two effects.

First, no distinction is made by the Board on a 'per vacancy' basis – all of the suitable applicants are recommended. Second, in the later period of this study, the Board stopped performing the role of a body that guided the government on the relative suitability of applicants. Applicants were now either suitable or unsuitable. But the legislation envisaged the Board performing a function that gave guidance or advice to the government on the relative suitability of qualified applicants by performing an exercise to determine the more suitable candidates among the qualified applicants. The Board was not intended to be a vetting unit. It was intended to narrow down the qualified judicial applicants and *advise* the government on the most suitable of these applicants. What is interesting is that there was no response by government to this change in the function of the Board. This conspicuous silence suggests the government either did not notice or acquiesced in this institutional drift.

The hybrid model of judicial selection system in Ireland had certain unexpected effects on the institutional functioning of the JAAB over time. Its strength was that it provided a quality screening system for government in judicial selection. This was especially important for appointments to the lower courts. It is clear that, although the Minister was not obliged to refer vacancies to the JAAB, this was the dominant practice.

However, the institutional design of the JAAB had certain weaknesses that may not have been anticipated. This capacity for institutional drift was facilitated by the drafting of the legislation which provides that the JAAB is to recommend at least seven names in respect of each vacancy. This allows a broad range of interpretations which may emerge as a consequence of the variation of individual members of the JAAB. The capacity for individuals to influence this process to such a degree is problematic, as the JAAB is a statutory process for recruiting constitutional office-holders with significant powers.

Institutional design matters because of its impact on institutional functioning over time. The flexibility of the institutional design in Ireland, along with the manner of its implementation by the Board, resulted in a shift of emphasis that arguably had not been originally envisaged.

In summary, the problems with the institutional design were:

1 no limits were placed on the number of candidates who could be recommended by the JAAB to government,
2 broad enabling powers for the JAAB to determine their own processes,
3 no review of the implementation of institutional change by government.

Institutional design is important for the functioning of the institution over time. The most crucial moment of institutional change is the critical juncture at which the institutional change takes place. The moment of initiating the design of the institution is not the final word on how that institution will function over time. Elements of institutional design may allow for institutional drift. This may result in a functional shift of the operation of the institution that may then need to be reviewed as the implications become clear.

The immediate trigger for changing the judicial appointment system in Ireland in the mid-1990s was to overcome a political problem between coalition partners. The new model introduced in the course of this crisis was one that was deliberately designed not to bind government in judicial selection, but to require government to choose between three and five recommended candidates. This was replaced by a model which, by increasing the number of names to be recommended, had the effect of widening the discretion of government. The implementation of this model by the JAAB resulted in a further widening of the discretionary powers available to the government.

Institutional change in Ireland achieved its purpose – a solution to a political problem. The design of the model and its implementation by the JAAB ensured that government discretion is not constrained by the existence or the operation of the JAAB. However, the creation of the JAAB deflected political attention from the institutional weaknesses in the model of judicial selection that permit extensive scope for executive appointment. It created a veneer of reform by adopting an alternative model that, on the surface at any rate, appeared to separate politics from judicial selection more thoroughly than was really the case.

In Chapter 1 it was observed that a range of judicial selection models were used in common law countries. Some governments made a decision to retain full control of judicial selection. In these cases government would remain accountable for the decision they made in relation to the selection of judges. Similarly, the creation of judicial selection commissions in England and Wales, Scotland and Northern Ireland was accomplished in a way that delegated nearly all of the government's discretion to the commission, because of the very tight constraints on the government and the number of recommendations made by the commissions. While acknowledging that there are concerns with both systems, both clearly delegate responsibility and accountability for judicial selection to some extent.

The difficulty with the Irish model is that it arguably provides neither transparency nor accountability in judicial selection. So long as the government chooses candidates that have been recommended by the JAAB, the government has political security or, we might say, political 'cover', for the decisions it makes in nominating individuals for appointment by the President. If the appointment turns out to be a bad appointment, the government can deflect accountability to the JAAB, which has all of the statutory powers necessary to assess the suitability of people for judicial office and make a determination that everyone on a specified list of persons was qualified. The existence of the JAAB absolves the government from political accountability in the selection of judges.

However, the JAAB cannot be held to account either. It is operated by the most senior judicial office-holders in the state and operates under confidential processes. In the interests of professional confidentiality, it is not subject to freedom of information processes. If accountability for judicial selection is genuinely to be vested in the JAAB, it is important that its functioning should be more transparent.

APPENDIX 1

Interview codes

Interviews were conducted with a total of forty individuals. These included two Taoisigh, nine Attorneys General, six Ministers for Justice, nineteen members of the JAAB other than those members who were Attorneys Generals. It also included three Cabinet members of the Fianna Fail/Labour government and two senior government advisers to that government. Data from these interviews was cross-checked with other relevant government advisers and politicians of the period, though these are not formally included in the data set.

Interviewees are coded in three ways – whether they were an office-holder before 1995 or after 1995; what position they held and the chronological sequence of interviews with that group of office-holders. In this way, 'Post-1995/AG/2' is the second Attorney General who was interviewed in the course of this study and who held office after 1995. It is important to identify whether they held office before or after 1995 because part of the analysis concerns whether things changed for the individual office-holders as a result of institutional change in 1995.

Some of the individuals held more than one position – for example, an Attorney General could also have held the role of Minister for Justice or been a member of the JAAB in a judicial capacity. Where this occurs – and a quote is attributed to them – it is attributed under the relevant code. For example, if an Attorney General is speaking about their role in government, they are expressed under the AG code. If that Attorney is speaking in their capacity as a JAAB member about the JAAB, they are expressed under their JAAB code. So it could be the case that, purely for illustrative purposes, Pre-1995/AG/1 might also be JAAB/2.

Interviews were also conducted with members of government who did not hold one of these offices (or senior government advisers) but who are, or were, centrally involved and familiar with the institutional changes that took place in 1994 and 1995. These are expressed as POL. This category is not split into pre- or post-1995.

TAO	Taoiseach
AG	Attorney General
MJ	Minister for Justice
JAAB	Member of the JAAB
POL	Member of Government or Senior Government Adviser

All interviewees were assured of absolute confidentiality. In giving this assurance, I was able to draw on the successful study of the senior judiciary which I undertook in 2004 where similar guarantees of confidentiality had been given and anonymity was carefully protected by ensuring that any quotes did not reveal the identity of interviewees.

Two interviewees are quoted directly in the study with a named attribution for which their permission was sought and received. This occurs in Chapter 2 and Chapter 5 and the reason is that they were so centrally involved and their contributions so important to understanding the institutional change process that it warranted making an exception to the usual provisions of anonymity.

APPENDIX 2

Interview with Alan Shatter regarding purpose of Review of Procedures for Appointment as a Judge

'The statutory mechanisms for JAAB had been there for a lot of years, I thought the time had come to review how it works, to get a perspective from other people. There were things about the way the system was working, that I saw from the inside, that I thought were not satisfactory. I had one particular understanding of how it was working before I became Minister, but then my perception of it changed. I was also concerned that, and I had no great complaint about this, that it was a lawyer dominated process, which I thought in principle wasn't unreasonable because it was practising lawyers and those involved in law that would have some insight into the capacity of applicants. But I was concerned about the position of lay people on JAAB. I was always in favour of lay person involvement, but I was concerned that they were – and I don't mean this disrespectfully to either current of former lay members – but I was concerned that they should be in a position to make a substantive contribution to the selection process but because, by dint of the system, they wouldn't know the personalities, they wouldn't know the professionalism or expertise of the individual applicants, all they could possibly know about the individual applicants was what was contained on the CV. It became absolutely apparent and clear that despite the power to do so, JAAB had never at any stage since its formation interviewed anybody. The only way a non-lawyer might have got some perspective was through some form of interview process. An interview process is not a unique and definitive basis for selecting someone to be a member of the judiciary any more than it is for selecting someone for any other position, there are some people who excel at interviews but are not necessarily good at whatever the job is they have applied for …

'I was also very conscious of the fact that there were always allegations made that the appointments were political and the reality of course was that JAAB proposed names and that there was a wide area of discretion of the approved candidates who might be selected. I approached the matter on the basis of, not simply who were the best lawyers for the District Court, Circuit Court, High Court or whatever, but where were the gaps in the judiciary – if a member of the judiciary who had retired had two or three particular specialties on that particular court – criminal law, commercial law – I tried, and I would religiously read all of the CVs that came through of the recommended persons, and as a former practising lawyer I would have some degree of insight into some of the applicants. Of course I didn't know all of the applicants, but I was concerned that when JAAB were making recommendations that wasn't part of what they consider and should that not be part of what they consider? For example, if a very good judge retired that was primarily involved in commercial law or in judicial review and constitutional law, then there was something of a disconnect in that JAAB would just recommend whatever names were ok, but it wasn't really part of their remit to consider where the expertise gaps were on the court. When I was recommending appointments to government I was always very conscious of those gaps. It happened at all the different levels of the court, where particular judges retired, some of them were generalists and some of them were specialists; where they were specialists I tried to make sure we filled that particular gap.

'With all of this going on, I felt the time was right to see if there was a better way of doing it. I came to the consultative process with certain preconceptions, which were that the Constitution should not be changed and I deliberately said we would do it within the constitutional parameters. I thought that it was very important. I was very interested to see what would come out of this, but my inclination was that ultimately government or a government minister had to be accountable to the Dáil for the appointments that were made. I didn't buy in, and having read the submissions that came in, I still didn't buy in to the idea that it would be a superior form of appointments system if you had an independent quango that was accountable to no one in real terms but based on some insider engagement whether it be lawyer insiders or some lay people who would still have difficulty working out why you would appoint X instead of Y. I didn't buy into the narrative that we should have some free floating independent quango who would appoint all of the judges or the government would simply rubber stamp, without any consideration, whatever names they produced because I thought that was a completely undemocratic system, there would be no true parliamentary accountability if a really appalling appointment was made and instead of allegations being made of appointments being political it could have become a group who appointed people that who they liked to play golf with or lawyers of whom they particularly approve and I don't think that the system should become judicially dominated, because there are all sorts of good and bad reasons why judges may or may not favour particular members of the profession.'

25 June 2015

Bibliography

PRIMARY SOURCE MATERIAL

Australia

Commonwealth of Australia Act 1900.
High Court of Australia Act 1979.
House of Representatives, 25 October 1978.
Commonwealth of Australia, *Report to the Senate, August 1984*.
Mabo v. Queensland (No. 2) (1992), 175 CLR 1.

Canada

Supreme Court Act 1985.
Canada. House of Commons. (2004) 'Improving the Supreme Court of Canada appointments process: Report of the Standing Committee on Justice, Human Rights, Public Safety and Emergency Preparedness'. Available at http://www.parl.gc.ca/HousePublications/Publication.aspx?DocId=1350880&Language=E&Mode=1&Parl=37&Ses=3 (accessed 16 Jan. 2014).
Canada. Department of Justice. (2013) 'Ad hoc committee on the appointment of Supreme Court of Canada justices'. Available at http://www.justice.gc.ca/eng/news-nouv/ja-nj/2013/doc_32972.html (accessed 16 Jan. 2014).
R. Morgentaler [1988] 1 S.C.R. 30.

England and Wales

Constitutional Reform Act 2005.
Crime and Courts Act 2013.
Human Rights Act 1998.
United Kingdom. Ministry of Justice. (2012) *Appointments and diversity: a judiciary for the 21st century*. Available at https://www.justice.gov.uk/downloads/publications/policy/moj/judicial-diversity-taskforce-annual-report-2012.pdf.pdf (accessed 16 Jan. 2014).
United Kingdom. House of Lords Constitution Committee. (2012) *Twenty-fifth report: judicial appointments*. Available at http://www.publications.parliament.uk/pa/ld201012/ldselect/ldconst/272/272.pdf (accessed 16 Jan. 2016).
United Kingdom. Lord Chancellor's Department. (1986) *Judicial appointments: the Lord Chancellor's policies and procedures*. London: Lord Chancellor's Department.
United Kingdom. Judiciary. (2010) *Report of the advisory panel on judicial diversity*. Available at http://www.judiciary.gov.uk/Resources/JCO/Documents/Reports/advisory-panel-judicial-diversity-2010.pdf (accessed 16 Jan. 2014).

Ireland

Courts (Supplemental Provisions) Act 1964.
Courts and Court Officers Bill 1994.
Courts and Court Officers Act 1995.
Courts and Court Officers Act 2002.
Courts of Justice Act 1936.
Office of the Director of Public Prosecutions Annual Reports 2005–12.

Ireland. Constitution Review Group (1996) 'Report'. Dublin: Stationery Office. Available at http://archive.constitution.ie/publications/default.asp?UserLang=EN (accessed 16 Jan. 2014).

Ireland. Fair Trade Commission (1990) *Report of study into restrictive practices in the legal profession*. Dublin: Stationery Office.

Ireland. Judicial Appointments Advisory Board. (2002–13) *Annual Reports*. Dublin: Courts Service. Available at www.jaab.ie (accessed 14 Jan. 2014).

Ireland. Houses of the Oireachtas. (1994) *Report of the Sub-Committee of the Select Committee on Legislation and Security*. Dublin: Stationary Office.

Israel

Basic Law: The Judiciary (1984).

Judges Act 1953.

Law and Administration Ordinance 1948.

Public Committee Against Torture v. State of Israel HCJ (Israeli Supreme Court) 5100/94, 15 July 1999.

New Zealand

Judicature Act 1908.

Supreme Court Act 2003.

New Zealand Ministry of Justice (2004) *Appointing judges: a judicial appointments commission for New Zealand? A public consultation paper.* Wellington: Office of the Attorney General.

Northern Ireland

Northern Ireland Office, Secretary of State Ireland. (2000) *Review of the criminal justice system in Northern Ireland.* Belfast: Northern Ireland Office, Secretary of State Ireland. Available at http://cain.ulst.ac.uk/issues/law/cjr/report30300.htm (accessed 16 Jan. 2014).

Justice (Northern Ireland) Acts 2002 & 2004.

Justice (Northern Ireland) Act 2009.

Scotland

Judiciary and Courts (Scotland) Act 2008.

Scotland Judicial Appointments Board Annual Reports, 2002–13.

Scotland. Judicial Appointments Board for Scotland (2009) *Framework document.* Available at http://www.judicialappointmentsscotland.org.uk/Publications/Corporate_and_Business_ Plans2/Framework_Document.pdf (accessed 16 Jan. 2014).

Scotland. Scottish Government. (2000) *Judicial appointments: an inclusive approach.* Available at http://www.scotland.gov.uk/Publications/2000/04/5626/File-1 (accessed 16 Jan. 2014).

Scotland. Scottish Government. (2007) *Proposals for a Judiciary (Scotland) Bill.* Available at http://www.scotland.gov.uk/Publications/2007/02/13115213/0 (accessed 16 Jan. 2014).

Scotland. Scottish Government (2006) *Strengthening judicial independence in a modern Scotland.* Available at http://www.scotland.gov.uk/Publications/2006/06/13143517/0 (accessed 16 Jan. 2014).

United States

Constitution for the United States of America, article 2, section 2.

Newspaper Articles

Associated Press (1981) 'Reagan ends Carter's judge selection system', *The Telegraph*, 7 May. Available at http://news.google.com/newspapers?nid=2209&dat=19810507&id=NqkrAAAAIBAJ&sjid=IPoFAAAAIBAJ&pg=5485,1473422 (accessed 15 Jan. 2014).

Browne, V. (1994) 'Spring's opposition made Whelehan all the more determined', *Irish Times*, 18 November.

Carroll, J. (1994) 'FF strongly opposes attempts to block Whelehan as next High Court President', *Irish Times*, 20 September.

Clark, H. (2003) 'Nation ready for its own highest court', *New Zealand Herald*, 10 October. Available at http://www.nzherald.co.nz/nz/news/article.cfm?c_id=1&objectid=3527954 (accessed 15 Jan. 2014).

DeBreadun, D. (1994) 'Legacy of the programme for government may still be passed on', *Irish Times*, 18 November.

Editorial. (2003) 'Not too late for poll on new court', *New Zealand Herald*, 17 September. Available at http://www.nzherald.co.nz/nz/news/article.cfm?c_id=1&objectid=3523814 (accessed 15 Jan. 2014).

Harkov, L. (2011) 'Likud MKs promote bills to reform judicial selection system', *Jerusalem Post*, 11 November. Available from http://www.jpost.com/National-News/Likud-MKs-promote-bills-to-reform-judicial-selection-system (accessed 15 Jan. 2014).

Harkov, L. (2013) 'Bill ensures women will be on judicial selection panel', *Jerusalem Post*, 12 March Available at http://www.jpost.com/Breaking-News/Bill-ensures-women-will-be-on-judicial-selection-panel-333857 (accessed 15 Jan. 2014).

Kelly, D., O'Regan, M. and O'Halloran, M. (1994) 'Reynolds accepts "wider" responsibilities', *Irish Times*, 16 November.

Kennedy, G. (1994) 'Taoiseach says Whelehan is "only nominee" for High Court post', *Irish Times*, 5 October.

O'Toole, F. (1994) 'Labour's real beef against Harry Whelehan', *Irish Times*, 7 October.

Rozenberg, J. (2012) 'Jack Straw on judicial appointments: "Labour went too far"', *The Guardian*, 4 December. Available at http://www.theguardian.com/law/2012/dec/04/jack-straw-judicial-appointments-diversity (accessed 15 Jan. 2014).

Ziegel, J. (2003) 'Disrobe this process: let's update our 19th-century system for appointing Supreme Court judges and make it transparent', *The Globe and Mail*, 27 November.

SECONDARY SOURCE MATERIAL

Abraham, H. (1996) *The judiciary: the Supreme Court in the government process*. New York: New York University Press.

Allan, J. (2006) 'Judicial appointments in New Zealand'. In: Malleson, K. and Russell, P.H. (eds) *Appointing judges in an age of judicial power*.

Armytage, L. (1996) *Educating judges*. The Hague: Kluwer.

Ashenfelter, O., Eisenberg, T. and Schwab, S. (1995) 'Politics and the judiciary. The influence of judicial background on case outcomes'. *Journal of Legal Studies*, 24(2): 257–81.

Bacik, I., Costello, C. and Drew, E. (2003) *Gender injustice: feminising the legal profession*. Dublin: Trinity College Law School.

Balkin, J.M. (2001) 'Bush v. Gore and the boundary between law and politics' *Yale Law Journal*, 110: 1407–58.

Bartholomew, P. (1971) *The Irish judiciary*. Dublin: Institute of Public Administration.

Beaud, O. (2012) 'Conceptions of the State'. In: Rosenfeld, M. and Sajó, A. (eds) *The Oxford handbook on comparative constitutional law*. Oxford: Oxford University Press.
Bell, J. (2006) *Judiciaries within Europe.* Cambridge: Cambridge University Press.
Besselink, L. (2013) 'The proliferation of constitutional law and constitutional adjudication, or how American judicial review came to Europe after all'. *Utrecht Law Review*, 9(2): 19–35.
Beth, L. (1952) *Politics, the Constitution and the Supreme Court*. London: Harper and Row.
Bickel, A. (1975) *The morality of consent*. New Haven: Yale University Press.
Bogdanor, V. (1988) (ed.) *Constitutions in democratic politics*. Oxford: Gower.
Byrne, R. and McCutcheon, P. (1996) *The Irish legal system*. 3rd edition. Dublin: Butterworths.
Byrne, R. and McCutcheon, P. (2009) *The Irish legal system*. 5th edition. Dublin: Butterworths.
Burbank, S. and Friedman, B. (eds) (2002) *Judicial independence at the crossroads: an interdisciplinary approach*. California: SAGE Publications
Cameron, C., Cover, A. and Segal, J. (1990) 'Senate voting on Supreme Court nominees: a neo-institutionalist model'. *American Political Science Review*, 89: 525–34.
Carroll, J. (2005a) 'You be the judge: a study of the backgrounds of Superior Court judges in Ireland in 2004'. *Bar Review*, 10: 154.
Carroll, J. (2005b) 'You be the judge: politics and processes of judicial appointments in Ireland'. *Bar Review*, 10: 212.
Carroll, J. (2007) 'The right stuff: judicial appointments, solicitors and the ambiguity of section 8'. *Law Society Gazette*, August/September 2007: 32.
Casey, J. (1988) 'Changing the Constitution: amendment and judicial review' in Farrell, B. (ed.) *De Valera's constitution and ours*. Dublin: Gill and Macmillan.
Casey, J. (1996) *The Irish Law Officers: roles and responsibilities of the Attorney General and the Director of Public Prosecutions.* Dublin: Round Hall, Sweet & Maxwell.
Casey, J. (2000) *Constitutional law in Ireland.* 3rd Edition. Dublin: Round Hall, Sweet & Maxwell.
Casper, J. (1976) 'The Supreme Court and national policy making'. *American Political Science Review*, 70: 50–66.
Chubb, B. (1978) *The Constitution and constitutional change in Ireland.* Dublin: Institute of Public Administration.
Chubb, B. (1991) *The politics of the Irish Constitution*. Dublin: Institute of Public Administration.
Chubb, B. (1992) *The government and politics of Ireland*. 3rd edition. Harlow: Longman.
Cicchillo, R. (1990) 'The Conseil Constitutionnel and judicial review'. *Tocqueville Review*, 12 (1): 3–82.
Coakley, J. and Gallagher, M. (2004) *Politics in the Republic of Ireland.* 3rd edition. London: Routledge.
Coen, D. and Thatcher, M. (2005) 'The new governance of markets and non-majoritarian regulators'. *Governance*, 18(3): 329–46.
Collier, R. and Collier, D. (1991) *Shaping the political arena: critical junctures, the Labor movement and regime dynamics in Latin America.* Princeton: Princeton University Press.
Collins, N. (1999) *Political issues in Ireland today*. Manchester: Manchester University Press.
Corder, H. (2004) 'Judicial authority in a changing South Africa'. *Legal Studies*, 24(1–2): 253–74.
Cornes, R. (2004) 'Appealing to history: the New Zealand Supreme Court debate'. *Legal Studies*, 24: 210–27.

Courtney, J. and Smith, D. (eds) (2009) *The Oxford handbook of Canadian politics*. Toronto: Oxford University Press.

Cullen, P. (2002) *With a little help from my friends: planning corruption in Ireland*. Dublin: Gill & MacMillan.

Dahl, R. (1958) 'Decision-making in a democracy: the Supreme Court as a national policy maker'. *Journal of Public Law*, 6: 279–95.

Dahl, R. (2000) *On democracy*. New York: Yale University Press.

Davis, R. and Williams, G. (2003) 'Reform of the judicial appointments process: gender and the bench of the High Court of Australia'. *Melbourne University Law Review*, 27: 819

De Cruz, P. (1999) *Comparative law in a changing world*. 2nd edition. London: Cavendish.

DeSmith, S. and Brazier, R. (1971) *Constitutional and administrative law*. 6th edition. London: Pelican.

Delany, V. (1975) *The administration of justice in Ireland*. 4th edition. Dublin: Institute of Public Administration.

Domingo, P. (2000) 'Judicial independence: the politics of the Supreme Court in Mexico'. *Journal of Latin America Studies*, 32: 705–35.

DuBois, P. (1980) *From ballot to bench: judicial election and the quest for accountability*. Austin: University of Texas Press.

DuBois, P. (2006) 'Judicial selection in post-apartheid South Africa'. In: Malleson, K. and Russell, P.H. (eds) *Appointing judges in an age of judicial power: critical perspectives from around the World*. Toronto: University of Toronto Press.

East, P. (1995) 'A judicial commission'. *New Zealand Law Journal*, 189: 190–1.

Edelman, M. (1994) 'The judicialization of politics in Israel.' *International Political Science Review*, 15(2): 177–86.

Edelman, M. (2001) 'The judicial elite in Israel'. *International Political Science Review*, 13: 235–48.

Epstein, L., Knight, J. and Shvetsova, O. (2001) 'The role of constitutional courts in the establishment and maintenance of democratic systems of government'. *Law & Society Review*, 35: 117–64.

Epstein, L., Knight, J., and Shevtsova, O. (2002) 'Selecting selection systems'. In: Burbank, S. and Friedman, B. (eds) *Judicial independence at the crossroads: a comparative perspective.* London: Sage.

Epstein, L. and Segal, J. (2005) *Advice and consent: the politics of judicial appointments*. New York: Oxford University Press.

Epstein, L., Lindstadt, R., Segal, J. and Westerland, C. (2006) 'The changing dynamics of Senate voting on Supreme Court nominees.' *Journal of Politics* 68(2): 296–307.

Finlay, F. (1998) *Snakes and ladders.* Dublin: New Island.

FitzGerald, G. (2003) *Reflections on the Irish state*. Dublin: Irish Academic Press.

Frankenberg, G. (2012) 'Democracy'. In: Rosenfeld, M. and Sajó, A. (eds) *The Oxford handbook on comparative constitutional law*. Oxford: Oxford University Press.

Gaille, S. (1997) 'Publishing by United States Court of Appeals judges: before and after the Bork hearings'. *Journal of Legal Studies*, 26: 371–6.

Gardbaum, S. (2013) *The New Commonwealth model of constitutionalism*. Cambridge: Cambridge University Press.

Gee, G., Hazell, R., Malleson, K. and O'Brien, P. (2015) *The politics of judicial independence in the UK's changing constitution*. Cambridge: Cambridge University Press.

Gerhardt, M. (2000) *The Federal appointment process: a constitutional and historical analysis*. Durham: Duke University Press.

Gilardi, F. (2002) 'Policy credibility and the delegation to independent regulatory agencies: a comparative empirical analysis'. *Journal of European Public Policy*, 9(6): 873–93.

Goldman, S. (2005) 'W. Bush's judiciary: the first term record'. *Judicature*, 88:244.

Grimm, D. (2012). 'Types of constitutions'. In: Rosenfeld, M. and Sajó, A. (eds) *The Oxford handbook on comparative constitutional law*. Oxford: Oxford University Press.
Giles, M. and Walker, T. (1975) 'Judicial policy-making and Southern school segregation'. *Journal of Politics* 37: 917–36.
Hagle, T. (1993) 'Strategic retirements: a political model of turnover on the United States Supreme Court'. *Political Behaviour*, 15(1): 25–48.
Hall, K. and McGuire, K. (2005) *Institutions of American democracy: the judicial branch*. New York: Oxford University Press.
Hall, P. and Taylor, R. (1996) 'Political science and the three new institutionalisms'. *Political Studies*, 44(4): 936–57.
Hall, P. (2009) 'Historical institutionalism in rationalist and sociological perspective'. In: Thelen, K. and Mahoney, J. (eds) *Explaining institutional change: ambiguity, agency, and power*. Cambridge: Cambridge University Press.
Hamilton, J. (2008) 'The accountability of the Director of Public Prosecutions in Ireland', Seminar on Accountability in the Public Sector: organized by Mason Hayes and Curran. 14 November. Dublin: Office of the Director of Public Prosecution. Available at http://www.dppireland.ie/filestore/documents/Seminar_on_Accountability_in_the_Public_Sector_organised_by_Mason_Hayes_&_Curran_141108.pdf. (accessed 15 Jan. 2014).
Handsley, E. (2006) 'The judicial whisper goes around: appointment of judicial officers in Australia'. In: Malleson, K. and Russell, P.H. (eds) *Appointing judges in an age of judicial power*.
Hart, H. (1994) *The concept of law*. 2nd edition. Oxford: Oxford University Press.
Hodder, J. (1974) 'Judicial appointments in New Zealand', *New Zealand Law Journal*, 80: 82–5.
Hogan, G. and Whyte, G. (2003) *J.M. Kelly: the Irish Constitution*. 3rd edition. Dublin: Butterworths.
Hogan, G. (2000) 'The Supreme Court and the reference of the Offences Against the State (Amendment) Bill 1940'. *Irish Jurist*, 35: 238–79.
Hogan, G. and Morgan, D.G. (1991) *Administrative law in Ireland*. London: Sweet & Maxwell.
Johnson, T. and Roberts, J. (2004) 'Presidential capital and the Supreme Court confirmation process'. *Journal of Politics* 66(3): 663–84.
Kelsen, H. (1942) 'Judicial review of legislation: a comparative view of the Austrian and American constitutions'. *Journal of Politics* 4: 183.
King, G. (1987) 'Presidential appointments to the Supreme Court.' *American Politics Quarterly*, 15: 373–86.
Kirby, M. (1999) 'Modes of appointment and training of Judges – a common law perspective'. Legal Institutions in Transition. 8 June 1999. Belfast: High Court of Australia. Available at http://www.hcourt.gov.au/assets/publications/speeches/former-justices/kirbyj/kirbyj_judicial2.htm. (accessed 15 Jan. 2014).
Kokott, J. and Kaspar, M. (2012) 'Ensuring constitutional efficacy'. In: Rosenfeld, M. and Sajó, A. (eds) *The Oxford handbook on comparative constitutional law*. Oxford: Oxford University Press.
Koopmans, T. (2003) *Courts and political institutions: a comparative view*. Cambridge: Cambridge University Press.
Labour Party (1995) *Access to justice: Labour's proposals for reforming the civil justice system*. London: Labour Party.
Lee, H. (ed.) (2011) *Judiciaries in comparative perspective*. Cambridge: Cambridge University Press.

Lewis, O. and Steinmo, S. (2012) 'How institutions evolve: evolutionary theory and institutional change'. *Polity*, 44(3): 314–39.

Majone, G. (19994) 'The rise of the regulatory state in Europe'. *West European Politics*, 17(3): 78–102.

Malleson, K. (1999) *The new judiciary: the effects of expansion and activism*. Aldershot: Dartmouth.

Malleson, K. and Russell, P. (eds) (2006) *Appointing judges in an age of judicial power: critical perspectives from around the world*. Toronto: University of Toronto Press.

Maltese, J. (1995) *The selling of Supreme Court nominees*. Baltimore: John Hopkins University Press.

March, J. and Olsen, J. (1984) 'The new institutionalism: organizational factors in political life'. *American Political Science Review*, 78: 734–49.

McGrath, J. (1998) 'Appointing the judiciary'. *New Zealand Law Journal*, September 1998: 314–18.

Moraski, B and Shipan, C. (1999) 'The politics of Supreme Court nominations: a theory of institutional constraints and choices.' *American Journal of Political Science*, 43(4): 1069–95.

Morgan, D.G. (1997) *The separation of powers in the Irish Constitution*. Dublin: Round Hall Sweet and Maxwell.

Morgan, D.G. (2001) *A judgment too far? Judicial activism and the Constitution*. Cork: Cork University Press.

Morgan, D.G. (2004) 'Selection of Superior Judges'. *Irish Law Times*, 22: 42.

Morton, F. (2002) *Law, politics and the judicial process in Canada*. Calgary: University of Calgary Press.

Nemacheck, C. (2008) *Strategic selection: presidential nomination of Supreme Court Justices from Herbert Hoover through George W. Bush*. Charlottesville: University of Virginia Press.

Nevill, P. (2005) 'New Zealand: the Privy Council is replaced with a domestic Supreme Court'. *International Journal of Constitutional Law*, 3(1): 115–27.

North, D. (1990a) *Institutions, institutional change, and economic performance*. New York: Cambridge University Press.

O'Toole, F. (1995) *Meanwhile back at the ranch*. London: Random House.

Overby, L., Henschen, B., Walsh, M. and Strauss, J. (1992) 'Courting constituents? An analysis of the Senate confirmation vote on Justice Clarence Thomas'. *American Political Science Review*, 86: 997–1003.

Palmer, G. (2002) *Judicial administration issues*. Wellington: Office of the Attorney General.

Paterson, A. (2006) 'The Scottish Judicial Appointments Board: new wine in old bottles?' In: Malleson, K. and Russell, P.H. (eds) *Appointing judges in an age of judicial power*.

Peters, G. (2000) *Institutional theory in political science: the new institutionalism*. London: Continuum.

Peters, G., Pierre, J. and King, D. (2005) 'The politics of path dependency: political conflict in historical institutionalism'. *Journal of Politics*, 67: 1275–1300.

Rader, R. (1989) 'The independence of the judiciary: a critical aspect of the confirmation process'. *Kentucky Law Journal*, 77:767.

Raz, J. (1979) *The authority of law*. Oxford: Oxford University Press.

Rhodes R., Binder, S. and Rockman, B. (eds) (2008) *The Oxford handbook of political institutions*. Oxford: Oxford University Press.

Roesler, S. (2007) 'Permutations of judicial power: the new constitutionalism and the expansion of judicial authority'. *Law and Social Inquiry*, 32: 545.

Riddell, T. (1994) 'The Canadian Charter of Rights and Freedoms: a descriptive analysis of the first decade 1982–1993'. *National Journal of Constitutional Law*, 5: 1

Russell, P. and Ziegel, J. (1991) 'Federal judicial appointments: an appraisal of the first Mulroney's governments appointments and the New Judicial Advisory Committee'. *University of Toronto Law Journal*, 41(4): 4–32.

Salzberger, E. (2006) 'Judicial appointments and promotions in Israel'. In: Malleson, K. and Russell, P.H. (eds) *Appointing judges in an age of judicial power.*

Scheppele, K. (2002) 'Declarations of independence: judicial responses to political pressure'. In: Burbank, S.B., & Friedman, B. (eds) *Judicial independence at the crossroads: an interdisciplinary approach*. California: SAGE Publications.

Segal, J. and Spaeth, H. (2002) *The Supreme Court and the attitudinal model revisited* Cambridge: Cambridge University Press.

Shapiro, M. and Stone, A. (1994) 'The new constitutional politics of Europe'. *Comparative Political Studies*, 26: 397.

Shapiro, M. (1980) 'Comparative law and comparative politics'. *Southern California Law Review*, 53: 537–42

Shapiro, M. (1986) *Courts: a comparative and political analysis.* Chicago: University of Chicago Press.

Shetreet, S. (1994) *Justice in Israel: a study of the Israeli judiciary.* Dordrecht: Martinous Nijhoff.

Slapper, G. and Kelly, D. (2013) *The English legal system.* 14th edition. London: Routledge.

Squire, P. (1988) 'Politics and personal factors in retirement from the United States Supreme Court'. *Political Behaviour*, 10(2): 180–90.

Stone, A. (1992) 'Where judicial politics are legislative politics: the French Constitutional Council' in Volcansek, M.L. (ed.) *Judicial politics and policy-making in Western Europe.* London: Frank Cass

Stone, A. (2000) *Governing with judges. Constitutional politics in Europe.* Oxford: Oxford University Press.

Stone, A. (2007) *The politics of constitutional review in France and Europe. Icon* 5 (1): 69–92.

Stone, A. (2012) 'Constitutional Courts'. In: Rosenfeld, M. and Sajó A. (eds) *The Oxford handbook on comparative constitutional law*. Oxford: Oxford University Press.

Strauss, D. and Sunstein, C. (1992) 'The Senate, the Constitution and the confirmation process'. *Yale Law Journal* 101: 1491.

Szmer, J. and Songer, D. (2005) 'The effects of information on the accuracy of presidential assessments of Supreme Court nominee preferences'. *Political Research Quarterly*, 58: 151–60.

Tate, C. and Vallinger, T. (eds) (1995) *The global expansion of judicial power*. New York: New York University Press.

Thatcher, M. and Stone, A. (eds) (2003) *The politics of delegation*. London: Routlegde.

Thelen, K. and Streeck, W. (eds) (2005) *Beyond continuity: institutional change in advanced political economies*. Oxford: Oxford University Press.

Thelen, K. and Mahoney, J. (eds) (2010). *Explaining institutional change: ambiguity, agency and power*. Cambridge: Cambridge University Press.

Thomas, C. (1997) *Judicial Appointments Commissions: a critical review of practice and implications for the creation of the Judicial Appointments Commission in England, Wales and Northern Ireland*. Lord Chancellor's Department Research Series No. 6/97.

Thomas, C. (2005) *Judicial diversity in the United Kingdom and other jurisdictions. A review of research, policy and practice*. London: Commission for Judicial Appointments.

Tolley, M. (2006) 'Legal controversies over Federal judicial selection in the United States'. In: Malleson, K. and Russell, P.H. (eds) *Appointing judges in an age of judicial power*.

Tushnet, M. (2008) 'Comparative constitutional law'. In: Reimann, M. and Zimmerman, R. (eds) *The Oxford handbook of comparative law*. Oxford: Oxford University Press.

Volcansek, M. (1982) 'The effects of judicial selection reform: what we know and what we do not know'. In: DuBois, P. (ed.) *The analysis of judicial reform*. Lexington: Lexington Books.
Volcansek, M. (1992) 'Judges, courts and policy-making in Western Europe'. *Western Europe*, 15(3): 1–8.
Volcansek, M. (2007) 'Appointing judges the European way'. *Fordham Urban Law Journal*, 34 (2007), 363–85.
Zander, M. (2004) *The law-making process*. Cambridge: Cambridge University Press.
Ziegel, J. (2005) 'Merit selection and democratization of appointments to the Supreme Court of Canada'. *Choices*, 5(2): 3.
Ziegel, J. (2006) 'A new era in the selection of Supreme Court judges?'. *Osgoode Hall Law Journal* 44: 547.

Index